C000253856

The Propensity of Things
Toward A History of Efficacy
in China

François Jullien

ZONE BOOKS · NEW YORK

1999

The publisher would like to thank the French Ministry
of Culture for its assistance with this translation.

First Paperback Edition

Originally published in France as *La propension des choses:
Pour une histoire de l'efficacité en Chine* © 1992 Editions
du Seuil.

Printed in the United States of America.

Distributed by The MIT Press,
Cambridge, Massachusetts, and London, England

Library of Congress Cataloging-in-Publication Data

Jullien, François, 1951–
    [La propension des choses. English]
    The propensity of things : toward a history of efficacy
in China / by François Jullien; translated by Janet Lloyd.
        p.   cm.
    Includes bibliographical references.
    ISBN 0-942299-95-7 (pbk.)
    1. China–History–Philosophy. I. Title.
DS736.5.J85   1995
951'.001–dc20   94-30660
                                                    CIP

Contents

To my mother,
The last summer
Guillestre, 1990

Translator's Note

In the original French text, François Jullien frequently uses the word *disposition*, which I have usually but not invariably translated as "disposition" (in the sense of arrangement or configuration, *not* as in the phrase "he was of a nervous disposition"). He also frequently uses the French word *dispositif*, the usual meaning of which is "tool," "instrument," "device," or "means": that is, something that can be used to produce an effect, which is indeed sometimes and/or partly what is meant by it in this work. However, the sense is often closer to that of *disposition*. The *dispositif esthéthique* is how things are disposed aesthetically so as to be effective, *dispositif stratégique* is how things are disposed strategically so as to be effective, *dispositif historique* is how things are disposed historically so as to be effective, and so on. *Dispositif* refers to the efficacy of a *disposition* (whether strategic, aesthetic, etc.), its capacity to function spontaneously and inexhaustibly. Every configuration or disposition possesses an inherent potential or propensity that is fulfilled by the *dispositif*. In other words, a *dispositif* is a "setup," a colloquial expression to which I have often resorted in preference to longer, heavier phrases such as those above. However, it has not proved possible to settle for a single term to translate *dispositif* in all contexts. For example, the term has been translated as "instrument" (p. 158), "deployment" (p. 16), "configuration" (p. 78), "tool" (p. 33), "setup" (p. 129), and "How Chinese aesthetics work" (figures 14 and 15). On page 16, Jullien discusses the difficulties of translating the Chinese term *shi*. My difficulties in translating his *dispositif* have been similar.

Introduction

Between the Static and the Dynamic

We start with a distinction. On the one hand there is the disposition of things — their condition, configuration, and structure. On the other there is force and movement. The static versus the dynamic. But this dichotomy, like all dichotomies, is abstract. It is a temporary means for the mind to represent reality, one that simplifies as it illuminates. The question we should thus ask is: What of that which, stranded between these two terms of the dichotomy, is consigned to inconsistency and, as a result, remains largely unconceptualized even though we sense that what is at stake here is everything that really exists?

However much our logic fends off the question, it will not go away: How can we conceive of the *dynamic* in terms of the *static*, in terms of "disposition"? Or, to put it another way, how can any static situation be simultaneously conceived in terms of historical movement?

A Confusing Ambiguity: The Word Shi

A single Chinese word, *shi*,[1] will serve as our guide as we reflect on this matter, even though it is a relatively common term generally given no philosophical significance. The word is itself a source of confusion, but it was out of that confusion that this book emerged.

Dictionaries at times render the term as "position" or "circumstances," and at other times as "power" or "potential." Translators and interpreters, except in the clearly defined domain of politics, tend to compensate for imprecision by drawing attention to its polysemy but attaching no importance to it, as if it were simply yet another of the many imprecisions in Chinese thought (insufficiently "rigorous" as it is) that must be accepted and to which we must accustom ourselves. It is a simple, practical term, forged initially for the purposes of strategy and politics, used largely in stereotyped expressions, and glossed almost exclusively by a handful of recurring images: nothing bestows on it the consistency of a proper concept – of the kind that Greek philosophy has taught us to insist on – that can be used for a neutral, descriptive purpose.

It was precisely the *ambivalence* of the term that attracted me, in that it insidiously disrupts the carefully constructed antitheses on which our own Western representation of things rests. Because the term openly oscillates between the static and the dynamic points of view, it provides us with a thread to follow, sliding between the different levels in which our own analysis is trapped. However, even the status of the term is provocative. For although the word defies unequivocal interpretation and remains incompletely defined regardless of its context, we also sense that it plays a determining role in the articulation of Chinese thought. Its function in Chinese thought is usually discreet, rarely codified, and seldom commented on, but in fulfilling this function, the word seems to underpin and justify some of the most important Chinese ideas. I was thus also led to reflect on the *usefulness* of this term.

This book thus begins by wagering that *shi*, a disconcerting word because it seems torn between points of view that are apparently too divergent, *is* nevertheless a *possible* word with a discoverable coherence or – better yet – with an illuminating logic. And it is not merely Chinese thought that might be illuminated – that is, the whole spectrum of Chinese thought which we know has focused since its origins on perceiving reality as a process of transformation. The logic of *shi* could even pass beyond peculiar cultural perspectives and thereby illuminate something that is usually difficult to capture in discourse: namely, the kind of potential that originates not in human initiative but instead results from the very disposition of things. Instead of always imposing our own longing for meaning on reality, let us open ourselves to this immanent force and learn to seize it.

Convergences between Fields: Potentiality at Work in Configuration, Functional Bipolarity, and a Tendency toward Alternation

I have accordingly decided to make the most of the fact that we have in *shi* a word that can serve as a tool, even though it may not correspond to any global, defined concept with a ready-made framework and preestablished function. This fact will give us a chance to undermine the system of categories in which our Western minds are always in danger of becoming mired. But while that chance seems worth taking, we should not underestimate the difficulties entailed. The term never gave rise to any coherent, general analysis among the Chinese themselves (even on the part of Wang Fuzhi, in the seventeenth century, although he came closest). As already mentioned, it does not figure among the major concepts (the "Way," *Dao*; the "organizing principle," *li*; etc.) that provided themes for Chinese thinking; to grasp its importance, we will be forced to track it from one field to another – from the field of war to that of politics, from the aesthetics of calligraphy and painting to the theory of literature, from reflection on history to "first philosophy." One by one, we will have to consider all

13

these diverse modes of conditioning reality, even though they lead us in apparently disparate directions: first, to the "potential born of disposition" (in strategy) and the crucial nature of hierarchical "position" (in politics); next, to the force working through the form of a character in calligraphy, the tension emanating from the disposition of things in painting and the stylistic effects of the configuration within literary texts (*dispositif*); and finally, to the tendencies resulting from particular situations in history and the propensity that governs the overall process of nature.

As we proceed, we will be led to reflect, through this term, on the logic of these major fields of Chinese thought. That reflection will raise more general questions: Why, for example, did ancient Chinese reflection on military strategy, as well as one faction of ancient Chinese political thought, steer clear of counting on personal, human qualities (e.g., the courage of soldiers, the morality of rulers) in pursuing a desired result? What, in the eyes of the Chinese, determined the beauty of a piece of calligraphy? What justified mounting a painting on a scroll? What was the origin of the realm of the poetic? And finally, how did they interpret the "meaning" of history, and why did they not need to posit the existence of God to explain reality?

Above all, by forcing us to move across domains, this word makes it possible for us to discover many overlapping areas. Common themes emerge: an *inherent potentiality at work in configuration* (whether in the deployment of armies on the battlefield, the configuration of an ideogram set down in calligraphy and a painted landscape, or established by literary signs); *a functional bipolarity* (whether between a sovereign and his subjects in a political situation, between high and low in aesthetic representations, or between the cosmic principles "Heaven" and "Earth"); and a *tendency* generated *sponte sua* simply through *interaction*, which proceeds to develop through *alternation* (whether, again, it involves the course of a war or the unfolding of a work, a historical situation or the process of reality as a whole).

All these themes, as they corroborate one another, can teach us much about the Chinese tradition. But can we really still speak simply — indeed naively — of a "tradition" once we have become aware that an important school of thought in the human sciences, particularly since Michel Foucault, has rendered such a representation suspect? Might we not be overinfluenced by Chinese civilization itself, which depends so heavily on references to the past and pays such attention to the transmission of tradition? Or was Chinese civilization indeed more unified and continuous than were others? (Even though we know that its impression of "inertia" is only an illusion, since it too has evolved a great deal.) Might it not instead be that *our external perspective* on this culture — that "heterotopic" point of view mentioned by Foucault at the beginning of *The Order of Things* — makes us able, as outsiders, to perceive modes of permanence and homogeneity that do not appear so clearly to those within the culture, who look upon the "discursive configurations" that continuously replace one another?

There is thus a second bet to be made as we embark on this study. A term like *shi*, while somewhat disappointing from the perspective of a conceptual history of Chinese thought, is well worth studying to help *illuminate* such thought. For at the intersection of these various domains, we sense the same underlying intuition that seems to have been taken for granted as generally self-evident for centuries: namely, that reality — every kind of reality — may be perceived as a particular deployment or arrangement of things to be relied on and worked to one's advantage. Art, or wisdom, as conceived by the Chinese, consequently lies in strategically exploiting the *propensity* emanating from that particular configuration of reality, to the maximum effect possible. This is the notion of "efficacy."

A Word Indicative of a Culture

The intuition of efficacy is common enough in China that it fails to give rise to any abstract reflection, and so widely disseminated that individual instances of it are hardly noticeable. Deeply embedded in the language as it is, it constitutes *a common basis of understanding* that is all the more solid since, being so integral, it is unnecessary to comment on it. This intuition is never at the fore in literary commentaries, nor does it surface completely in any particular term, but it can be glimpsed — definitely, if fleetingly — in the word *shi*, which always reflects this intuition about efficacy in one particular domain or another as a privileged idea. The term does not fully express this common basis of understanding on its own, but it does allow us to detect its presence and to sense the logic behind it.

Starting from this word, then, and working backward, as I intend to, let us try to understand this intuition of efficacy, draw it from its silence, and elaborate a theory about it. Certainly, none of our ready-made concepts will suffice to grasp it as it slips, unquestioned, through Chinese discourse. That difficulty is not because any consensus of thought exists among us, as it does among the Chinese, but because the intuition of efficacy entails that we resist the urge to separate conceptual fields that we customarily set in opposition because those very oppositions help to structure our thought. (One characteristic of the word *shi*, as noted earlier, is its tendency in translation to fall between the static and the dynamic.) To begin our dialogue, our only hope is first to alter the focus of our vision and attack the problem obliquely, falling back on conceptualizations that, although of minor importance up to the present, nevertheless offer a possible new point of departure through what they hint at. The terms we will use to help convey this idea of the intuition of efficacy are, first, "deployment" or "setup" (in the sense not only of how things are disposed but also how they can be used [*dispositif*]) and, second, "propensity" or "tendency"; we hope to illuminate the force of the Chinese word through the interaction of these terms. Although they may be marginal to our Western philosophical language, these expressions will establish the conceptual framework that will progressively allow us to come to terms with the difference between Chinese culture and our own.

A Possible Alternative to Philosophical Preconceptions

To the Chinese, the idea of *shi* seems self-evident; but it may never occur to us in the West. Yet the fact that there is an overlapping of different domains in Chinese thought reveals a common model that runs through the entire culture, namely, of a configuration or disposition of things operating through opposition and correlation, and which constitutes a working system. This model has the effect of challenging a number of Western categories that have served as a basis for our own thought but have now ceased to be relevant: in particular, the relational category of means to ends or, better yet, of cause to effect. We will become aware of a certain prejudice in Western philosophy, whose "traditional" nature, now seen from the outside, will also appear by contrast more marked: we will see that it is based on what is hypothetical and probable rather than on what functions automatically, that it favors a single and "transcendent" pole rather than interdependence and reciprocity between two poles, and that it values liberty more than spontaneity.

When compared with the elaboration of Western thought, the originality of the Chinese lies in their indifference to any notion of a *telos*, a final end for things, for they sought to interpret reality solely on the basis of itself, from the perspective of a single logic inherent in the actual processes in motion. So let us once and for all discard the Hegelian prejudice according to which Chinese thought had remained forever in its infancy, never able to evolve beyond the cosmological point of view common to all ancient civilizations toward the more "self-conscious" and therefore superior stages of development, represented by "ontology" and "theology." On the contrary, let us recognize the extreme coherence that underlies the Chinese mode of thought even though it never valued conceptual formalization at all. Finally, let us use this new appreciation to decipher from the outside our own intellectual history — now so familiar to us that we can no longer see it as it is — so as to reveal our own a priori assumptions.

Retracing Our Path beyond Our Questions
From the beginning, it is true, the self-imposed project of Western philosophy (always in quest of more emancipated thinking) has been to question freely the foundations that underlie its own activity. But at the same time we know that alongside the questions that we ask, that is, the questions we *can* ask, is also all that *which prompts us* to ask those questions. It is this realm that we are not capable of questioning, namely, the fabric of our thought that is woven by Indo-European languages, informed by the implicit categorizations of speculative reason, and oriented by a characteristic aspiration toward "truth."

Thus, this proposed excursion through Chinese culture also seeks to measure the extent of our conditioning more accurately; not, I hasten to say, through any naive yearning for escapism or fascination for the exotic, nor to justify Western feelings of guilt or the new dogmas of cultural relativism (which, in truth, are just another side of ethnocentrism). Rather, this detour is simply an attempt to deepen our own comprehension of the state of things, to renew the impulse to question, to rediscover the joys of inquiry.

Notice to the Reader

This book is a sequel to my earlier essay, *Procès ou création*,[1] in particular the last chapter ("Un même mode d'intelligibilité"). However, my angle of approach here is almost the reverse. In that earlier work, I begin with the thought of a single author, Wang Fuzhi (1619–92), seeking to analyze its coherence; in this study, in contrast, the Chinese term that I intend to explain will lead us from one domain to another, encompassing more than fifty writers (from Antiquity to the seventeenth century). However, the spirit of my research remains the same. Whether it is a matter of a single *œuvre* or of the word *shi*, my constant concern is to rediscover, in concentrated form, the logical, if underlying, features of an entire culture. And in this study the thought of Wang Fuzhi again circumscribes my concerns.

Likewise my intention remains unchanged. There are two reefs on which I must not founder: first, the sealed and sterile realm of speculative sinology; second, its opposite, a popularization that distorts its subject and renders it inconsistent on the pretense of making it accessible. The only possible course is to steer the narrow course between these two toward the elaboration of a theory. I must work at once as a philologist and a philosopher, reading both extremely closely (to plumb the individual nature of the text and how it works) and from the greatest distance (against a background of difference and by putting things into perspective), to avoid two common mistakes: naive assimilation, according to which everything can be directly transposed from one culture to another, and equally simplistic comparativism, which proceeds as though ready-made, suitable frameworks existed for apprehending the differences in question. The more prudent course adopted in this study is that of a tentative entrée, based on the progression of our understanding.

A number of methodological decisions have shaped this study. In the presentation of each of the areas of Chinese culture, I observe historical connections and use them to underpin the argument but do not follow them up simply for their own sake. The reason for this stricture is to allow the logical connections to emerge fully and to keep purely sinological discourse to a minimum (the contextual references are given in the notes) to make it more accessible for the nonspecialist. Similarly, comparisons are not made at the outset, in the form of parallels, but are instead introduced as hypothetical conclusions, indicators of the differences that the work seeks to reveal: the Chinese position is thereby made more meaningful, even if the space devoted to the two traditions under comparison is not equally divided (since I have assumed that the references to China will be new to the reader, whereas those to Western philosophy will already be familiar and may be mentioned in a more allusive fashion).

A number of plates are incorporated in this volume to help the uninitiated reader grasp the aesthetic dimension of *shi*. The glossary of Chinese expressions at the end of this volume is designed to help sinologists check certain characteristic occurrences of the terms used in the text.

Finally, the omission of an index is deliberate.

My prime purpose has been the pleasure of following up an idea.

The numerical superscripts in the text direct the reader to the notes at the end of the work (pp. 267ff.); the letters that precede them direct the reader to the glossary of Chinese expressions, also to be found at the end (pp. 307ff.).

PART ONE

CHAPTER ONE

Potential Is Born of Disposition in
Military Strategy

The reflection on the art of warfare that developed in China at the end of Antiquity (between the fifth and third century B.C., in the period of the warring states) went far beyond its actual subject. Not only did the particular systemization characterizing it constitute a remarkable innovation from the point of view of the general history of civilizations, but the type of interpretation to which it gave rise projected its form of rationalization on reality as a whole. Warfare has often seemed the domain of the unpredictable and of chance (or fatality) *par excellence.* However, from early on, Chinese thinkers believed that they could detect in warfare's unfolding a purely internal necessity that could be logically foreseen and, accordingly, perfectly managed. This radical concept betrays the effort that must have accompanied its elaboration; as a result, Chinese strategic thought stands as a perfect example of how one can manage reality, and provides us with a general theory of efficacy.

Victory Is Determined before Engaging in Battle
An intuition serves as our starting point: war is a process that evolves only in relation to the force it puts into play. The task of a good general is to calculate in advance and with accuracy every

Sunzi
4th century B.C.

25

factor, so that the situation develops in a way as beneficial as possible to him: victory is then simply a necessary consequence – and the predictable outcome – of the imbalance that operates in his favor and that he has been able to influence. No "deviation" is possible in these circumstances, for an advantageous result follows ineluctably when the appropriate measures are taken.[a1] The entire art of the general thus consists in seeing that those measures are taken before the confrontation itself takes place, and in recognizing early enough – in the opening stages – all the factors, so that he can influence the situation even before it has taken shape and become a reality. For the sooner this favorable orientation is imposed, the more easily it will take effect. If a good general's "action" is taken at the ideal moment, it is not even detectable: the process that leads to victory is determined so far in advance (and its development is so systematic and gradual) that it appears to be automatic rather than determined by calculation and manipulation. It is thus only seemingly paradoxical to say that a true strategist always wins "easy" victories;[b2] these victories appear easy because victory, when it comes about, no longer calls for tactical skills or great human effort. True strategical skills pass unnoticed; the best general is the one whose successes are not applauded: the common people praise neither his "valor" nor even his "wisdom."

Sunzi   The crucial point in this strategic thinking is to *minimize the armed engagement*, an idea expressed best in the following remark: "The victorious troops [i.e., those bound to be victorious] seek confrontation in combat only after they have already triumphed; whereas the vanquished troops [i.e., those bound to be defeated] seek to win only once battle commences."[3] He who seeks victory only at the last stage of armed conflict will probably always be defeated, no matter how talented he may be. Instead, everything should be played out at an earlier stage in the determination of events, when dispositions and maneuvers, at this point still solely dependent on our own initiatives, can be adjusted at will. Interlocking and reacting logically, the process is always efficacious. (It has a "spontaneity" or "logic." As we will see below, the two terms mean the same thing from two different perspectives.) It becomes possible to retain such control over the later course of developments that it may not even be necessary to join battle:[4] a good general, Sunzi tells us, "is not bellicose." Let there be no mistake, however. This ideal of nonconfrontation is not prompted by any moral concern, nor does it stem from any abstract idea, for, on the contrary, attention is focused on determining most precisely and at the earliest stage the future orientation of events. All that matters is to act in a way to ensure one's victory, by making it predetermined. Ultimately, every ideal outcome depends "simply" on getting the operative and controlling effect in any given situation to work toward its achievement. This idea is common in Chinese Antiquity. The *Laozi*, the founding text in the Daoist tradition, states that "it is easy to control a situation before any symptoms have manifested themselves" (para. 64). Further, "the good warrior is not bellicose," and "he who does not engage in battle is likely to defeat the enemy" (para. 68).

The Notion of Potential Born of Disposition

As a result of this perspective, the concept of a *potential born of disposition* emerged for the first time. In the context of military strategy, this is usually conveyed by the term *shi*.[5] The whole art of strategy can be more precisely recast through use of this term: to say that "skill" in warfare "depends on the potential born of disposition" (*shi*)[c6] means that a general must aim to exploit, to his own advantage and to maximum effect, whatever conditions he encounters. This dynamism, which stems from the configu-

Sun Bin
4th century B.C.

27

Sunzi ration of things and must be harnessed, is represented well by the flow of water: if a wall retaining a large amount of water is breached, the water can only rush down,[7] and in its impetuous surge forward, it carries everything in front of it, even boulders.[8] Two features characterize such causality: it results only through some objective necessity and, given its intensity, it is irresistible.

But from a strategic perspective, what is included in the "disposition" that generates the potential? For one cannot interpret it simply, as in the comparison above, in relation to the configuration of the lay of the land — even if the terrain of operations is certainly one determining factor, since a general must make the most of the character of the land, distant or close, low-lying or elevated, accessible or difficult to reach, open or closed in, as the case may be.[9] But equally important is the moral disposition of the protagonists, whether they are enthusiastic or dispirited, and

Huainanzi all the other "circumstantial" factors also count — whether the
2nd century B.C. climate is favorable or unfavorable, whether the troops are well organized or scattered, in good shape or exhausted.[d10] Whatever the factors involved, the situation can, and must, exert its coercive effect in two ways: positively, by encouraging the troops to

Sun Bin invest all their energy in the offensive,[e11] and negatively, by sapping the enemy troops of all initiative and reducing them to passivity. Because of *shi*, they will not be in a position to resist, no matter how numerous.[f12] Mere numerical advantage gives way before these superior, more decisive conditions.

It is well known that the use of the crossbow (a Chinese invention dating to circa 400 B.C.) contributed significantly to revolutionizing the conduct of warfare through both the accuracy of its straight trajectory and its formidable force. The "activation" of its "mechanism" thus naturally served to symbolize the sudden

Sunzi unleashing of an army's energy:[13] *shi* is like a "crossbow stretched to its maximum."[g14] Apart from its pertinence to the theme (the image of the bending of the bow being used to convey potential), the technological innovation represented by the crossbow reflected progress comparable to the capacity to exploit *shi* rigorously at the strategic level. In fact, it is possible to develop this image even more precisely: the advantage peculiar to the cross-bow is that, "while the point from which the bolt departs is very close (between the shoulder and the chest), one can kill people more than one hundred paces away, without their companions realizing from where it was fired."[15] The same applies to the good general who, by using *shi*, manages with minimum effort to achieve the maximum effect from a distance (either temporal or spatial), simply by exploiting the factors in play, without common knowledge of how the result was achieved or by whom.

Sun Bin

One final image, which once and for all captures the various aspects of *shi* and conveys the theme particularly well: if one uses logs and stones on level ground, they remain stable and therefore immobile, whereas on sloping ground they begin to move. If they are square, they stop; but if they are round, they roll down. "For a man who is expert at using his troops, this potential born of disposition may be likened to making round stones roll down from the highest summit."[16] *Disposition* includes the particular shape of the object (round or square) as well as the situation at hand (on level or sloping ground). Maximum potential is conveyed by the differing nature of the gradient.

Sunzi

Power Relations Are More Important than Human Virtues and the Debunking of All Supernatural Determination

The above comparison reveals yet more. The fact that the round stones ready to roll down from the top of the slope serve as an image for troops that are maneuvered in the most skillful fashion suggests that what matters is not so much the personal quality of the soldier as his deployment. The oldest treatises on military

29

Sunzi art make the point openly: a good general "expects victory from the potential born of disposition, not from the men placed under his command."[h17] The objective propensity that stems logically from the situation, as it is managed, is the decisive factor, not the willing efforts of individuals. An even more radical formulation of the same point runs as follows: "courage and cowardice are a matter of *shi*."[i] The commentary adds, "if the troops have *shi* [i.e., if they benefit from the potential born of disposition], then the cowardly are brave; if they lose it, then the brave are cowardly"; and again, "courage and cowardice are variations of *shi*."[18] These laconic statements are designed to convey purely practical information; however, they contain considerable philosophical significance for us. They imply powerfully that human virtues are not intrinsic, since the individual neither initiates nor controls them, but are the "product" (even in the materialistic sense of the word) of an external conditioning that is, for its part, totally manipulable.

Such a point of view could become established only at the cost of strenuous rationalization prompted by the most rigorous of exigencies, namely, practical efficacy. The warring-states period was a time when warfare between rival principalities all aspiring to hegemony escalated to unprecedented levels. The fighting unto death in which they engaged – in perfect accord with the principle of "development to extremes" that our modern theorists have used when elaborating their notion of "absolute" war – left no room for simple religious belief or even for the least "idealism," at least in this particular domain. But the tendency then was precisely that it was becoming impossible to consider war as a "particular" domain, since it had continued (over the course of two centuries) to take on an increasingly costly importance, becoming the only thing that mattered. Under these circumstances, it was logical that strategic thinking should play its part

30

in prompting a more general line of thought, and that its extreme commitment to penetrating the real nature of all determining factors and doing away with all possible illusions should have resulted in making the notion of *shi*, the potential born of disposition, the keystone of the theory.

It should be remembered that in the immediately preceeding period (up until about 500 B.C.), not only had warfare been regarded more or less as a ritual, ruled by a whole code of honor and played out in seasonal campaigns that drew the line at radical extermination, but no venture was ever undertaken without the diviners commenting on its propitious or unpropitious nature. Now, however, not only was "*shi* superior to men"[j][19] and the tactical disposition of things more important than moral qualities; ideas of transcendent or supernatural determination, too, were banished and replaced solely by strategic initiative. Of all the factors to be considered, only *shi* was truly decisive.[20] Whoever took up an ax to cut wood did not need to worry about whether the date was suitable and the day auspicious. But if he had no handle in his hand with which to impress his force, he would produce no results, no matter how favorable the omens.[21] As this example illustrates, it is only through *shi* that one can get a *grip* on the process of reality. Similarly, choosing a precious wood to make an arrow and decorating it artistically contribute nothing to the arrow's range. All that matters is the drawing of the crossbow. Only from *shi* can a real effect be expected.

Huainanzi

Variability according to Circumstances and the Renewal of the Strategic Mechanism

Now let us examine more concretely how this efficacy works. In general, strategy aims, through a series of factors, to determine the fixed principles according to which one evaluates the prevailing power relations and plans operations in advance. However,

warfare, consisting of action and, moreover, regulated by reciprocity, is known to be the domain par excellence of unpredictability
and change, and thus it always remains more or less beyond the
scope of theoretical predictions. All this has often been regarded
simply as a matter of common sense, imposing *practical* limits on
any strategy. However, for the same reason that they rely on the
Sunzi   notion of *shi* to resolve the contradiction, the Chinese theorists
of war do not seem bothered by this *aporia*. The point is clearly
stated: "Once one has determined the principles that are advantageous to us, favorable dispositions [endowed with efficacy: *shi*]
must be created for them, in such a way as to assist whatever
reveals itself [at the time of the operations] to be external [to
those principles]."[k22] We are led to the following definition,
which we will come across again in many other domains in the
Chinese tradition: "*shi* [in as much as it is a concrete deployment
or setup] consists in organizing circumstances in such a way as
to derive profit from them."[l] These statements, central to the
opening chapter of the earliest Chinese treatise on strategy, effect
a transition from the preliminary determination of abstract and
constant elements (the "five factors" and the "seven evaluations")
to the description of a tactic based on simulation, which follows
in that same text. As such, all the efficacy of the tactic arises from
being specifically devised to evolve along with the situation and
to overcome the enemy all the better because it manages to adapt
itself constantly to him. Through *shi*, whatever stems from the
circumstances and seems to elude one's initial calculations naturally finds itself again contained by them.

But the main strength of Chinese strategic intuition lies not
so much in this intermediary concept making it possible to combine what is constant and what is changing (theory and practice,
principles and circumstances); rather, it is that it demonstrates
pertinently how the evolution of circumstances, inseparable from

the course of any war, in fact constitutes a general's major tactical trump card, allowing him to renew the *potential* and hence the efficacy of the strategic deployment. The art of the military commander is found in leading the enemy to adopt a disposition that is relatively fixed and therefore easy enough to reconnoiter, which enables the general to get a grip on his opponent. At the same time he constantly revises his own tactical disposition so as to take the enemy by surprise, always misleading him and catching him off guard and thereby depriving him of any control over the situation.[23] In this way, the military commander becomes as unfathomable as the great process of the world itself in all its infinity (the *Dao*) that, never settling into any particular disposition, is bound to be unique, and offers no clues to its reality.[m][24] *Huainanzi*
Let us return, then, to the image of water, considering it now, however, as it flows along in a level, peaceful manner. "Just as the *Sunzi* disposition of water is to avoid all heights and to flow downhill, similarly the disposition of [well-led] troops is to avoid the strong points of the enemy and attack the weak points; just as water determines its course in relation to the terrain, similarly the troops determine their victory in relation to the enemy."[25] Through its extreme variability (stemming from its radical adaptability), *water*, which stands opposed to rigidity, is used as a symbol of the most penetrating and unstoppable force.

Thus, a disposition is effective by virtue of its renewability; it is a *tool*. To say that *shi*, as a strategic tool, must be as mobile as flowing water[n] and that "victory is gained only through transformation and adaptation to the enemy"[26] means more than merely saying that the ability to adapt is necessary or purely a matter of common sense. What is involved is the deeper intuition that a particular disposition loses its potentiality when it becomes *inflexible* (or static). For is it not precisely the fundamental objective of all tactics to ensure that dynamism continues to operate to one's advantage (meanwhile draining the opponent of initiative and reducing him to paralysis)? And how better to reactivate the dynamism inherent in any disposition than to open it up to alternation and reversibility? It is here that strategic theory coincides *Sunzi* with the most central idea of Chinese culture: the perpetually renewed efficacy of the course of nature, illustrated by the succession of days and nights and the cycle of the seasons. Ultimately, because the absolute causality constituted by the *Dao* never becomes immobilized in any one disposition, it remains forever inexhaustible.

A Major Chinese Originality: Dispensing with Confrontation

The concept of potential born of disposition, which lay at the heart of ancient Chinese strategic thought, ultimately passed into wider usage[27] and the entire later tradition never detached itself from this point of view.[28] In the twentieth century, even Mao Zedong resorted to this concept to explain the tactics most appropriate to a war of resistance – the "long" war – against Japan:[29] this was a tactic of "alertness" and spontaneous reaction to all occasions and situations. This strategy became all the more effective since it precluded immobilization, or being "blocked" in a predetermined disposition from which there would soon be no escape.[30]

The perspective operative here is of a process that can evolve to our advantage if we make opportune use of its propensity. Reading the ancient Chinese literature on strategy, one begins to realize the extent to which the type of representation it embodies is opposed to any heroic or tragic vision (and also why ancient China remained so disinclined to such a vision). For confrontation lies at the heart of that vision, a confrontation carried to the crisis point in a situation offering no escape. In contrast, anyone who knows how to exploit strategically the potential born of disposition can *lead* the antagonism to resolve *itself* thanks to this perfectly controllable internal pattern. Whereas tragic man clashes irrevocably against superior powers, resisting all surrender (*eikein* is the crucial word in Sophoclean drama), the Chinese strategist prides himself on his ability to manage all the factors in play, for he knows how to go along with the logic behind them and adapt to it. The former *fatally* discovers, all too late, his "destiny"; the latter knows how to anticipate the propensity at work so that he has it at his own disposal.

From a more strictly military point of view, one finds this same opposition between Chinese theoretical thinking based on *shi* and the "Western model of warfare" bequeathed to us by the Greeks (on which John Keegan and Victor Davis Hanson have recently shed new light).[31] As we have seen, Chinese strategy aimed to use every possible means to influence the potential inherent in the forces at play to its own advantage, even before the actual engagement, so that the engagement would never constitute the decisive moment, which always involves risk. In contrast, after the time of the skirmishes and duels described by Homer, the Greek ideal was the "all or nothing" of pitched battle. The fifth-century Greeks gave priority to the heavily armed hoplite infantry rather than the formations of lightly armed peltasts and cavalry, ascribing more importance to the immediate use of forces drawn up and facing each other on the battlefield than the art of harassment, evasion, or any other maneuvers designed to wear down the enemy. They thus reached a concept of warfare in which the *head-on clash* of the two phalanxes, deliberately engineered by both sides, constituted the determining element, that is, hand-to-hand fighting in broad daylight (according to Quintus Curtius, Alexander refused to achieve victory "through the wiliness of brigands and robbers whose sole desire is not to be noticed"). Combat was also relatively brief, since it was totally concentrated in the destructive clash and left no possible outcome other than a rout or death. "To win a battle before it had even started," Hanson tells us, "was to allow...one side to 'cheat' in a victory achieved by some means other than their own bravery in battle."[32] The spear was both instrument and symbol of this heroic confrontation. Projectile weapons, on the other hand, were generally despised in ancient Greece, because they killed from a distance and without regard to the personal merits of the fighting men. Nothing could be further from the high value placed on *shi*, symbolized by the crossbow, the most highly perfected of all projectile weapons.

Decisive and *direct* confrontation in battle is central to modern European concepts of war, particularly in the writings of Carl von Clausewitz. Clausewitz's fame rests on his being the first Western thinker to attempt an overall, theoretical account of the realities of warfare. He reacted simultaneously against "pedants" for whom military knowledge was simply a matter of practical questions of weaponry and supplies, and who believed that war could be conceived as an exact science based on angle calculations and immutable principles (Prince von Bülow and Henri de Jomini are among the most famous of these theorists), and against those who denied that warfare, considered simply as a human and thus "natural" function, could be theorized at all. For Clausewitz, the only possible way of "thinking through" warfare was to conceive of its conduct as *art*. In doing so, he envisaged it logically, according to an idea that had become traditional in Western philosophy, namely, the Aristotelian relation between *means* and *ends*, *Mittel* and *Zweck* (final end) or *Ziel* (intermediate end). In other words, he conceived of warfare as using the most appropriate means for achieving a predetermined end. Even that objective could take the form of an intermediate stage leading up to a more general, ultimate goal, political in nature (in accordance with the rule that Clausewitz in his youth had formulated in terms of a Kantian maxim: "You will aim for the most important goal, the most decisive one that you feel you have the strength to attain; to reach that end, you will choose the shortest path that you feel you have the strength to follow").[33] By contrast, in ancient Chinese strategic thought, the relation between means and end is never made explicit; in it is replaced by notions of a setup and its efficacy.[P]

Because Clausewitz conceives of warfare from the perspective of *finality*, he not only ascribes maximum importance to direct confrontation (as a goal), but he is also forced to recognize the intrinsic importance of unquantifiable moral factors, such as courage and determination. He is thus led to think of war in terms of probability – the means used are simply those with the greatest chance of leading to the desired result. As we have already seen, this in no way relates to the attitude of the Chinese theorists of warfare, for whom war is conceived from the perspective of *propensity* and a *shaping of effect*. They place the greatest store in what Clausewitz, for his part, disdainfully regards as "simply indirect destruction," a preliminary operation that proceeds by dint of paralysis and subversion (whereas the pitched battle – *die Schlacht* – which is essential for Clausewitz, is for them no more than a final stage). Furthermore, the logic of Chinese strategic thought also leads them to treat the moral qualities that are essential to warfare as simply being *involved* by the situation rather than as factors in themselves, as Clausewitz regards them. Under these circumstances, the Chinese can conceive the process of warfare as "ineluctable" and "automatic" rather than in terms of probability.

Finally, it is well known that Clausewitz's theory of *friction* plays an important role in his thought. This theory was conceived as a means to account for a troublesome gap in Western strategic thought: the disparity between the plan drawn up in advance, which is of an ideal nature, and its practical implementation, which renders it subject to chance. The Chinese concept of *shi*, inserting itself into the distinction between what Westerners have opposed as "practice" and "theory," and thus collapsing that distinction, shifts "execution" toward something that, given the propensity at work, operates of its own accord and excludes any uncertainty or inadequacy: neither deterioration nor friction is involved.

For the Chinese *shi* is most important; for Clausewitz "means" and "end" are. The disparity between these categories results in a fundamental structural difference. In particular, the contrast between these concepts of strategy cannot fail to be reflected, on both sides, in the domain of politics. The choice of the head-on clash in hoplite battle, representing a direct, immediate, and unequivocal means of obtaining a decision, is closely linked with another Greek invention, the vote in the assembly. Likewise, the attention paid to propensity, the efficacy that stems from disposition, is reflected, even more overtly, in the Chinese concept of authority.

CHAPTER TWO

Position as the Determining

Factor in Politics

Efficacy Does Not Depend on Personality

Strategy and politics both lead back to the same fundamental problem: What is the source of the efficacy that will allow us to manage the world as we wish? The capacities of individuals or the power relations in play? A subjective – moral, intellectual – input or an objective tendency imposed by the situation? Chinese thought in late Antiquity (the fourth to third centuries B.C.) encourages us to set up an opposition between these two possibilities and regard them as mutually exclusive, because this thought pushes each possibility to its theoretical extreme – particularly the idea that the course of things is determined by some force that has nothing to do with personality.

This line, handed down by Chinese wisdom, is disseminated in its most general form (according to the Daoists): allow the propensity of things to operate outside you, as their own disposition dictates; do not project values or desires on them but adapt constantly to the necessity of their evolution. For the very disposition of things results in a trend that never falters or deviates and can neither be "chosen" nor "taught."[1] Things "tend" of themselves, infallibly, with no need for "effort."[a] Allowing subjectivity to intervene is always mismanagement, which, by intro-

Zhuangzi
4th century B.C.

39

ducing human assumptions and calculations, puts obstacles in the way of that impeccable tendency. The terms of the opposition illuminate each other through their mutual incompatibility: the activity of conscious planning is contrasted with the natural spontaneity of things happening immediately as a simple reaction within the system. The initiative seems to lie totally with the world, just as, in Western cultures, people may passively place themselves completely at God's disposal. Instead of seeking to manage the world imperiously by our own actions, we should let ourselves be carried along as the world pleases; instead of wishing to impose our own preferences on it, we should let ourselves go with the flow of things, adopting the line of least resistance. As the Chinese say, "He advanced only if pushed, came only if pulled"; "as the wind blows," "as a feather spins," or "as a millstone turns."

When we transfer this reductive view of reality as a play of potentials to the political level, we find it there too, within society, as a kind of hierarchical "position." Here too, as in the world itself, we find an arrangement or *disposition* which infallibly gives rise to a certain *tendency*.[2] The term *shi* is used to designate the configuration of power relations in politics in the same way it denotes a strategic setup. Just as wisdom was conceived as the ideal of allowing the propensity inherent in reality to operate of its own accord and to maximum effect, it can be argued that the political order is similarly determined in a purely objective way and proceeds "necessarily" from the prevailing relations of authority.

From the start, two aspects to any potential effectiveness stem from hierarchical positioning. First, it does not depend on the personal merit of the individual using it, and certainly not his *moral* merit. Second, the individual may or may not use it but can never do without it entirely. Such effectiveness is a "support" in a purely instrumental sense but also one with an absolutely deci-

Shen Dao
4th century B.C.

40

sive effect. Take the cases of a chariot, a drug, or an ornament: each of these different examples demonstrates the indispensable nature of what may initially appear to be no more than an aid.[3] One example cited is the following: if you take the most beautiful women and dress them in the most beautiful finery, they will be attractive to everyone, but if you strip them of that finery and clothe them in rags, you will drive everyone away. The wind provides yet another popular example of the effectiveness of such "supports." Because it is supported by the wind, the bolt of the crossbow can soar into the air; by allowing itself to be carried along by the wind, a blade of grass can be transported far away. In a mythical rendering of the same theme, the dragon flies majestically along, riding the clouds, but if these are dispersed, it will find itself grounded, like a worm, for it will have lost the *shi* that bore it up in its soaring ascent.

Now let us interpret these images in political terms. Even the wisest man cannot be sure of influencing other men, however close to him they may be, if he does not enjoy the *support* of a position (*shi*). Conversely, if the most worthless man has the benefit of such support, he can force even the greatest sages to obey him.[b] Just as what counts in strategy is not so much the large number of troops or pure brute force but rather exploiting the potential born of disposition, in politics likewise a governor "depends" not on his "force" but on his "position."[c4] This opposition of force and position is particularly significant. Indeed, one would imagine the two terms to be associated. Yet the notion of force has negative connotations of personal investment, of being insufficiently liberated from all innate human capacity. The notion of position, on the other hand, can automatically explain the totally external nature of the determining factor in any situation.

Because philosophical argumentation is less developed in ancient China than in ancient Greece, we might mistakenly be

Shang Yang
4th century B.C.

led to believe that it had no place in China at all. As it happens, quite apart from all the examples that illustrate it, this political concept of the effectiveness of the support which is inherent in a given position gave rise to a theoretical debate, summarized here.[5] The refutation of the thesis that position is a determining factor, proceeded as follows. First, even if "position" does intervene as a factor, it cannot be sufficient since personal attributes also contribute. For instance, the example cited above can be reversed: no matter how dense the clouds, an earthworm – unlike the dragon – could never be supported by them and rise into the air. Second, given that it can operate just as negatively as positively, the factor of position turns out to be neutral and thus makes no difference in the situation: it allows a good sovereign to rule well, just as it allows a bad one the worst kind of tyranny. Third, since human nature is in general more bad than good, the trump card provided by position overall threatens to do more harm than good. Hence, in the last analysis, everything depends on the abilities of the individual involved. The state is like a chariot, and the "position of authority" resembles the team of animals that pulls it:[6] in the hands of a good driver it will go fast and far; in the hands of a bad driver, the result will be the opposite.

Hanfeizi
3rd century B.C.

The refutation seems commonsensical and free of any particular cultural biases. As a result, the systematic critique it in turn gives rise to is all the more interesting, since the radical line it adopts lends originality to the concept of *shi* at use here.[7] But this refutation of a refutation itself is possible only because it involves first a displacement of what is at stake and second a distinction in meaning: the political order envisaged in this response is not the ideal moral order dreamed of by all utopianists; rather, it is the order of a state machine functioning like clockwork.[d] Furthermore, it makes it necessary to distinguish between *shi*

Hanfeizi

42

as a natural disposition and *shi* as an "institutional" relation of
authority if the latter is to provide the basis for a truly political
framework.[e] In fact, in history, the first *shi* (i.e., *shi* as a natural
disposition) is only at play, for better or worse, in altogether extreme and exceptional situations – that is, either a golden age or a
time of calamities. Such situations deny man the room to maneu-
ver that normally allows him to remain in control. Yet even in such
extreme situations, both saints and tyrants owe their emergence
not to their own good or bad qualities but to the conditioning
of necessity. Meanwhile, in normal times hierarchical position,
instituted as positive power, operates on its own as a determining factor sufficient to make order reign among everyone.

It is not even feasible to claim, as at the start of the first thesis, that the factor of personal ability coexists alongside this factor
of position. These two suggested determining factors are mutually exclusive, according to the Chinese notion of "contradiction."
This contradiction is illustrated by the image of a man selling a   *Hanfeizi*
spear and a shield who boasts that the one is capable of penetrating anything while the other is impossible to penetrate. In sum,
it is pointless to hope for a savior-sage; the odds of such a reign
are one in a thousand. Rather, the best strategy, here and now, is
to make the arrangement of authority work as effectively as possible, thus ensuring that the state runs smoothly. The existence of
a hierarchy suffices on its own to generate order. As a result, the
image of the chariot of the state should be reversed: if the chariot is solid and the team is good (with the latter, as before, illus-
trating the effectiveness that results from position), it is pointless
to wait for a supremely gifted driver. All that is necessary are relay
posts set at regular intervals to ensure that even an ordinary driver
can drive fast and well. These relay posts let the teams of horses
operate to full capacity as they travel from one stop to the next.
In explicit terms, the governor's only task, working from his dom-

inant position, is to erect enough political "relay posts" to preserve the full impetus stemming from his authority.

Political Position Operates as a Power Relation

The debate above pitted those supporting the factor of personal merit against those ascribing efficacy solely to position. In the China of late Antiquity, this debate opposed the partisans of "Confucianism" and those traditionally described as "Legalists." The two sides agreed on at least one point, namely, the monarchical form of power — one essential difference between China and the West is that no form of political regime other than royalty was imaginable. The difference between the two sides of the debate lay in their understanding of that form of power. The Confucians regarded it as an essentially moral authority, the expression of a "heavenly mandate" operating through the exemplary influence of the sage-king. For the Legalists, in contrast, royalty was not the manifestation of any superior will; its authority stemmed purely from the pressure exerted by the monarch's position.[8] The opposition between the two groups was occasioned by two different social and cultural environments in ancient China, two different mentalities even, and thus involved a primarily ideological difference. On the one side were those who belonged, at least in spirit, to the ancient court circles, attached to the values of ritual and tradition, and acting as *literati* for the princes; on the other were those open to the influence of the world of enterprise and trade (at this time undergoing an extraordinary surge in China) and who projected their realist and aggressive vision on the management not only of power but of the entire social body. However, this was not a "class" difference, nor did it oppose progressivists and conservatives; for despite their modernist ideas, the Legalists, far from encouraging claims to new rights, were characteristically concerned with positive efficacy solely for the benefit

44

of despotic imperialism. They were theorists of *authoritarianism* and *totalitarianism* rather than "legalists" in the true sense of the term (despite the usual translation, which is based, in fact, on false pretenses), for Chinese political thought was usually concerned with power but not with rights, and this category of thinkers helped entrench that tendency by radicalizing it rather than seeking to modify it.

Thus, the sovereign's position counted above all. Even if the influential position of great families or powerful ministers sometimes became an issue,[9] the only theory – in terms of *shi* – elaborated in Chinese political thought related to the *royal position*, precisely by resolutely eliminating any other position that might detrimentally affect the sovereign's position. The Chinese Legalists perceived the prince and his subjects in a strictly antagonistic relationship. For if sovereignty only exists by virtue of position,[g][10] it should not count on sentiments of love or devotion on the part of the people to establish its authority (a view clearly in contrast to the Confucians' paternalism). Strictly speaking, this power could only be based on rewards and punishments, forcing everyone (except the sovereign) to subject his own ambitions to the authority of one man.[11] Under these circumstances, political position constitutes a complete and sufficient mechanism since it operates positively and negatively at the same time, both inciting and repressing. For the sovereign to "occupy" his position fully,[h] he must above all delegate to no one his twin control over fear and self-interest. If he does let himself be dispossessed of his *shi* by others, he will inevitably come under their control and be manipulated by them.[i] And this will eventually become the source of sedition and revolt aiming not to topple the throne but to usurp it, simply by taking its occupant's place. The risk of this occurring is even greater since, as we have seen, the setup functions regardless of the personal moral qualities of whoever con-

Guanzi
3rd century B.C.

45

trols it, for that reason passing just as easily into other hands.

Thus conceived, the monarchy becomes the object of permanent – if mostly latent – conflict, in which the despot is opposed
Hanfeizi by everyone else: in the first place, of course, his nobles, ministers, and advisers, but also his wife, mother, concubines, bastards,
and son-heir. The theory of position goes hand in hand with a subtle psychology of the seizure of power: the prince must be on
guard above all against those who anticipate his wishes and regularly embrace his cause, for in this manner they are building up
Guanzi reserves of trust that will one day give them power over him.[j][12]
In fact, the authority of the ruler increases in proportion to the
distance he manages to maintain between himself and his subjects, just as wild beasts continue to daunt us precisely because
they usually lurk unseen in the forests.[13] The privilege of position should not be diluted or shared,[14] and favorites and those
on familiar terms are worse than insubordinates. The sovereign's
position is exclusive and monopolized and must not be the object
of rivalry.

Lüshi Chunqiu　　Within a feudal framework, the same applies to the relation-
3rd century B.C.　ship between a sovereign and his subjects.[15] The sovereign's task,
faced by his vassals, is to weaken them as much as possible so
they will bend easily to his will. It is not out of the goodness of
his heart that he distributes fiefdoms among them, but to establish his own preeminence better, and the farther away they are,
the smaller those fiefdoms must be, to compensate for the sovereign's resultant loss of control. In general, power can be wielded
even better (i.e., more easily, from the sovereign's point of view)
the greater the inequality of positions and the greater the resulting imbalance.[k] The sovereign's task, like that of the general's
noted above, is to make the relation of forces operate to his advantage, reducing all others to subordination. Indeed, as applied
in their respective domains, political and strategic theories fre-

quently overlap:[16] the best card a ruler holds vis-à-vis his external enemies (his strategic *shi*) is the power base provided by his
position of authority (his political *shi*) inside his realm, through
his own subjects.

Hanfeizi

The Position of the Sovereign as an Instrument of Totalitarianism

But a position of sovereignty should not be conceived purely as
defensive, the warding off of possible encroachments from all those
who threaten it. It is also effective in itself, especially concerning information, for it enables the sovereign to obtain knowledge
of everything occurring in his empire. The authoritarian aspect
of the sovereign's position, which is a common feature in the
ancient world, is joined here by a totalitarianism reminiscent of
our own times, if pushed to an extreme degree of systematization.

Even in their earliest speculations on the subject, at the end
of Antiquity, the Chinese theorists of despotism were intelligent
enough to see clearly that political power depended essentially
on the all-enveloping knowledge that could be acquired about
people and on the resulting transparency in which those people
were forced to live. In this, the theorists drew their inspiration
from the Mohists before them, who had already questioned the
importance that the Confucian tradition placed on the moral intuition of conscience in the domain of knowledge and were the first
to attempt to define the conditions of scientific knowledge based
on inquiry, experience, and verification.[17] In Chinese thought,
one does not encounter the metaphysical doubt in the face of
appearance and reality that has so profoundly marked our own tradition. Chinese thought is, however, quite aware that individual
knowledge is doomed to remain fragmentary, incomplete, and
therefore marred by subjectivity. Individual knowledge needs
help from other quarters; as the proverb puts it, "Two eyes are

47

better than one." If objectivity is to be attained, knowledge must become both all-encompassing, must be put to the test. To the theorists of despotism, who set more store in coercion than unanimity, a position of sovereignty was ideal for the acquisition of such knowledge.

Hanfeizi

Precise knowledge of the facts was converted into a marvelous tool for controlling people. Once established at the center of the functioning of the state, the position of the sovereign can make information converge from all sides and appear in front of him. Through the power of the position, information can be extracted even from the recalcitrant and, when false, detected. To achieve this, all the ruler need do is systematically use the two-fold procedure of *dissociation* and *solidarization*.[l] By dissociating bits of information, the prince methodically investigates the exact source of each individual item, comparing them and making their respective authors personally responsible for them. At the same time, by forcing solidarity on people, he gets them to betray individual characteristics that distinguish them, a quality that encourages denunciations. In this fashion, the prince can flush out self-interested attitudes instead of letting them flourish with impunity under the anonymous cloak of common deliberations. Meanwhile, by brandishing the threat of collective punishment, he will be able to nip in the bud any partisan cliques.[18] Through a subtle operation both contrasting and complementary in manner, these two methods are all that is necessary to turn the sovereign's position into a veritable *intelligence machine*.[m] Through the enforced collection and meticulous sifting of all information, the sovereign, from deep within his palace, manages to "see" and "hear" everything. By now his strength is not really physical; it lies simply in being able to place others where they can watch for him and, in consequence – since his subjects are bound to watch each other too – also be seen by him. His strength is thus politically sufficient, for he can detect any sign of revolt in ample time and annihilate it in embryonic form, simply by discovering it, without even needing to go to the trouble of meting out punishments. The sovereign himself is not expected to be moral but, through his position, "enlightened."[n19]

The sovereign's position thus rests on two foundations. One is clearly visible, and the law imposed on every subject forces them to respect it. The other, which is carefully concealed, is constituted by the meticulous division of society into separate sections. The sovereign's position thus combines the two pillars on which Chinese despotism is founded: the public, draconian "norm," equal for everyone, which fixes rewards and punishments, and the subterranean political "technique" that proceeds via parallel lines of investigation and loaded misinformation, criticism, confrontation, and cross-checking.[o] This combination makes it possible to command openly and manipulate secretly.

We now have a more precise and definite understanding of the notion of the support inherent in the position of the sovereign. The art of a ruler lies simply in getting everyone else to contribute toward the maintenance of his own position[p20] – not by committing *himself* to the endeavor but by getting others to toil on his behalf. A prince perceives little purely through his own senses. If he had to draw on his own capacities, he would soon exhaust himself and prove unable to rule. Thus, princes should aim to economize their efforts in proportion to their own status. "An inferior prince thoroughly uses his own ability, a prince of the middle rank thoroughly uses the strength of others, an excellent prince thoroughly uses the intelligence of others."[21] Everyone else helps the sovereign rise, just as, in the earlier example, the clouds helped the dragon soar into the air. Or, one could say that the prince is borne along by the masses as a boat by water. He is like a tree surveying the valleys from a mountaintop.[22] The height of

Huainanzi
2nd century B.C.

Hanfeizi

49

the tree is irrelevant; what counts is the altitude of the mountain on which it is perched.

A theoretical question on the art of governing is whether a prince is wrong to leave his capital on a whim and retire to the seashore. The Chinese theorists of totalitarianism answer negatively, for the prince might perfectly well remain conscientiously in his palace, at the center of his states, yet still not be properly occupying his position.q[23] Conversely, he could withdraw to the sidelines yet retain his hold on the structures of power and remain in control of everything. In other words, his position is filled not by his personal commitment but *technically*. It depends not on physical presence, which is local and limited, but on the handling of command. For this reason it can claim to exert total power, through and through.

Automaticity of the Mechanism of Power

The nature of the setup constituted by the position of sovereignty can thus be reduced to two essential features. First, it is purely a product of human invention, for it emanates from no transcendent design but is technically organized by man. Second, this kind of power functions autonomously and automatically, regardless of the qualities of the person using it, provided it is totally at his disposition and unobstructed. It is artificial and yet operates at the same time *naturally*; and its usefulness rests on the combination of those two aspects.

Its naturalness is itself twofold. As concerns the prince's subjects, the two means of command upon which his position as sovereign depends, and which he grips as firmly as a haft or handle,[r] provoke two basically opposite and instinctive reactions in his subjects: punishment spontaneously excites repulsion, while rewards produce attraction.[24] The prince merely has to occupy his post of command and allow it to operate: there is no need for zeal or

Hanfeizi

50

even the slightest effort on his part. For just as fruits ripen naturally in season with no need for anyone's effort, in the prince's
position the renown of "merit" accrues spontaneously "with no
need for him to strive for it."[s25] Just as water always tends to flow
and a boat tends to float, from the sovereign's position stems a
natural – and therefore inexhaustible – propensity for his orders to
be punctiliously executed. By occupying his position, the prince
rules men as though he himself were "Heaven" (or Nature) and
makes them function as if he were part of the invisible reign of
the "spirits."[t26] In other words, simply by allowing the power
that stems from his position to work, he is unable (as are the
movements of the heavens) to deviate from the regularity of his
conduct or, consequently, to provide any room for criticism.[27]
Furthermore, since he (like the spirits) invisibly haunts the human
world, he never has to "make an effort," since his subjects feel
themselves to be determined, not by some external causality, but
simply by their own spontaneity.[28] They are activated just as if
they were activating themselves; they lend themselves to manipulation as though it were impulsive. Accordingly, if "the position
functions," it will encounter no obstacle, no matter how harsh
the authority."[u29]

According to the subtle analysis of ancient Chinese thinkers,
the whole strength of totalitarian authoritarianism lies in the following in no way paradoxical fact: oppression carried to extremes
will no longer be seen as oppression but as its opposite, something spontaneous, natural, and requiring no justification. This
is the case partly because such pressure creates a long-term *habitus*
that becomes second nature to the individuals subjected to it.
More fundamentally, human law, *in becoming inhuman*, takes on
the characteristics of natural law. Insensitive and hence equally
pitiless and omnipresent, it imposes its constraints on everyone,
at every moment. As the Chinese Legalists saw it, the law they

establish is a perfect extension to the *Dao* and accords with the logic of things: it merely translates the inherent order of nature into social actuality. In this way they conceive the sovereign's position as essentially a rigorous power over life and death, to be exercised at all times over every subject – a power that, above all, the prince alone must possess. He decides who should live and die, with all the inexorability of fate. Because the prince, through his position, reproduces exactly the conditions of possibility in nature, the social body becomes completely permeable to the dictates of his authority, and these are consequently in no danger of being deflected or lapsing. The effect of the prince's position is uniform, and for this reason he appears as the very embodiment of the great regulating process of reality in the political sphere. His position constitutes the precise, unique point anchoring the human level in the original dynamism (the influence of "Daoist" philosophy is, of course, detectable here[30]). In this way, the prince can harness an efficacy equal to the totality of things, simply by occupying his position, and the mechanisms of manipulation operate of their own accord, without his needing to apply any pressure at all.

Hanfeizi   All this makes it easier to understand the conflict that sets these Chinese theorists of despotism against Confucian moralism. As the former see it, the extreme ease with which power can be exercised from a position of sovereignty proves the superiority of their brand of politics. A man who governs in the name of morality is, on the contrary, forced to make ever-increasing efforts without ever achieving any indubitable and definite success. He resembles one who sets off on foot in pursuit of the fastest of animals: the chase is exhausting, and, at the end of the day, the effort will more than likely prove to have been fruitless. In contrast, if one rides in the chariot of state, letting oneself be drawn along by its team of horses (which, again, is a symbol of the efficacy of position), one arrives naturally at the intended result and, furthermore, with minimal effort.[v31] The Confucians themselves recognized that even Confucius, the greatest of sages, managed to attract only seventy disciples despite his great efforts, whereas Duke Ai, his sovereign, a no more than mediocre man, had no trouble at all as a prince in subjecting everyone else, including Confucius.[w32] The Confucians' first mistake was to place too much faith in morality and, in particular, to confuse the attitude appropriate for subjects with the attitude appropriate for disciples.

But they made an even graver mistake as well. By preaching goodwill and clemency to the prince, the Confucians upset the functioning of the power that stems from the sovereign's position and derailed it from its regular course. For even the love between parents and children, which the Confucians adopt as a model when they root their political paternalism in nature, is by no means unaffected by exceptions and revolts. Besides, what is goodwill if not the granting of rewards to those who have not earned them? What is clemency if not exempting from punishment those it is just to punish? If a sovereign demonstrates either virtue, he will certainly enjoy a good conscience but society, for its part, will meanwhile careen into disorder.[33] The sovereign's subjects will no longer feel obliged to devote all their energies to serving him and will soon think only of their own private interests. As for the prince, as soon as he embarks on a path of "humanity" and "compassion," he will be operating in no more than a purely human fashion and will accordingly find himself competing with many other rivals in this domain: he will have slipped from his position.

Hanfeizi

To strive for morality is thus harmful, and those who preach morality are corrupt, since it introduces slackness into what would otherwise run tightly on its own. The only correct way to use the sovereign's[x] position is to recognize that it works *automatically*.[34]

One with such a system at his disposal, far from drawing attention to himself by his favors, like the Confucian king, conceals himself behind his machinery, becoming indistinguishable from its cogs. He who is all-seeing offers no glimpse of himself, forcing transparency on others but protecting himself through his own opacity.[35] All-powerful, he passes unnoticed (and the better his position operates, the less visible he is). He is, like the *Dao*, the ultimate term in the great process of things, of which nothing is known except that "it exists."

The Radical Nature of the Chinese Concept

The dehumanization of power could hardly be pushed further. As Léon Vandermeersch's analyses have admirably shown, of all the Chinese thinkers of Antiquity, the theorists of despotism advanced political thought the most, by reaching for a more abstract notion of the state – particularly at the level of administration, which came to be regarded as purely functional and totally free from the old ruling aristocracy. However, owing to the absolute domination of the monarchical principle in China, the limitation of their system lay in its failure to dissociate totally the state from the prince in similar fashion. This accounts for the extreme *depersonalization* of the sovereign, the logical conclusion, which reduces him to nothing but his *position*: the political setup operates rigorously, but, centered as it is on the prince, it cannot transcend the apparatus that the prince embodies. By its own logic, it thus becomes altogether monstrous.[36]

The thought of these Chinese authoritarians is commonly compared today with that of Machiavelli. Political reflection in both is presented as disguised advice addressed to the prince and aimed at achieving the only important end, namely, the reinforcement of his power. In *The Prince*, too, we read, "The point is to maintain one's authority."[37] In both cases, political thought is precisely liberated from morality and from finalist justifications, and power is seen simply in terms of what Machiavelli calls "effective truth": it proceeds slowly from human institutions, is interpreted as a pure clash of interests, and bears only upon the reality of relations of force. In a way unheard of until that period of Western thought, Machiavelli, like the Chinese thinkers, makes no distinction between legitimate and illegitimate forms of power: his concept of a *principe* deliberately confuses the monarch and the tyrant. The comparison ends here, however, because Machiavelli has no intention of reducing the prince to his position. Far from seeking to depersonalize him, Machiavelli, as a man of the Renaissance, appeals strongly to the sovereign's personal qualities. But instead of conceiving him in moral terms, as in all the other "mirrors for princes" of his day, Machiavelli goes so far as to assess him from the perspective of the efficacy of his *virtù*. For him, politics is the art of grappling with *la fortuna*, not the regular operation of a setup valued for its automaticity. Machiavelli cleverly and subtly perceived the secret principles of authoritarianism, but he still had no idea of how totalitarian politics might operate.

In Western thought, the ideology of an absolute reign of surveillance appears, rather, in what Foucault describes as the control one might imagine imposed in a town quarantined because of the plague.[38] The entire territory is carefully divided into sections, and individuals are constantly tailed and identified so that, with even the tiniest details of existence strictly regulated, the workings of power can be utterly all pervasive. Similarly, perhaps the closest Western approximation of the effect of position is Jeremy Bentham's famous *Panopticon* described by Foucault.[39] On the periphery is a ring-shaped building divided into individual cells, each of which stretches from the inner rim of the edifice to the outer and has a window at either extremity so that the light sweeps through the cell. In the center of this ring stands a tower with windows facing the inner wall of the ring. The men in the cells are kept under constant surveillance and are at the same time constantly aware of their visibility. In the tower a guard observes them all the time but is never observed by them, to the point that the effect of surveillance persists even if he happens to leave his post. In both Bentham's and the Chinese system, the functional dissymetry is identical: on the one hand the enforced transparency of those who are observed, on the other the opacity of the observer, whether prince or guard. As noted earlier, in the Chinese theory the sovereign could continue to occupy "his position" perfectly well even if he left his palace.

Foucault comments that this is "an important mechanism, for it automatizes and disindividualizes power."[40] No better definition of the political *shi* could be imagined: this mechanism, which improves the exercise of power by making it swifter, less cumbersome, and more efficient, "has its principle not so much in a person as in . . . an arrangement whose internal workings produce the relation in which individuals are caught up."[41] An individual confined to "the field of invisibility" of the panopticon – and likewise one placed in such transparency by the position of the sovereign – who is conscious of such incarceration, assumes responsibility for the constraints of power and "makes them work spontaneously upon himself" in such a way that "the external power may shed its physical pressure." The more this power "tends to the noncorporal, the more constant, profound, and permanent are its effects." Bentham, the inventor of this panoptic system, congratulated himself on discovering "a great and new instrument of government," a way of obtaining power "in a hitherto unexampled quantity." Foucault, for his part, saw the invention as a symbol of a historical transformation, one characteristic of modernity in that it led to the emergence of the disciplinary society. In China, meanwhile, such an invention had been rigorously elaborated as early as late

Antiquity by the theorists of *shi*, and not simply on the cautious, modest scale of a prison but on a scale that controlled the whole of humanity.

CHAPTER THREE

Conclusion I:

A Logic of Manipulation

Analogies Between the Strategic and Political Mechanisms
The conduct of warfare and the management of power: we can
push the affinity between the two, but there also seems to be a
reluctance, in the West, to define more closely what they have
in common. We hesitate to pass beyond the simple metaphor
("political strategy") and interpret them by the same criteria.
"Manipulation" is generally restricted to the sciences of nature,
and there is a reluctance – or resistance – to embarking on the
elaboration of a theory of human manipulation.

However, some of the ancient Chinese thinkers felt no such
reluctance or qualms. The heavy emphasis on ritualistic and moral
attitudes in ancient China was matched, during the social and
political crisis at the end of Antiquity, by an equally determined
and radical reaction provoked by the undermining of those earlier attitudes. As we have seen, the common "kernel" of *shi* now
provided the deep underlying basis for both strategy and politics.
The aims of both were, after all, the same. For Chinese strategists (by which I mean the *theorists* of strategy), it was most important *not* to aim to exterminate the enemy – this would be a loss
and, besides, warfare should not be murderous – but to force the
enemy to yield while preserving as many of their troops as pos-

sible for conversion to the victor's own use. Similarly, for Chinese theorists of despotism, the only goal of politics is "to subject others to oneself," and they repeatedly point out that every subject should be regarded as a potential enemy. Whether the other be subject or enemy, everything must be designed to paralyze *his* plans and wishes and to force him to work, despite himself, toward fulfilling the aims imposed on him. The procedure in both fields is identical, through exploitation of the inherent play of forces. Anything that might modify or obscure that stark constraint is to be avoided, while anything that might strengthen the imposed coercion without arousing the opposition's suspicion (such as cunning, traps, and dissimulation) is to be encouraged. For this reason, whether in the conduct of warfare or the management of power, the mechanism's use is basically the same. In one case one sets out to destroy, not the enemy, but his powers of resistance; in the other, one is prepared to exterminate any subject once he becomes an obstacle.

Furthermore, in war or politics, the mechanism involved presents the same functional characteristics. First, its processes are totally automatic: if the strategist or general knows how to operate the mechanism he controls, his victory over the enemy is assured before the battle, just as the prince can be sure of imposing obedience on his subjects without even having to constrain them. Results follow automatically, for they are simply effects. Such a mechanism is inexhaustible, since it functions "naturally"; its propensity makes it constantly renew itself on the battlefield as well as in politics, and the nature of this kind of power is to issue orders ad infinitum without wearing out.

Another point of similarity is the inconspicuous nature of the manipulator, doubly so in the case of a good general: firstly from a purely tactical perspective in that he does not reveal his own dispositions while forcing the enemy to reveal his; secondly from a strategic perspective in that he never displays his clairvoyance and courage, even though they would certainly attract admiration, but instead makes it appear that victory was inevitable. The same is true of a knowing prince: in his immediate relations with others, he carefully conceals anything concerning his innermost preoccupations while forcing total visibility on his subjects, and he guards against manifestations of clemency and generosity in his use of power, even though they would reflect on him advantageously as "virtues" in the eyes of his people. Meanwhile, he scrupulously avoids upsetting the self-regulation of the social body, which is maintained by the impartiality of his acts of retribution. In both cases, behavior is based on the same analysis: on a practical level, to let oneself be visible gives others a hold over one and puts them in control; on a theoretical level, the true manipulator becomes one with his position and vanishes from view. In each case, the same consequences follow: moral behavior becomes the product solely of manipulation. A soldier is brave and a subject loyal thanks not to the fine virtues they are supposed to possess but simply because they have no option. Efficacy proceeds from an objective determination or, more precisely, a dispositional determination, and success stems from this alone too; the more discreetly it does so, the more infallible it will be.

Moralists versus Realists

Predictably enough, the notion of *shi* as a mechanism that works is spurned by the moralists as much as it is valued by the strategists and theorists of despotism. One group views it as negatively as the other rates it positively, since, after all, morality is per se an affirmation that values are invariably more important than the fickleness of circumstance and that subjective factors are more important determinants than the pressure exerted by relations of force. As Chinese thought matured in late Antiquity with the flowering of the "hundred schools," one principal debate involved the "realists," that is, the theorists of *shi*, and the moralists, a.k.a. the Confucians.

In the domain of warfare, the moralists ignore *shi*, since strategy does not interest them at all. According to them, wars resolve themselves thanks to the moral influence emanating from the good sovereign. Accordingly, warfare need not be considered as a thing in itself and from a technical perspective, but simply as a consequence of politics, itself a consequence of morality. If a sovereign truly encourages the stirrings of virtue innate in his conscience, even the most distant, hostile peoples will "infallibly" be won over by his goodness and spontaneously throw open their gates to him and flock to welcome him to enjoy the beneficence of his reign.[1]

Mencius
4th century B.C.

Meanwhile, in the social and political domain the moralists preach total indifference to the power attached to position, doing so in the name of the superiority of moral values (but not, of course, with any intention of criticizing the social hierarchy, for which the Confucians have a greater respect than anybody). Mencius tells us that "the sage-kings of Antiquity loved the Good and set no store by the power attached to their position (*shi*).[a] How could wise *literati* possibly have done otherwise? They were committed to their own particular Way and took no account of the power attached to the position of anyone else."[2] He continues: "If the kings and dukes did not show them the greatest respect and did not perform all the rites due them, they were not allowed to pay men of letters frequent visits. Accordingly, if it was up to the princes to make frequent visits to the *literati* and if they were permitted to do so frequently, how could the princes have made the *literati* their subjects?" This paragraph is extremely revealing: first because it harks back to an idealized past (in total contrast to the Legalists' characteristically realistic attachment to

the present), but above all because of the rhetoric used to justify
the recalcitrance of the *literati*, namely, their refusal to submit
and thereby leave themselves powerless. The passage begins inno-
cently enough, introducing the scholar in the shadow of his
prince; but by switching things around, it ends up completely
reversing their roles. Along the way, an inverse gradation is suggested: the king simply "loves" the Good, while the *literati* "delight
in" their own particular Way. Finally, instead of *literati* visiting and
paying tribute to the king (as they clearly do in reality), it is the
princes of the world who are said to hope to be worthy to come
and pay tribute to the *literati*.

Characteristically enough, this kind of reversal operates even
with respect to *shi* once it is appropriated by the moralists. Whereas
it normally denotes the consequences stemming naturally from
disposition, it apparently here means the opposite. This is true
even of the theme of water, the spontaneous flow of which is nevertheless retained as an image of propensity. It is a characteristic
of human nature to tend toward the good, Mencius tells us, just   Mencius
as water tends naturally downhill. But if one strikes the surface
of the water, it will splash higher than one's brow, and if one bars
its course and forces it to turn back on itself, it can be blocked
on the summit of a mountain, not from its own nature but from
shi,[b3] understood here as a violent pressure artificially exerted.
This is altogether contrary to normal usage, but once one adopts
the moralists' perspective, it becomes perfectly logical. From
the perspective of a theory of despotism, what is conceived and
exploited as an effect stemming naturally from position is seen
by a scholar subjected to that position to be an arbitrarily imposed
constraint. From one point of view it is an internal propensity
(stemming from the mechanism of power); from the other it is
an external force of coercion (opposed to our natural inclination). Thus, the ambivalence mirrors the antagonism between

63

two different perspectives; the semantic paradox reflects the social contradiction.

Theoretical Compromises and Fundamental Convergences

Nevertheless, faced with the rise of these theories of strategy and despotism, the moralists found that they had to take greater account of their opponents' concept of *shi* and accept the latter's meaning. If they were not to founder in utopianism, they had no choice but to react to realism. For example, they now drew a clear distinction between two types of war: the "royal" war, the ideal kind engaged in by the ancient forebears who could operate without striking a single blow, thanks to their moral prestige; and the war of hegemony, such as was the reality of the time, in which military strength came into play and tactics became necessary. But from the perspective of its efficacy this second kind of war was definitely inferior to that of the ancient sovereigns, for whom a punitive expedition against a bad ruler became a mere parade, so confident were they of the unanimous support of their own people and the enthusiasm of formerly hostile peoples who, won over by their goodness, would flock to offer their submission.[4]

The same applies in the political domain, where at least a minimal place was now granted to the position of authority, if only as a starting point. As such, it was useful to the first sovereigns when it came to forcing acceptance of what was good on their peoples, who were still so uncivilized that they were recalcitrant to moral influences.[5] It was also useful to the founders of empires. For them, the support provided by their fiefdoms, however modest, made it possible for them to launch themselves into their undertakings.[6] Finally, it was useful to society as a whole in that it provided the basic condition for the smooth functioning of the hierarchical system that alone could guarantee cohe-

Xunzi
3rd century B.C.

Xunzi

sion and tranquility.[c7] Nevertheless, the moralists insisted, the only true choice that could decide the fate of states was a purely moral one. As every case of a fallen sovereign attested, however powerful his position might be, it could not prevent a prince who displeased his people through his immorality from hastening his own downfall and ending up in a position less enviable than that of the least of his subjects.[8] Power is not an end in itself, and the *Dao* of wisdom is definitely superior to *shi*.[9] While the moral ascendancy based on the gratitude and goodwill of the prince's subjects guarantees him "peace and strength," power obtained by force, by intimidation and surveillance (according to the methods recommended by the theorists of despotism), procures only "weakness and danger."[10] The submission of the prince's subjects, which even to the moralists is certainly the condition of good political order, will be real only if spontaneous: from which one must conclude that a position of authority cannot cause the submission but, on the contrary, can only be maintained as a result of it, as a consequence and effect of that submission.[d11]

However, even if the two sides find themselves increasingly and explicitly opposed in terms of *shi*, the strategists and theorists of despotism nevertheless agree with the moralists concerning the logical basis of their rival arguments, for both recognize the superiority of a tendency operating *sponte sua*, through pure propensity, as a means of determining reality. Their only real divergence is over the nature of the tendency they privilege, even to the point of excluding all else: namely, the propensity stemming from the relation of forces or the propensity emanating from the exemplary lesson of moral conditioning. The objective "ineluctability" at which the strategist and theorists of despotism claim to aim is countered by "the impossibility of not responding" to the subjective stimulus influenced by wisdom:[e] morality spontaneously gives rise to morality, not so much because people strive to emulate it but through the spontaneous attraction it exerts on everyone and the homogeneous reactions it causes. Superiority is thus claimed on the same grounds for each option: namely, that it operates perfectly smoothly, without encountering the slightest resistance and without even the awareness of those whom it affects. Whether from the propensity of the situation or the inspirational force of virtue, the efficacy immanent in the process spontaneously and logically resolves all tensions and antagonisms, provided it can come fully into play and thus become totally binding. To the moralists too, any war they support will inevitably lead to triumph even before confrontation, to the degree, indeed, of making any such confrontation totally unnecessary. According to Xunzi them, it is only by resorting to tactical cleverness and cunning that one puts oneself on the enemy's level, for he can do likewise, rendering the outcome of the clash uncertain.[12] A good sovereign never even dreams of attacking people who might resist, for if they are capable of doing so, they must possess a measure of moral cohesion, which he can only applaud. Similarly, as the moralists see it, the reign of virtue is infinitely preferable because only moral example can spare the prince the effort and bother to which all despots are doomed, for such an example elicits unanimous support and reintroduces spontaneity into positive behavior, whether innate or acquired. In the last analysis, ritual itself, the basis of Chinese civilization as a whole and Confucian morality in particular, can be considered purely as a mechanism.

The Historical Compromise and the Originality of the Chinese

Of course, the prince who managed systematically to conquer all his rivals and impose his domination over all China, thereby ending centuries of struggles for hegemony, did so by strictly applying the authoritarian and totalitarian theories that were championed over the moralist tradition. All the same, to ensure the centralized operation of the state, the source of its strength, this new empire needed the support of an increasingly sophisticated bureaucracy, which could only be recruited from the ranks of the *literati*, heirs to the Confucian tradition. Hence an ideological compromise soon became detectable between the two rival factions, providing the basis for the entire subsequent tradition.

First, in the domain of warfare two moralist principles once again gained acceptance: the superiority of a just, punitive war, provoking spontaneous submission, over a war of self-interest and conquest, entailing armed conflict, and the desirability of moral unanimity between a prince and his subjects.[13] At the same time, with the decrease in the emphasis on an ideal kind of war, tactical theories, and the crucial importance of the potential stemming from disposition, were resuscitated and elaborated.[14] In politics, in contrast, the authoritarian and despotic attitude provided the framework, and the theory of position became the keystone of the imperial system: the sovereign prevailed over everyone through his *shi*, both eliminating all competition and compelling others to expend their total effort in his service. His position established him as the pivot of the whole world and the source of all regulation.[15] But even though the constraints of the inequality in these relations of force were maintained, the relationship between the sovereign and his ministers was no longer perceived in purely antagonistic terms. Appeals for cooperation were now made and the relationship became "humanized." The customary metaphor of the "chariot of state" underwent a revealing change: instead of the state representing the chariot and the team of horses the position, position was now represented as the chariot and the ministers as the team of horses.[16] A good driver became one who knew how to handle the horses, remaining always alert to their

Huainanzi
2nd century B.C.

reaction to his pressure on the reins. In this way the Confucian ideals of reciprocity and harmony were reintroduced, along with the role of the moral model and its educative mission. Even as morality without the support of position was pronounced ineffective, in accordance with Legalist beliefs, the privilege of position was hailed as the method for the sovereign to impose his will as a norm and to transform the behavior of his people by his influence,[17] a surreptitious rehabilitation of the moralists' ideal.

The one type of efficacy at last seemed to combine with the other. Of course, this compromise could also be seen as a subterfuge: enforced submission was transformed into voluntary cooperation and tyranny was disguised by the fine trappings of consensus. But all this further confirms the strange affinity we may already have detected between these rival tendencies: whether efficacy proceeds from the transforming influence of morality or from the relationship of force established by position, social and political reality is always conceived as a setup to be manipulated. In itself the ideal of "order" shared by both sides imposes the vision of a purely functional human world. The merit of spontaneous regulation is unanimously invoked as the ultimate argument in defense of opposing policies without ever provoking the least distrust on either side. Social and political "processes," appreciated for their predictability, must be impeded by no obstacle or friction – by no claims for rights, no recognition of any freedom of conscience, no "liberty."

For whether efficacy stems from moral example or from the mechanism created by a power relation, it always operates *indirectly*, through the situation, and replaces confrontation – either armed or argumentative. The logic of manipulation presupposes an ideological view of our relation to others that rests on the postulate of having other peoples' minds at one's sovereign disposal, instead of treating them themselves as an end (the reverse of the

Kantian position). This logic also implies the rejection of all efforts at persuasion, for it rests on profound distrust of the power of words, a distrust characteristic of the ancient Chinese world (in contrast to the Greek world). Admittedly, rhetoric can also be regarded as an art of manipulation.[18] However, it involves at least turning toward others, addressing them, and seeking to convince them; which gives them a chance to reply, defend themselves, and argue the opposite case. An argument may not always bring forth the truth, but it at least lets one react consciously: conflict too grants the other a chance, for it at least enables one to rebel. And, as we realize from the contrast provided by Chinese civilization, from that face-to-face *agon* in the agora — a symmetrical reflection of the field of battle — Greek democracy was born.

The Art of Manipulation

Manipulation, not persuasion, was the Chinese way. This telling feature of Chinese tradition, characterizing as it does a logic of both individual and collective behavior toward others, is not limited solely to the political and strategic domains. It would be interesting to know how it worked more generally, in other fields besides politics and strategy, as a social and moral phenomenon at the level of day-to-day life. It would be interesting to study it in ordinary lives, so as to understand how manipulation can become a generally accepted principle at work in human relations; how this strategy of indirectness can be useful not just in warfare but also in daily life; and how this policy of conditioning affects not only the management of power but also the most common patterns of behavior. However, it was perceived so intuitively and shared so universally that it never became the subject of any theoretical discourse in Chinese civilization. Because of the consensus and acceptance it found, no one ever thought to investigate the logic behind it. Something that strikes us, from the *outside*, as such an obvious trait finally escapes our grasp, is never fully explained for us, but is simply taken for granted.

We therefore have to seek another basis for our analysis. Since we cannot expect explanation at this stage from the Chinese thinkers, we will resort to our remaining resource: direct experience. Let us consider the kind of stories told about manipulation, in other words, the evidence provided by the novel.

A single anecdote will suffice. One of the great novels of the Chinese tradition, *The Water Margin*, tells how the hero Fine-Beard was banished to a distant fortress for assisting the escape of a comrade-in-arms who had been unjustly condemned to death.[19] There, his magnanimity won him the trust of the local prefect, who gave him the task of escorting his own son in the streets of the town one festival evening. Unexpectedly, the man who owed him his life turned up with a group of comrades. They drew him aside for a moment to invite him to join their outlaw band committed to rectifying wrongs. Out of loyalty to the prefect, the hero refused, but when he went back to look for the child, the boy had disappeared; when he followed the tracks of the outlaws out of town, he found the boy dead: they had deliberately killed him. In fury, he set off in their pursuit and they led him further and further away, until finally the stratagem to which he had fallen victim became harshly clear to him: everything, including the child's murder, had been planned in advance to make him give up his ideal of loyalty, since he had no way to return, and to force him to join their camp.

A critic struck by the literary qualities of the story comments alongside the text as follows: "Every stroke of the brush combines to create a *shi* of terrible specters who seize the man in their talons,"[f20] striking terror in the reader. For everything that happened did so without our hero being able to intervene, to make

The Water Margin
14th century

Jin Shengtan
17th century

autonomous decisions, or to put up any resistance. And when the others, falling at his knees, finally beg his pardon, Fine-Beard is still forced to do exactly as they had decided from the start, in disposing of him in this sovereign fashion. His conscience has not been won over, but his hands are tied by the situation. Moreover, not one of these fine fellows shows the slightest remorse at having abused a friend who was also a benefactor or indignation at the murder of an innocent child for the sake of the cunning plot. Manipulation is an art enhancing the standing of these heroes.

As it happens, this type of manipulation was not only applied to the management of human relations, but also corresponded to an artistic effect. As such, it played a role in the aesthetic ideas of the Chinese. In calligraphy, painting, and poetry as well, the efficacy of disposition is crucial and we must recognize its role to understand the full potential of this Chinese way of representing reality. Of course, we need not seek some kind of artistic justification (as though there could possibly be one) for what we as Westerners reasonably (from our perspective) regard as an unacceptable factor of political oppression in China. Instead, we must broaden our investigation because the only hope we have of grasping the coherence of a culture is by investigating it in its totality. We must, then, pursue our theme, tracking it through every domain, from that of the manipulation of military strategy to the most disinterested of creative artistic processes.

Part Two

CHAPTER FOUR

The Force of Form, the Effect of Genre

Absence of Mimesis: Art Conceived as the Actualization of Universal Dynamism

The dislocation of the empire (at the end of the second century A.D.) and the fragmentation of China over several centuries sped the collapse of the system of unified thought, at once cosmological, moral, and political, that had prevailed until then. Instead, it favored the emergence of an autonomous aesthetic mindset that had previously been buried in that system. The conditions that enabled the development of artistic criticism as a distinct line of thought emerged at last.

But from the start this mode of thought never conceived of artistic activity as the West initially did, that is, as *mimesis* (the reproduction or imitation of a particular kind of "nature" at some level more "ideal" or more "real," either more general or more specific, than nature is normally understood to be).[1] Rather, artistic activity was seen as a process of *actualization*, which produced a particular configuration of the dynamism inherent in reality. It operated and was revealed through the calligraphy of an ideogram, through a landscape painting, or a literary composition. The particular disposition that receives form can potentially express the universal dynamism. This potential must be maximally exploited: it lies in the tension that animates the various elements of an ideogram set down in calligraphy, in the force and movement of forms in a painting, in the effect created by a literary text. The ancient strategic model thus also serves as a basis for aesthetic theory; art too can be conceived in terms of *shi*, as a possible setup.

The Force of Form in Calligraphy

The transition between military art and the art of writing is explicit: "When they discussed calligraphy, the Ancients stressed the paramount importance of *shi*. . . . Calligraphy is a study that rests on the configuration [of ideograms]. Now, once there is a configuration, there is a potential stemming from that configuration.[a] Strategists ascribed the greatest importance to the positioning [of the troops on the battlefield] and to the potential [born of that disposition]: as soon as one obtains the advantage constituted by that potential [*shi*], one holds the key to success."[b2]

Kang Youwei
end of
19th century

The Chinese art of calligraphy can be considered a prime example of dynamism at work within a configuration because, in the case of each ideogram copied, a particular gesture is converted into a form, just as a particular form is equally converted into a gesture. In this schema the figure produced and the movement producing it are equivalent; one can speak of the *shi* of the brush that delineates the ideogram just as one speaks of the *shi* of the ideogram that it traces.[c] The same force is at work, apprehended at two separate stages or, as it were, in two different "states." Thus, *shi* can be defined overall as the *force* that runs through the *form* of the written character and animates it aesthetically.[3] "When *shi* comes, do not stop it; when it departs, do not hinder it," we are advised in a treatise believed to be one of the earliest on the theory of calligraphy.[4] On the one hand there is the "configuration" (of the various elements making up the strokes

Cai Yong
2nd century A.D.

76

in the ideogram), on the other, the "potential"; on the one hand, one "considers" the "form" of the character from the perspective of its appearance, on the other one "pursues" the *shi* through the lines traced, appreciating the effects of tension produced by the alternation of different strokes.[5] The "body" of the character is seen as evolving: "If the *shi* is harmonious, the body will be well balanced."[6] But the *shi* of the writing is simultaneously distinct from the overall body of characters, each of which is regarded as a particular written form: "One and the same *shi*, whatever the body [form] of the writing used."[d7] *Shi*, the determining factor in calligraphic art, thus serves to unify the strokes set down, however varied they may be.

Wang Yizhi
3rd century A.D.

Wei Heng
3rd century A.D.

However, it would be a mistake to believe that Chinese aesthetic thought developed through careful discrimination between terms, resorting to precise conceptualizations and definitions in the Greek, particularly Aristotelian, manner. Rather, the terms operate through networks of affinities, one constantly implying another through allusion. They interact more through contrast than in terms of the separate fields they denote. Instead of proceeding from preestablished, methodical distinctions (inevitably abstract and also very convenient), they frequently convey their meaning through the interplay of parallelisms and correlations made possible by their infinitely rich evocatory powers. Aesthetic phenomena are expressed more through a series of polarities than through concepts.[8] The *shi* of calligraphy can thus be likened to an ideogram's internal "skeleton," which provides the character's structural consistency, and it is thereby opposed to the enchanting grace of a mere flourish.[9] However, it may be equally opposed to the rigid and fixed structure essential to the nature of writing, and is absorbed in this sense into the delicate form of the line.[10] It is an in-between term, at times relating to the invisible, subjective, and cosmic energy pervading and operating through the

Yang Xin
3rd–4th
centuries A.D.

77

activity of calligraphy, at other times relating to the shape or form of the individual ideograms at the definitive stage when each is set down; in the latter case it tends to be fused with that particular configuration.[e]

But even when *shi* is simply understood as the configuration of a written character, it suggests the breath that lives in that character and that makes itself felt through it – here again, the oscillation between two poles. "In default of any other term bequeathed by the tradition,"[11] *shi* may be explained metaphorically as a leap, a soaring, a bound. For example, a particular specimen of writing on a seal is described as "stretching out its neck and contracting its wings, its *shi* aspiring to reach the clouds."[12] In general, it is *shi* that "gives life"[f13] and makes the slightest dot or stroke vibrate, as if we were reliving the moment of its execution.[14] *Shi* thus always enhances what would be mere empty representation without it, for *shi* gives depth to a representation and exceeds its concrete limitations by revealing, within the actualized static form, a dimension of perpetual, soaring flight. *Shi* is not only the internal energy from which that form has proceeded; it is also the effect of the tension this energy produces. The "form" is seized on in all its *propensity*, which means it should be seen not merely as "form" but also as a continuing process.

But what is the concrete source of this effect of tension forever animating the various elements of the character in calligraphy? In other words, how can this character function efficaciously as a configuration? Zhang Huaiguan tells us that the first rule for handling a brush is that "*shi* must be achieved, both for dots and for strokes, through the creation of tension between top and bottom, lowering-lifting, separating-gathering together."[g15] The logic of the dynamism at work depends on contrast and correlation. Each element composing the configuration of the ideogram must either attract or repel another, either "turning to face another"

Wei Heng

Zhang Huaiguan
8th century

Jiang Kui
12th century

Zhang Huaiguan

78

or "turning its back on another."[h] A line at the top bending down-ward is complemented by one at the bottom curving upward; and the tip of the former implicitly prefigures and initiates the lat-ter. In similar fashion, one stroke turns heavily back on itself while another carries on into a free-flowing tip; here the ink is thicker, there thinner. Separation gives rise to closeness, opposi-tion to balance. Polarity engenders reciprocity and conversion. In this way the elements in the painted figure play off each other to an advantage, as if by "mutual reflection"[i16] allowing their common pulse to circulate freely among each other with no "bleeding" at any point. This produces the ideogram's *shi*, at once "vigorous in a male fashion and charming in a feminine way."[j17] The vari-ous elements in the configuration of the written character thus create a magnetic field of maximum intensity and perfect har-mony. The ideogram set out in calligraphy becomes a living sym-bol of the great process of the world, constantly maintaining its equilibrium at the center as a seat of plenitude, yet constantly dynamic because it is self-regulated.

Tension at the Heart of Configuration in Painting

This formula applies equally well to the other art of the brush: in painting as in writing, one must always strive to "obtain" or "achieve" *shi*, since it is easily "missed" or "lost."[k] The two pos-sibilities in these two common pairs of terms echo the ancient Chinese political concept of the efficacy of position, which one either occupies or abandons. When the term *shi* entered the domain of painting theory (an extension of calligraphy theory), so far as the depiction of people and horses was concerned the term still wavered between the interrelated meanings of "dispo-sition" and "impulse."[18] But with respect to the elements compos-ing a landscape, the term truly came into its own. For example, describing the mountain that provides the setting for a religious

79

Gu Kaizhi
4th century A.D.

scene (and here, for the first time, the setting matters more than the human subject), the artist shows he is sensitive to the effect produced by a narrow crest of rock snaking up through the surrounding crags: it creates a "dynamic configuration" (*shi*), thanks to its line "snaking and weaving like a dragon."[19] Facing this first peak, another rises proudly, a bare rock face that merges into a cinnabar escarpment, the foot of which plunges into a ravine. This escarpment must be painted in flaming red, Gu Kaizhi tells us, to heighten the dynamic configuration (*shi*) created by this dangerous precipice.[120] The lines of the painting that depict this vertiginous drop achieve the greatest possible tension. Similarly, the line that runs down to the other edge of the picture, where it then tails off, completes the composition by producing a carefully created effect of suspension.

The mountain is the central element in the Chinese aesthetics of landscape painting and is also the place par excellence for *shi*, for it allows the most diverse tensions to operate together at the heart of its configuration. When painting a mountain, an artist can exploit all the possibilities of height and distance: the pin-

Zhang Yanyuan
9th century

nacles that rise, sharp and straight, on the horizon produce the effect (*shi*) of the encrusted, comblike spine of a rhinoceros.[21]

Huang Gongwang
14th century

One need only add a trail of clouds or mist clinging to the side of one of its slopes to confer on the mountain an effect (*shi*) of measureless height;[m22] similarly, by simply blurring the lines a little, greater distance is imparted to the *shi* of the mountain.[23]

Da Chongguang
13th century

The painter can also exploit the possibilities of alternation and contrast. The curved flank of the mountain, now convex, now concave, "opens" and "closes," spreads out then folds in, making "the mountain's *shi*" "twist" and "undulate";[n] the peak rises, then falls, and the mountain "moves" as it stretches.[24] Like the shape of an ideogram, the mountain too is conceived of in all its propensity and the tension is heightened by the contrast between its slopes: one rises, another falls. Meanwhile the animation of a village is countered by expanses of solitude.

Similar contrasts can be found in the overall landscape where water complements mountains and vice versa.[25] Though their natures are fundamentally opposed, at the same time the qualities of the two elements discreetly interact: even as the mountain represents stability, it appears "to become animated and to move" through the diversity of its aspects; and even as it flows, water seems "to become compact" through the mass of its waves. To emphasize the *shi* of the water, it should be painted as contained by a deep gorge, rushing straight down or swirling around the rocks. Every drop of water is in motion, thus turning it into "living water." It should not be painted too "soft," for that would diminish its *shi*, or too "stiff," like a plank, or too "dry," like dead wood:[26] if done correctly, the force of the propensity imprinted in its lines will then make it seem to strive "to splash the walls."[o][27]

This quest to depict tension can be sensed in the other elements of the landscape as well. This is particularly the case with rocks, whose *shi* is conveyed by emphasizing their tendency to pile up at the foot of a mountain, "pressed one against another,"[p] as after a rock fall,[28] and in the trees, particularly the pines, in which we detect the same lofty aspiration of the mountain peak. A pine tree should also be painted in isolation, "dangerously" rearing its knotted trunk, like a rippling peak, "up to the Milky Way," while its lower branches droop toward the ground.[q][29] The same applies even to the light and supple willow, to which *shi* can be imparted simply by feathering the delicate tips of its branches.[30]

As with the calligraphic ideogram, the logic of this dynamism is one of contrast and reciprocity. The theme of the copse illustrates this best.[31] To confer *shi* on a copse, the most important principle is that of "irregularity," achieved by having the trees spread out in some places and not in others:[r] the branches should

Tang Zhiqui
17th century

Wang Zhideng
16th–17th
centuries

Gu Kaizhi

Jing Hao
10th century

Mo Shilong
16th century

Fang Xun
18th century

not extend from the trunk at even intervals, and they should inter-
lace sparsely in one place, with a single dead bough suspended
amid the trunks, but in another place more densely and bushily:
"It must be assessed with *shi* in mind, if it is to be successful."[s32]
Such irregularity is dynamic because it is produced by an alternation between straight lines and curved ones (the constant preference for curves, that of common tastes, becomes monotonous),
between what is intricate and what is more "coarse" and careless,
and between compact, closely crowded clumps and spaces con-
taining no more than a scattering of trees. The principle behind
all these contrasts is the opposition of emptiness and fullness, a
principle that is as central to Chinese aesthetics as it is essential
to their vision of the world: "To bring into play this opposition
between emptiness and fullness will be enough to achieve *shi*."[t]

Shitao
17th century

What must be done is group together pines, cedars, old acacias,
and old juniper trees in clumps of three or five, in such a way as
to emphasize their *shi*: "Then they will begin to dance with heroic
and warlike energy, some lowering their heads, others tossing
them aloft, now bending low, now stretching straight up, undulating yet balanced."[33] As with the strokes and dots that compose
an ideogram, here too the aesthetic configuration, whose operation is achieved by means of attraction, tension, and interchange,
is completely efficacious.

The Aesthetic Setup

We know that the history of Chinese aesthetics as a whole is an
evolution from the initial primary concern for external resemblance to a desire to transcend the purely "formal" representation of reality through a "spiritual communion" with it and finally
convey the "intimate resonance" that animates it. The effect of

Li Rihua
16th–17th centuries

tension characterized by *shi* occupies an intermediate stage in this
process. While a formal configuration ("round, flat, or square")

82

can be caught by a brush, the effect of tension imparted by the *shi* that imbues it, "through twisting or broken-off movements and by indicating tendency and direction," though possible to capture with a brush, cannot be rendered fully, for "it has to do with mental representation" and "something in it is bound to elude the brush."[34] The effect of tension imparted by *shi* is responsible for ensuring that the aesthetic process progresses from the merely figurative to the spiritual.

Even at the level of artistic method, the distinction can be seen to be fundamental to Chinese pictorial technique, for it is reflected in the different natures of ink and brush. While the ink "spreads out the configuration of the mountains and rivers," the brush "shows their different *shi* in turn"; at the heart of the landscape, "the ocean of ink surrounds and sustains" the line of the mountain painted by the brush, but this line instead "directs and leads."[35] The ink spreads out and fills the space, but the brush informs and imparts dynamism. Among the elements that make up a landscape, the tension imparted by *shi* can be seen in symbolic terms to possess an affinity with *wind*. Similarly diffused through forms and thereby animating them, it too is a physical reality, but an evanescent one manifested only in its effects.[36] The tension is all the more powerfully conveyed since it is never totally actualized: hence the value of the brush stroke that is all the more forceful when remaining inchoate, barely suggesting a line of eternal suspense.

Consider a frail skiff painted in the middle of an expanse of water. Because it is so far away, the sail sheet is not detectable; even so, "if one does not paint it at all, the representation will lack *shi*." The solution is to paint only the bottom corner and not show the precise spot at which the boatman's hand holds it, which the distance makes it impossible to see.[37] *Shi* thus creates its effect of tension at the exact boundary between the visible and

Shitao

Gong Xian
17th century

83

the invisible, where the explicit nature of the configuration becomes more richly charged with implicit meaning, emptiness
becomes allusive,[u38] and the finite and the infinite illuminate and
reinforce one another. *Shi* starts out as a painterly technique; but
it also and inevitably provokes emotion. By rendering form in an
effective way, it immediately conjures up a lifelike impression.
And the effect produced is of crucial importance, for *shi* is responsible for opening up that which is concrete to that which lies
beyond it, and for conveying through what is represented the sug-
gestion of something "beyond," an effect essential to art. Through
shi the visible configuration evokes the infinite: the world of
representation accedes to a spiritual dimension and, at the edge
furthest from the visible, gestures toward the invisible.

Literary Configuration and the Propensity for Effect

The kinship between calligraphy and painting is obvious in China.
But the common model provided by strategy can serve as a basis
for developing an analogy between the Chinese art of writing and
the more general art of literature. Just as for troops "there is no
constant disposition on the battlefield," for the ideograms rendered by calligraphy "there is no single way, always the same, of
actualizing their configuration"[v]: as with water and fire, there are
multiple potentialities stemming from their disposition (*shi*), and
these are "not determined once and for all."[w39] Literature benefits from a comparable variability. Because of the diversity of what
texts need to express, they are composed in different ways, in
each case producing the type of potentiality that stems as a literary effect from the particular form of the composition (*shi*).[x40]
It is up to the writer to determine (and exploit) this potentiality
most effectively.[y] A text should also be regarded as a particular
configuration (of words) that can be used to good effect, as seemingly demonstrated by one chapter of the Chinese tradition's finest

Yu Shinan
6th–7th centuries

Liu Xie
5th–6th centuries

84

work of literary thought, the *Wenxin diaolong*, whose exceptional profundity is only today being rediscovered, after more than a millennium of obscurity.

Let us consider the text to be a particular actualization, a literary configuration, and *shi* to be its propensity for effect. Various themes from strategy stress the "natural" character of such a propensity,[41] modeled after the tendency of a bolt projected by a crossbow to fly straight, or water confined to the bottom of a ravine to swirl about: the propensity for the text's effect emanates from its constitution just as a spherical body tends to roll and a cubic one remains still. The propensity can produce both good and bad effects, and in literature these are brought about by both content and form. From a positive perspective, someone taking the canonical texts as a model will "spontaneously" achieve a classical elegance; equally, a writer inspired by works of the imagination (the *Lisao*, as opposed to the *Shijing*) will "necessarily" produce the charm of the unexpected. Negatively, however, if the thoughts are put together superficially or make little impact, the text will lack "implicit richness," and if its style is overlabored or too succinct it will lack "rhetorical abundance." In the same way, water carried swiftly along makes no ripples, and a dead tree casts no shade.

Liu Xie, the Chinese theorist of poetics, shows us that the propensity that leads to effect does not merely stem of its own accord from the constitution of the text. It also intrinsically reflects that constitution, as he explains, drawing an analogy with painting. In painting, the association of different colors produces a particular picture (whether it is a horse or a dog that is represented); similarly, in literature, the interweaving of everything being expressed produces different propensities for effect (which may be elevated or vulgar). The result depends on the specificity of the style employed. Thus, two contrary but complementary principles

Liu Xie

Liu Xie

85

should guide the writer in managing this propensity for effect: on the one hand, he should combine the most diverse possibilities, so as to confer the maximum efficacy on the text;[z] on the other hand, he should respect the text's overall unity, so as to preserve its necessary homogeneity.[aa] For example, instead of ruling out "magnificence" to promote nothing but "elegance," the writer should exploit the potentials of both those contrary qualities, just like a general who skillfully combines head-on charges with attacks from the flank. At the same time, though, each text belongs to a certain genre, which leads to a definition of the literary genres *stricto sensu*, divided by their aims ("classical elegance," "limpidity of emotion," "precision in expression," etc.). This is the source of the table of twenty-two genres, classified according to six applicable literary criteria, five of which cover four genres each and one that includes only two. The most appropriate analogy for a text will thus, in the last analysis, be of a brocade fabric that, despite the interweaving of threads of the most varied colors, still retains in each case its own "basic texture."

Liu Xie also suggests, however, that it is quite possible to reverse this perspective and consider a text's propensity for effect in relation to the individual identity of the author rather than the genre to which it belongs. In other words, its propensity depends on his taste and his habits, both of which are personal. From this perspective, such propensity might be likened to the surplus of energy and vigor that can spread "beyond" the text, but that would mean interpreting the propensity for effect too exclusively in terms of the energy that is put into literary creation as breath (*qi*). There is an interesting distinction between *effect* and *force*: "The propensity that supports the text"[bb] may tend equally toward gentleness or its opposite, and its expression need not be vigorous and vehement to have *shi*. Nevertheless, and even more subtly, although propensity is distinct from force, it will still be manifested as a *tension*, which should be made to operate neither too strongly nor too obviously. Hence, the factor of tension needs to be balanced by a contrary factor of diffuse and harmonious *saturation* that permeates the tension and brings about relaxation and enjoyment.[cc]

Since a literary effect is supposed to be *natural*, in that it emanates from a *propensity*, it is not hard to imagine what an "artificial" literary effect would be like. Such an effect would not stem from a setup suited to the text and its particular genre, for the text would have been motivated by the decision to strive for novelty. It is normal to aim for originality, concludes Liu Xie, but this should not be confused with eccentricity. Originality comes from the successful use of the inherent potential of the work, but eccentricity results purely from contrariness, contradiction, and a quasi-mechanical subversion of whatever is correct and expected.[dd] It produces no more than a false "air of originality" with no effect at all. To cut corners, violence has been done to the shaping of the text instead of the text being left to work on its own.

Liu Xie

Difference from the Idea of Style

As we can see, our starting point of strategic thought also serves as a dominant model in the interpretation of literary composition, since literary composition is also conceived as a way of managing and exploiting natural *propensities* which stem from the different types of texts suited to the diverse *situations* in which an author finds himself, and because the aim is always to produce the maximum (artistic) effect. Now what must be understood is how to grasp this Chinese perspective in a specifically literary context, beginning from our own concepts.

Applied to the domain of literature, this theory of propensity inevitably overlaps with our Western notion of "style," combining two major concepts that have been formative at different times in our own tradition. When Chinese thought relates *shi* to literary *genre*, it seems reminiscent of the "teleological" attitude of classical rhetoric, which regards style as a matter of effectiveness in discourse. Equally, when Chinese thought relates *shi* to the personality of the author, it coincides with genetic theories of style that first became influential under romanticism. These replaced the teleological interpretation with a causal one in which style expressed a particular individual or a particular period and was viewed as the "transmutation of a humor," to borrow Roland Barthes's phrase. Under the influence of Western ideas, contemporary Chinese literary critics tend to equate the theorization of *shi* with a Chinese theory of "style" — while recognizing with some embarrassment that there are in fact other ideas in this fifth-century treatise, as well as in other works in the Chinese tradition, that likewise conjure the idea of "style."[42] Is this just a matter of the vagueness of Chinese concepts and the failings of polysemy? Or might it not rather reflect a general difference of perspective on how literature was conceived, one that does not allow us, in the last analysis, to match up their ideas and ours?

The fact is that our own conception of style proceeds from a philosophy of "form" (as testified by the influence in this domain of the Aristotelian school). In Antiquity, this is "the specific form of a work as shaped by its function" (Pierre Guiraud); in the modern period, it is "form without destination" (Barthes, who suggests that the actual "writing" is "the moral of this form").[43] The efficient form is here understood in its relation to the material content. However, in Chinese thought, as in calligraphy, for example, the "form" through which the literary *shi* is realized is that of a particular configuration which itself operates spontaneously to create an effect. Thus, what we customarily translate as "form" in Chinese texts of literary criticism is not the opposite

88

of "content" but the end product of the process of "actualiza-tion," *shi* being the potentiality characterizing that actualization.

Once again, the Chinese perspective is of an ongoing process taking place between the zone of the visible and the invisible. This process leads from the author's initial (affective, spiritual) situation to a formulation specific to it, as well as from the ten-sion implied by the words of the text to the limitless reactions of its readers. In these circumstances, the writer's main task is to "determine" the propensity of that process, endowing it with greater effectiveness so that it produces a maximum impact. Such a determination remains general and unifying despite its variabil-ity from case to case, and it depends upon a logic that he must know how to exploit. In literature as in painting, *shi* is the decisive factor: it *circulates*, bestowing a particular orientation on the com-position and breathing vitality into it. And in literature as in paint-ing, it is explicitly compared to wind and associated with it.[ee44]

Shi involves energy and effect: it animates the configuration of the written signs and makes that configuration effective, just as it operates in a painted landscape. Let us now move further backward, toward the source of that efficacy. Let us see how this source operates in nature.

CHAPTER FIVE

Lifelines across a Landscape

Lifelines in Geomancy

Let us first take another look at "nature." We will not consider it as an object of science, formulated through demonstration and reasoning by distinguishing "principle," "cause," and "elements." This has been our usual procedure since the early work of the Greeks – the procedure of "historical" humankind, in Heidegger's terms, a humankind that always heeds the unchanging call to respond to Being, and whose destiny this may be.[1] Rather, we should here perceive nature intuitively, through the sensibility of our bodies and their activity, as the single common principle within and outside us that operates throughout reality and explains how the world is animated and functions. Let us imagine a new "physics" and stop thinking of nature abstractly in terms of fundamental opposites (matter and form, potentiality and actuality, essence and accident) or the terms later substituted for the canonical formulations (for Aristotle's *Physics* certainly was the seminal work for Western philosophy, lurking always in the background and thus never really "thought through").[2] Let us instead experience "physics" as the single "breath at the origin of things, forever circulating," which flows through the whole of space, endlessly engendering all existing things, "deploying itself con-

Guo Pu
4th century A.D.

91

tinuously in the great process of the coming-to-be and transformation of the world" and "filling every individual species through
and through."[3]

This "vital breath" is an inherent animating energy that never
ceases circulating and concentrating itself is at the origin of all
reality, and by circulating, it bestows consistency on reality. Not
only my own being, as I experience it intuitively, but the entire
landscape that surrounds me as well, is continuously flooded by
this subterranean circulating energy. The form and individual
aspects of the landscape are, as it were, condensed from this endless animation. The most glorious sites will consequently be those
where it is most densely accumulated, where the circulation of
this breath is most intense, its transformations most profound.
These are the places where, through the variety and heightened
richness of forms, all the buried energy surfaces; here, through the
peaking of the harmonious tension between every element present, one can glimpse an invisible regulating power. In such places,
"spirituality" is more "alert," saturated, as it were, quickened.

This other kind of physics also has practical uses and can be
exploited to achieve happiness – but in an immediate rather than
a technical fashion:[4] for example, if one buries one's ancestors
in such a special place, their remains will logically be endowed
with greater powers of self-preservation, and, through the vitality that thus affects their entire line of descent, the favorable
influence of that burial place brings profit to their lineage, just as,
if one mulches the roots of a shrub, even the tips of its branches
will thrive. Similarly, by rooting one's dwelling here rather than
elsewhere, one locks into the very vitality of the world, taps the
energy of things more directly, and infallibly ensures for oneself
and one's descendants all possible wealth and prosperity.

But just as it permeates the human body, this vital breath trav-
erses the earth along particular tracks: in the language of geoman-

cers as it developed from the first century on, the term *shi* refers to certain "lifelines" detectable in the configuration of the terrain.[5] "The vital breath circulates along the lifelines (*shi*) of the terrain and is concentrated at the points where they come to an end."[a6] Since the breath of life is itself invisible, it is only by attentively studying the ramifications of these lines which run over the terrain that one can ascertain where the breath of life passes and where its vitality is concentrated, its energy condensed. This is at the point where the "lifelines" end, and the art of a geomancer thus resembles that of a physiognomist[7]: as it crosses fields, rocks, valleys, and hilltops, a lifeline is both a "vein" along which the breath, like blood, circulates, and the "skeletal structure" giving the relief of the terrain its solidity.[b] Or again, it is the "spinal column" that snakes in an uninterrupted line from one end of the horizon to the other, rising and falling, curving and winding, constantly changing. It follows no rigid route or preestablished model (recall that in strategy *shi* was compared with the moving flow of water). However, it structures all space, permeating it with its dynamic power. It can thus only be recognized from a distance, when one stands far away from it, in contrast to individual sites, which can only be spotted close up: "The lifelines (*shi*) are visible from a thousand feet away, the particular configurations of the terrain from a distance of one hundred feet."[c] Furthermore, although the spot to which *shi* leads forms a static and unchanging configuration, the lifeline, for its part, never stops "approaching" it, bringing from afar, in its constant movement, the beneficial influx of power that saturates and gives life to the spot.

Thus, space, and hence any landscape, was also conceived by the Chinese as a perpetual setup which puts to work the original vitality of nature. Everything in the landscape, down to the slightest hollow in the ground, is through its own particular disposi-

Guo Pu

93

tion endowed with a particular, ever-renewed propensity one should rely on and exploit. We have already encountered other configurations (on battlefields, in political power relations, in calligraphic ideograms, or in literary signs). Topographic configuration is similar but prior to them all. It constitutes a magnetic field which the geomancer explores with his compass, charged with a regular and functional potentiality that organizes it into the various networks through which efficiency winds its way. Lifelines are also energy lines.[8] It is not difficult to see why the Chinese aesthetics of landscape painting were directly affected by this physical intuition. Under the painter's brush, as in nature, "the aspects of mountains and water are born from the interaction of vital breath and the given layout to which that force imparts dynamism."[d9] In China, the purpose of painting is to rediscover the elemental and continuous course of the cosmic pulsation through the figurative representation of a landscape, which explains the particular orientation of the Chinese aesthetics of landscape painting. The concept of *shi* directly influences it both philosophically – the importance of standing back to understand better both the scene and the expression of the Invisible animating the scene through the lines is emphasized – and, later, technically, when the importance of the outlines and contours as well as the overall movement of the composition are stressed.

*Jing Hao
10th century*

The Effect of Stepping Back and Aesthetic Reduction

*Zong Bing
5th century*

The first of these ideas is obvious enough, but Chinese aesthetics transforms it into a mystical intuition. As one of the earliest treatises on painting points out, if you are too close to a landscape you will be unable to take in its contours; however, the farther you move from it, the more easily its immensity can be encompassed by the narrow perspective of the pupil. And if one spreads a fine piece of silk in front of the mountains to make them seem

94

far away, even the most imposing of them will retreat by one inch.[10] Similar advice was later offered on the painting of bamboos: One of the branches should be reflected onto a white wall by the light of the moon so that its "true form" might emerge.[11] The painter's words recall those of the geomancer: "Contemplating a landscape from afar, one grasps its lifelines (*shi*); considering it close up, one seizes its substance."[e] From close up, as one enjoys the detail, it is impossible to explore the vital tension of the painted lines' interplay as they rise up or stop short.[f] Only when they are seen all together and in contrast provided by distance, can these lines express their dynamism. Distance thus not only makes it possible to take in a vaster landscape but also renders it more accessible to contemplation, for distance, as it were, rids the landscape of all the weight of inessentials and restores it to the simple movement that gives it form and existence.

Guo Vi
11th century

Of course, the farther away one moves, the more reduced in scale the landscape seems. But far from marring the resemblance between the painting and the scene, reducing the size reveals more about it. In the Far East, as Rolf A. Stein has shown, miniaturization — from the art of "bonsai" to the art of creating gardens — guides the viewer to an initiation of understanding.[12] This coincides with the Buddhist idea that smallness is identical to largeness and that the customary proportions between things are completely illusory. Every microcosm can be as vast as the greatest macrocosm: "The whole world can be carried in a gourd, a single speck of dust contains Mount Sumeru."[13] The earliest treatises on the art of landscape painting were open to this Buddhist influence, which was novel at the time. They stress the reality of equivalence, which can be so enhancing to painting: "A three-inch long vertical stroke is the equivalent of a height of a thousand paces; ink spread horizontally over a few feet gives body to a distance of a hundred leagues."[14] The tiniest space can contain every-

Zong Bing

95

thing and, by exploiting this magical shortcut, in a stroke a painter transcends all the unreality of things. Not only does he restore the world to us in all its freshness and "brilliance," he also opens it up to the "spiritual" dimension[15] (particularly that embodied in Buddhist law[16]), a living reflection of which lies in all the aspects of the world one can "savor."

But what distinguishes this miniature world revealed by landscape painting from the world of geographical maps? Confusion between the two would seem to be even more likely given that the technique of drawing maps was already highly developed in China by the early first century A.D. and that, according to ancient etymology, the Chinese term designating the act of painting originally meant "to delimit with lines" (the ideogram in question "represented the four edges of a field drawn by means of a brush").[17]

Wang Wei
5th century Wang Wei writes: "What the Ancients meant by painting was not making a plan of cities and frontiers, distinguishing between different regions and prefectures, indicating mountains and other features of the relief, and painting in lakes and rivers."[18] For a map reduces scale merely for practical ends, whereas the process of reduction undertaken in painting has a richly symbolic purpose. (Wang Wei's reference to the Ancients is, of course, really a reference to his own time, when the art of landscape painting was only just emerging. The Ancients are brought in to lend his statement authority, a common practice in Chinese rhetoric.)

Wang Wei We are told that the painter's art, thus distanced from objective map making, is, surprisingly enough, closer to writing. Not only is it akin to ideographic writing through the material means of its production and the various elements – lines and dots – that give it visible form, but it is also close to the earliest and most sacred writing, the series of hexagrams that were sufficient to account for the whole mystery of becoming, merely through the alternation of continuous and discontinuous lines. For one thing, picture writing is expressive: "With a rising stroke, Mount Hua is suggested; with a short, hooked one, you have a large nose!" (These two kinds of strokes, *po* and *wang*, are also used in calligraphy.) Furthermore, simply by tracing a line, picture writing can also give form to the "Great Void," and the incessant renewal of the lines can evoke the endless transformation of things. This kind of writing was superior and truly spiritual, for through various forms it could express the Invisible.

To celebrate a painting by one of his friends, the poet Du Fu inevitably drew attention to the immensity of the landscape encompassed:

Du Fu
8th century

> From Lake Dongting, close to Baling [in southwestern China], to eastern Japan,
> The river, between its purple banks, reaches as far as the Milky Way

His praise of the painted landscape culminates with the following analytic observation:

> He excels at rendering the *shi* of the distance and nobody since Antiquity can equal him:
> To be able, in the space of one square foot, to evoke a landscape of ten thousand leagues!g[19]

Both the beginning and end of this poem emphasize the striking impression of perfect truth emanating from the work (e.g., the last, somewhat humorous line, in a style later consecrated by the *chan/zen* school of Buddhism: "This river, I wish I had scissors to snip a bit off!"). This is because only a representation of a landscape with a horizon opening out onto infinity can produce a truly "realistic" effect. For, as in reality, it is the circulation of

97

vital energy that stretches the landscape out to its edges and animates it, at its center, with movements that are familiar to us: the clouds swirl in the sky like dragons, and fishermen make their way back to the shore as the trees bend before gusts of wind. This breath that comes from afar floods the smallest detail at close quarters, and the painted landscape perfectly expresses it, seizing all its force lines in an elliptical foreshortening. Through the potentiality of *shi*, the world is reduced to what is essential, that which — whatever it may be named (and as a rule Chinese scholars are not particularly dogmatic) — constitutes its capacity for energy and vitality.

The saying "to contain within one square foot a *shi* of ten thousand leagues" subsequently became a kind of truism for Chinese painters,[20] for in China a painting is only really worthy of the name when it represents the totality of things. We must now consider the practical influence of that precept on Chinese art.

The Overall Movement of the Landscape

The importance placed on the lifelines in a landscape is reflected, in the painter's work, by the primacy of the general structural lines. These became an object of particular attention especially in the Ming and Qing periods, when landscape artists tended to paint grander compositions and felt a need to react against banally illustrative pictures full of minute detail, a temptation now regarded as "decadent" in relation to their art's true aim.

At the level of technique, which in Chinese painting is principally graphic, the primacy of *shi* corresponded to the priority given to "contour lines" over "wrinkles." The contour lines defined the major masses and provided the general structure of the painting, while the wrinkles, which were drawn within them or spread from them, cut up the contour lines and imparted detail, rendering the relief, texture, and luminosity of things. In Chinese terminology, which tended to be anatomical, the contour lines constituted the "skeleton" of the landscape, while the wrinkles represented the "muscles that moved it." Even if the wrinkles gradually encroached on the contour lines to the degree that the latter almost completely disappeared, those contour lines – like the lifelines weaving through the lay of the land and giving it life – still constituted the framework indispensable for form.[21] Thus, the procedure in painting a mountain is first to make its contours loom upward, playing on the contrasts to capture the underlying tension constituting its dimension of "meaning," and only then to move on to the wrinkles.[22] Once the *shi* of a mountain or a rock has been determined, "the aesthetic success of that mountain or rock is simultaneously also guaranteed."[23] The opposite procedure, to begin by drawing the rocks in minute detail in some corner of the space and eventually conveying, by "accumulation," the greater features of relief, is deplored.[24] We should therefore return to the precepts of the "Ancients," who could capture their subject in a few quick strokes: "In their great paintings, although many parts were minutely worked, the guiding principle was to achieve *shi*."[h25]

It is crucial to achieve *shi* because the reality of things only exists – and thus only manifests itself – in a totality, through the force of propensity that links its various elements as a whole. Zhao Zuo explains in detail that only if one grasps the overall movement (the *shi*) will the mountain, despite its uneven and sinuous relief, be able "to allow the breath to pass through its veins"; only then can each tree, despite their irregular and contrasting silhouettes, "express its own particular vitality"; only then will the rocks "be fascinatingly strange yet not bizarre," "endearing in their simplicity without being commonplace." Even the slopes, although they face different directions, will not give the impression of disorder.[26] Things will be complex but not confused, for

Tang Zhiqi
17th century

Fang Xun
18th century

Mo Shilong
16th century

Zhao Zuo
17th century

this general, overall movement corresponds to the internal "coherence" of reality and reproduces its peculiar "logic."[i] And what is true at the level of individual elements is even more so at the level of their arrangement. The arrangement depends on an overall logic operating through alternation and variation, so that the various elements play off each other in a reciprocal and continuous fashion. Even the bridges and hamlets, towers and belvederes, boats and carriages, people and their houses, at times shown clearly, at times hidden, should from the beginning be determined by this general order. Otherwise these elements will remain random and unconnected. In the last analysis, the imperative need for *shi* merges with the need for the unity of composition that is seen as a source of dynamism. Without that unity the picture will seem merely "patched together." Thanks to this unity, the whole painting can be taken in at a glance, "as in a single breath," while also lending itself to a slow, attentive reading, which helps one savor all its invisible harmony.

It is all the more difficult to grasp this overall movement constituted by the *shi* of the landscape, the tension peculiar to its configuration, since such movement is always unique and depends on the angle from which it is seen. Once again a comparison with the human body proves revealing. Regardless of a man's posture, whether he is standing upright, walking, sitting, or lying down, each part of his body, down to the smallest joint, will be in harmony with that posture. And to push this analogy to its limit — as Chinese critics love to do — rocks are like the skeleton of a mountain, forests are its clothes, grass its hair, waterways its arteries and veins, the clouds its air, mists its complexion, and temples, belvederes, bridges, and hamlets its jewels. From a total perspective, depending on the ramifications of the pinnacles that are its limbs, the mountain will stand straight, be bent, or lean.[27] When a man is lying down, his hand appears longer if it is dangling down,

Tang Dai
18th century

shorter if it is bent next to his body; and when standing upright in full daylight, he only has to shift one foot slightly to change his whole silhouette, along with the shadow it casts. The same goes for the overall movement of the mountain, depending on whether it is seen close up or from far away, from the front or from the side: all the valleys and ledges of a mountain seen from the front are bound to harmonize with the mountain's full-face physiognomy, "communicating," as they do, across one side of the landscape to the other. Among the larger features, one mountain peak always acts as a guiding principle to the whole composition — dominating, imposing, and proud — while the others "salute it with respect," as if "paying tribute to it"; among the smaller features, even the slightest bush or blade of grass "has the same lifeline running through it."[j] The painter must be inspired, must possess a particularly sensitive consciousness, so that he can "unite in spirit" with this landscape and, by exposing himself to it and communicating with it, grasp in a stroke how the whole scene functions in its powerfully general and delicately detailed way. If his faculties lack this exceptional plenitude, the "great *shi*" of the landscape will elude him and his painting will remain lifeless.

The general movement of the landscape, then, should not be confused with a laboriously constructed plan of it. It belongs to an earlier, subtler, and less apprehendable stage of creation, when the surging revelation of the landscape's configuration endowed the painting with the strength of the propensity that gave it life (i.e., animated its aesthetic effect). Only when the painter, provoked by the very body of the landscape and the divisions through which its life pulsates, has intuitively apprehended its general movement, can the structure of the painting be planned in a more intellectual and controlled operation, a now seemingly effortless task: "When one seizes on the general movement (*shi*), one can arrange everything as one will, every corner comes out well;[k] but

Da Chongguang
17th century

if one fails to apprehend it, try as one may to impose order, everything is unsuccessful."[28] The *shi*, the absolutely determining factor in the work, is advanced at a stage "of uncertainty, when it is hardly detectable,"[1] only materializing during the stage of "observation and measurement." If we are later able to verify its accuracy, we will trace it to the initial uncertainties characterizing any creative act. *Shi* lies not only at the line where the visible and the invisible meet but also at the secret, particular point where the success or failure of the painting is decided. In other words, *shi* is what every landscape painting depends on for its "life."

The Effect of Distance within the Poetic Space

The Chinese produced landscape poetry as well as landscape painting, and their landscape poems are inspired by this same spirit. Like the painter, the poet reduces what lies in the distance and concentrates space, retaining only its most deeply etched lineaments. For example, Wang Shizhen tells us, from a mountaintop he may describe a panorama vaster than the one he can actually see, or, while traveling, he may lay claim to a destination farther away than what he can actually reach. But that does not mean that the landscape described is fictitious or that he has no authentic firsthand experience of it. On the contrary, because he communicates intimately with it, the poet can intuitively apprehend the landscape in its entirety, approaching it through its distant ramifications, opening it up to the infinity and the breath that gives it life. We pass beyond the landscape; it is sublimated. By extending the horizon beyond all limits and bringing the unattainable Beyond within our range, the poet at a stroke transcends common, "kilometric," banally objective perception and succeeds in apprehending the world in that invisible Beyond.[29] Just as for a painter, geography is more than topographic reality, so too for the poet, the landscape is enriched by the tension of symbolism.

Wang Shizhen
17th century

"It is said that Wang Wei used to paint banana trees in the midst of the snow; it is the same with his poetry."[30] The tension produced by what is impossible leads to a wilder vision than that of the quotidian, a vision that embraces dreams. Wang Shizhen cites an example:

> In Jinjiang maples: how many times will they turn green?
> In Yanzhou five lakes: a single white mark!

He comments as follows:

> The poet cites a string of names, such as the town Lanling, the outskirts of Fuchun, the city of Shitou, although in reality these places are separated from one another by vast distances. In general, earlier poets and painters jotted down only what they apprehended through the emotion thereby inspired, which transcended the materiality of things.[m] Whoever tries to attain his object by setting it down precisely fails in that principle.[31]

Starting from the idea of *shi*, this comparison between painting and poetry may be carried even further:

Wang Fuzhi
17th century

> According to those who write about painting, "the space of one foot contains a *shi* of ten thousand leagues." It is worth paying attention to this term *shi*. For if one does not consider the question in terms of *shi*, the reduction of a space of ten thousand leagues to the dimension of one foot would merely result in producing the map of the world that one finds on the first page of geography books.[32]

Unlike the cartographic reduction of space, which is proportioned in a pedestrian manner, the aesthetic perception strives to apprehend space, whether pictorial or poetic, through the ten-

sions expressed by its lifelines. This is why the signs representing that space are endowed with a kind of potentiality stemming
from their disposition (the precise meaning of *shi* in this context);
it is this that gives them their artistic effect. What "space" means
here is not just the "landscape" traditionally evoked in a poem; it
is also the *poetic space* that such a text itself constitutes within its
own dimensions, through the language it uses to create its effect.
It is an ideal space – a space of language, of consciousness – but
it is permeated as well by an aspiration to apprehend totality, itself
pervaded by the dynamism of the far distance. Poetic writing
operates through symbolic concentration and reduction, as does
the language of painting. A quatrain, the briefest form of Chinese
poetry, is cited as a prime example:

> – My lord, where do you live?
> – Your servant lives in Hengtang.
> Boats pause, just long enough to ask a question...
> And what if they were both from the same village?

The philosopher tells us that "the breath animating the ink reaches
the infinite in every direction, and even in the blank spaces of the
text the meaning is omnipresent."[33] He means that, in this space
represented by the poem, the "breath" inspiring it and running
through it (just as it runs through all reality, making it exist)
endows every word in the text with a maximum (semiotic) potentiality by exploiting the distance between them (you/me; here/
there): the poem thus conveys first the immensity of distance that
separates and dilutes and then, suddenly, as two skiffs pass on the
river, the fleeting hope of a coincidence, a connection. Extreme
brevity of both space and time is achieved (the Chinese text consists of only four pentasyllabic lines, just the time that it takes to
ask a question). The scene itself and the feelings involved are

merely sketched but are thus all the more meaningful. Thus, this poem too is reduced to its lifelines. But such concentration tends to make it extend beyond the literal; it has the effect of flooding all the "blanks" in the text with meaning and endowing the language with an infinite range. The tension established between the characters is extreme, the potentiality of the meaning is at its maximum: the efficacy of the poem's configuration is fully in play.

This art of effective arrangement, or disposition, pervades the entire Chinese tradition, and its application across a wide range of cultural practices has been minutely cataloged.

CHAPTER SIX

Categories of Efficacious Dispositions

Technical Lists

There are lists of many different kinds of *shi*: the *shi* of the hand or the body, the *shi* of topography, the *shi* of the development of a poem. In the most general and yet concrete terms, what is art if not to capture and put to work all the efficacy possible through gesture and arrangement? And how better to assess precisely this possibility than by enumerating each example, one by one? The purpose of these lists is to record in each domain a typology of the various ways to group things, the ways recognized to be the most appropriate and experience has handed down from master to disciple, through the generations, as a secret of expertise. These lists, the fruit of long experience and practical in purpose, are mostly found hidden away in technological texts, handbooks, and collections of precepts. Many were drawn up under the great Tang Dynasty (seventh to tenth centuries), when the Chinese first began to think more precisely about the processes of creation[1] instead of concentrating exclusively on the moral and cosmic impact of its "spirit." These lists constitute an altogether new type of literature for us. Regardless of their importance for mastering an art and their information about the "genius" of Chinese culture, such technological codification has not been the object of much study. And whether it recorded anonymous, common expertise or, on the contrary, esoteric and jealously guarded teaching, the scholars who were their authors never rated these texts highly enough to sign them. So undervalued were they that some were in fact lost in China and were preserved only through works compiled by some illustrious monk or famous doctor at the time of the earliest Japanese contacts with the Chinese, when Chinese civilization was at its zenith and Japan's still in its infancy. The Japanese responsible for the compilations were anxious to pass on expertise in these arts to their own compatriots on their return.[2] These records, deemed either too rudimentary or too theoretical in China to be enshrined in works of literary merit, served outside China as an extremely useful and reliable guide for the novices of an emerging civilization. And these lists, however obsessed they may at first seem with minutiae, remain valuable today for their introduction to many Chinese skills.

Efficacious Dispositions of the Hand and Body

The foremost art in China is that of the brush; in this domain "efficacious dispositions" relate to its handling. Their primary concern was originally calligraphy, which in turn influenced the art of painting. "The Nine *Shi*," believed to be one of the earliest texts on the art of calligraphy, notes nine techniques for using the brush tip that are considered sufficient for every possible situation.[3] The art lies in (1) properly constructing the character, successfully balancing and offsetting the relations between its upper and lower halves; (2) twirling the tip of the brush in a rounded movement so as to avoid jagged angles; and (3) making an initial movement in the direction opposite that in which the brush must travel, both at the beginning and at the completion of the ideogram, thus concealing the mark made by the brush tip at the start of the stroke through the technique of the "hidden

Cai Yong
2nd century A.D.

tip." A similar technique is involved in (4) "hiding the head," in which one manipulates the brush to force the tip making contact with the paper to remain constantly at the center of the stroke, and (5) "protecting the tail," in which one completes the figure with a forceful backward flourish. These general methods of handling a brush are complemented by a number of other techniques: (6) a "hurried" movement (as when imprinting a flurry of "dots" or "breaking figures apart"; (7) a "lifting" movement, in which the tip makes a series of rapid, concentrated dots; (8) wielding the brush to impart a harshness to the line, as though it must overcome some resistance; and (9) a movement that executes horizontal strokes with the uninterrupted density of a "scaly carapace" or creates vertical lines that maintain a tension "like a horse that one is reining in." If an artist has learned these nine techniques, the treatise concludes, it should be possible, even without the aid of a master, to "be in harmony with the genius of the Ancients" and rise to the subtlest heights of perfection: this collection of artistic procedures is supposed to encompass the whole essence of the art.

Skillful handling of a brush was matched by the skillful fingering of stringed instruments. In China, the lute was as much an object of scholarly thought as was calligraphy. The idea of a *shi* of the hands may date to the seventh century, but not until much later (mainly under the Ming) do we find among the manuals a table demonstrating the various positions of the hands.[4] They are individually explained (sixteen for each hand), with the aid of a sketch showing the positioning of the fingers in each case and a detailed description of the fingering beneath. Opposite each sketch is another, which depicts the pose of an animal or even a natural landscape corresponding in each case to the particular example of fingering. Finally, a short poem, positioned beneath this second sketch and facing the explanation, renders allegorically the state of mind suited to the posture or landscape depicted. These postures or landscapes constitute, as it were, various novel and quaint examples of *shi*: the *shi* of "the crane singing in the shade of a pine tree," "the solitary duck winging its way around the mountain to rejoin its brothers," "the dragon clutching the clouds as it flies," "the praying mantis snatching up a grasshopper," "the spring cascading through a remote valley," or "the wind accompanying light clouds." Diagrams, rubrics, pictures, poems: every method – intellectual, visual, emotional – is employed and every approach – analytic, intuitive, methodical, suggestive – used to convey the character, both physical and spiritual, of each hand position.

What was traditionally known as "Chinese boxing" (*taiji quan*) and is still practiced either individually or in pairs in parks in contemporary China, is also presented as a sequence of positions. In this case the positions are assumed by the body as a whole, and not simply by the hands and wrists, and one's breathing is given paramount importance – since, as in the world at large, breath is what ensures the harmonious vitality of our whole being. This is a young "art" (writings on it date from no earlier than the nineteenth century), but the logic behind it, in sharp contrast to Western combat techniques, represents a rich cultural tradition. In the "long boxing" style, which is one of the most common, "thirteen *shi*" are usually listed, in groups of eight (parrying, pulling back, pressing forward, fending off, twisting, twisting downward, striking with the elbow, and striking with the shoulder), and five (advancing, retreating, moving to the right, moving to the left, and keeping in the middle).[5] The first series of movements is related to the eight trigrams. According to the *Book of Changes* (the ancient treatise on divination on which the Chinese representation of the universe is based), these eight trigrams constitute a systematic and complete set of figures based on the alternation of continuous and discontinuous lines; through them one can interpret the future. The second series is related to the "five phases" (water, fire, wood, metal, and earth) and represents in its conjunction and alternation the fundamental relations of all things in traditional Chinese physics.[6] In an exercise performed by two people (the "pushing of hands"), this series of *shi* is more precisely imagined as an externalization of the "inner force," itself a dynamic manifestation of the "true breath" and represented for practical purposes as being coiled like a "silk thread,"[a] ready to spiral up into space. The second series of *shi* constitutes the sequence of figures produced by this "uncoiling," beginning from the central breath and then going through the whole chain of postures.

Even the "Art of the Bedchamber" had been minutely codified since early times in terms of *shi*. A Chinese treatise written in the Tang period (but certainly reproducing older material) lists precisely thirty positions for coupling and claims thereby to cater to every possible case.[7] Each of these "thirty *shi*" is described symbolically, again using images borrowed from the world of animals and nature: "the unwinding of silk" and "the coiled dragon"; "fluttering butterflies" and "ducks flying upside down"; "the pine tree covering with its branches" and "bamboos facing the altar"; "the flight of gulls," "the frolicking of wild horses," and "the galloping charger." Despite their variety, nearly all these expressions refer verbally to a potential and a latent energy in each of the different positions adopted by the body. Incidentally, the term *shi*, used alone, had designated from early on a man's testicles: to castrate a man, a common punishment in ancient China, was to "cut off his *shi*."[b]

Positions that Best Embody the Efficacy of Movement

As a cultural phenomenon, the compiling of a list could be considered one of the most neutral acts. The task of assembling different compatible cases is merely one of tabulation, a concise and discreet operation hardly even deserving to be so named. Nonetheless, these lists are somewhat disconcerting. Certainly, there are some lists that are utterly uniform and regular. But there are others that seem to push heterogeneity beyond the limit of "reasonable" compatibility. The nine *shi* of calligraphy indiscriminately juxtapose general and particular cases: occasionally, a single case incorporates the two following ones (e.g., no. 3 incorporates 4 and 5), and some are analyzed according to their own particular logic (cf. nos. 1 and 2). Others are explained in terms of their exceptional use (cf. no. 6), while still others are expressed in purely metaphorical terms (cf. no. 9). This profusion of imaginary representations itself poses an intriguing and fascinating question: Should one view these imagistic references simply as an emblematic decoration, or should they be interpreted symbolically as actually providing a guide to understanding? Finally, what is strangest is that some of these lists form a united whole in and of themselves through their simple enumeration, without the notion of *shi* ever being specified (except by a number), commented on, or justified, even though the word forms the title of these lists and provides the logical basis of each series. It is as if the Chinese using the lists would have no need to derive a more abstract concept from the material instances, as if they had no need for any theory over and above what they could themselves instinctively and actively feel to be the pertinence of *shi* through the cases listed. For them, *shi* was a "practical" – indeed the most practical – term and one to be considered as such. *Shi* is self-evident, permeating whatever field one considers, and as soon as one is *exerting* oneself effectively and educating oneself in an apprenticeship, the very idea of explaining *shi* becomes pointless, even harmful to anyone using it. To consider doing so would only occur to someone uncommitted, *unconcerned* (from the perspective of his own particular logic), someone merely reading the text.

But for us this gives rise to an urgent question. We noted at the outset that we have no equivalent for *shi* in our language (by which I mean any "Western" language of the Indo-European family, which is related to both Greek and Sanskrit and thus certainly seems, vis-à-vis the Chinese language, to belong to a unified group). When translators do gloss *shi*, they render it indiscriminately as "postures" ("positions") or "movements." But actually both "postures" and "movements" are simultaneously involved. On its own, "posture" seems inadequate because it implies immobility, however temporary: our notion of reason seems incapable of analyzing a disposition without petrifying it. But given that, in reality, one gesture follows into another, it is not possible to arbitrarily distinguish between one individual "position" and the movement that both stems from it and leads into it. For this reason the various *shi* in calligraphy are described apart from the purely graphic elements to which they correspond once the brush has done its work, for those graphic elements are by now visible and therefore static.[c8] It is also for this reason that handbooks on lute playing contain a technical and greatly detailed description of the fingering (according to Van Gulik, 150 to 200 examples are usually cited). This description is complemented by much shorter lists of instances of *shi* that affect not just the fingers but the hand as a whole,[d] and these capture as a whole the impulse and logic behind each movement necessary for a particular harmony. Significantly, Chinese musical notation does not indicate the sounds themselves with separate instructions as to their volume, pitch, and duration, as we do today, but simply the precise gesture required to produce them. These positions in movement (and of movement) defy thought cast in the mold of dichotomies. For us too, the only way to describe them is through metaphor, by resorting to a cinematographic technique, for instance, and envisaging these series of *shi* as so many "freeze frames." Alternatively, using the terms of graphic representation, one might liken them to "sections" made for a drawing of an object imagined as divided across planes; the series of *shi* could thus be thought of as so many different sections cut through a continuous movement. Each section reveals in itself a fixed plane, but one reads it (or would read it) as a "configuration" matching the dynamic force invested in it.

Another dimension must be considered (a different dimension in appearance only — as above — thanks to our Western incapacity to imagine two aspects of a single logic simultaneously): these dispositions are not only *dynamic* but also *strategic*. For these sets of *shi* represent not just any random slice of movement but those that most fully exploit the powers of this dynamism and that are the most potentially effective. Arrangement possesses its own potentiality, which it is precisely the task of art to capture. Each list of *shi* thus constitutes, as it were, a set of various ways to induce the efficacy to operate. For this reason, despite their amazing heterogeneity, these lists are generally presented as exhaustive and systematic wholes, marked by a particular number ("nine," "thirteen," etc.). The succession of positions in Chinese boxing, for example, can be broken down into many more movements than there are instances of *shi*, so any initiate to Chinese boxing learns to master a whole succession of fragments of movements that cannot be equated on a one-to-one basis with the various *shi* ("parrying," "pulling back," "pressing forward," etc.). Consequently, the series of *shi* that is actually named is that which most effectively puts into play oppositions and complementarities, continuity and alternation — just like the different phases of dynamism, with its peaks of plenitude and its stages that are both basic and transitory.

Symbolic description appears precisely at this point. The thirteen *shi* of Chinese boxing are explicitly associated with the eight trigrams (representing the eight cardinal and collateral points) and with the "five phases," and not purely because of the Chinese taste for analogy and the rhetorical tradition. Just as the figures in the *Book of Changes* relate to the future and the "phases" relate to "physics," those *shi* are considered to operate as veritable "diagrams" of the dynamism at work. In Chinese boxing, the essential goal is an increasingly perfect match between the gestures that translate movement and the internal movement of one's thought, a match that, as such, "creates" new states. At the same time, the reference to hexagrams, phases, and cardinal points gives these physical exercises their full cosmic dimension: when I push in this manner with my hands, I am pushing against the Invisible in its entirety.

The same point could be made concerning the bestiaries featured in other treatises. In the handbook on sex the role of the bestiary is not particularly metaphorical but exists to provide an ambiguous pleasure through emblems that are both naturalistic and beguiling.[9] However, the bestiary does seem more important when it comes to understanding the various *shi* of a hand on a lute. As we have seen in the case of landscape painting, what matters in each scene is the *overall movement*, which can only be grasped intuitively and in relation to the landscape as a whole, not in a concerted approach combining different perspectives from many different angles, but suddenly, all at once. An animal or scenic metaphor conveys the intrinsic unity of a melody by capturing our imagination and making us react directly to it.[10] Consider the example of the *shi* of "a famished bird pecking at the snow" (in which two notes are supposed to be produced on a single string in rapid succession);[11] the image of an emaciated crow perched on a bare tree or pecking at the snow in hope of finding something to eat is singularly evocative of that rapid, dry, fingertip touch, like a beak plucking at the string. And the nonchalant flick of a carp's tail (the image given when the index, middle, and third finger are to grip two strings at once, bearing first inward, then outward) conjures up just such a leisurely, wide sweep of the hand. Similarly, drawing on our inner sensitivity, we can imagine the *shi* of a sacred turtle emerging from the water (when seven notes are played on two strings: first two, then two pairs of two, more rapidly, and finally one, as the index and the middle fingers alternately pluck at the two strings). The *shi* of the turtle effortlessly evokes a brief but assured touch with a regular rhythm. Then there is the *shi* of the white butterfly fluttering at flower level (corresponding to a harmonic effect produced by the left hand, which, instead of putting pressure on the string, touches it lightly); it conveys better than any analysis "the floating sound" evoked. The corresponding poem runs as follows:

> White butterfly, at flower level:
> Light wings, delicate flowers.
> It wishes to leave but does not,
> It lingers but does not stay:
> It is my inspiration
> To describe
> The light touch of fingers.

Not only does this bestiary evoke subtly and sensitively the particular gesture; through the code of nature, it also represents that gesture to us at a stage of absolute perfection that could never be learned methodically and deliberately, a stage at which the positioning is harmonious, the dynamism pure, and the efficacy total, the ideal stage at which expertise is wedded to instinct and converted into spontaneity.

Strategic Dispositions in Poetry

But would it be equally possible to apply these terms of efficacious positioning to artistic procedures such as poetic creation,
which involve no gesture or physical movement but stem solely
from mental activity? The answer is that an exactly similar method
is employed for these practices as well. The poetic *shi* are also
represented to us by means of a most colorful imaginary bestiary.
Qi Ji, a late Tang period monk, lists ten poetic *shi*:[12] those of "the
lion whirling round, ready to spring," "the fierce tiger lying low
in the forest," "the cinnabar phoenix with a pearl in its beak,"
"the venomous dragon contemplating its tail," and so on. Under
each of these headings, a single couplet is cited as an example,
with no further explanation. For the last of these *shi*, that of "the
whale swallowing the vast ocean," the corresponding two lines
run as follows:

Qi Ji
9th–10th
centuries

> In my sleeve the sun and the moon are hidden,
> On the palm of my hand the entire universe fits!

In this case one certainly senses that an explanation for the
connection might be possible (on the basis of the Buddhist notion
mentioned earlier, i.e., that the immensity of the universe can
be captured in miniature). However, to attempt to analyze the
function of such an analogy more "objectively" might prove risky.
The "critical" decision to limit oneself to metaphor, ostensibly
forestalling any form of commentary, suggests a desire to break
away from discursive analysis and endless words, and a preference
for an internal, silent kind of intelligence. All but one of these ten
different cases are illustrated by a couplet of poetry (the exception may be an unintentional gap in the text or a deliberate, tan-
talizing omission). This self-sufficient system provides us with a
neat, almost perfect, little ten-sided figure. No doubt the teas-

ing author delighted in imagining his somewhat mystified readers wrestling with it. Fortunately, Wang Changling, the author
of another list of *strategic dispositions in poetry*, this one written more than a century earlier, resisted the temptation to be
so cryptic; his catalog is easier for us to learn from. In this list
we are not distracted by external examples of gesture and posture; the text itself says everything, and we need only interpret
it. It might be worth pausing to study it.[13] Seventeen *shi* are
listed below:

Wang Changling
8th century

Strategy (i.e., Strategic Disposition) 1: "Entering straight and fully
into the subject," as when, whatever the theme of the poem, it
is tackled directly, in the first line. The example provided is a
poem addressed to an absent friend, beginning: "That I am far
away from you we know full well . . ."

Strategy 2: "Entering into the subject by way of a general reflection," as when the first lines of the poem "consider the reason
for things" from a general perspective, and one reaches the main
point in the later lines (the third, fourth, and fifth). The example
given is a poem addressed to an uncle who is a high-ranking official: "Great sages can rise alone / When the opportunity arises,
they set up their plan / You, my uncle, have been endowed by
Heaven . . ." (The first two lines constitute a general reflection;
the subject of the poem is not tackled until the third line.)

Strategy 3: "When the specific subject is not tackled until the
second line, following a first line that is direct but unrelated."
In this case the first line "directly" (immediately) evokes a landscape or an event without linking it to the theme of the poem,
which is approached only in the next line. The example given is
that of a poem of the type "climbing up to ramparts and think-

ing of the past": "Forests and cold marshes into infinity / I climb up to the ramparts and think of the past..."

Strategies 4 and 5: The same as strategy 3, except that the initial theme continues through two or three lines, and only in the next line does one enter into the main subject. If the initial theme persists beyond this limit and runs to four lines or more, the poem risks disintegrating and being ruined.

Strategy 6: "Through an indirect entry, by way of an imagistic theme." The first lines "immediately" evoke a theme that itself relates metaphorically to the later development of the poem. For example, "In the blue a lonely cloud floats away / In the evening one has to return to the Mountain / The noble scholar poring over the Good / How long before he sees the Face of the Dragon?" (The lonely cloud of the first line symbolizes the solitary scholar of the third; the "Face of the Dragon" is clearly the emperor whom the poet hopes to interest in his own future. This case thus differs from the preceding three by the clearer metaphorical function of the initial theme.)

Strategy 7: "Through an enigmatic image." The metaphorical link in this case needs more interpretation. The example provided is that of lines for which the poet (the author of this list) himself supplies a commentary: "Grief at separation – Qin and Chu – so profound / From the depths of the river the autumn cloud rises." The author proceeds to tell us that the pain of separation is as deep as the regions of Qin and Chu are distant from one another, and the uncertainty of meeting again is comparable to the cloud rising into the sky, which finds itself blown about at the whim of the wind.

Strategy 8: "When the line following supports the line before it." If the sense is not expressed fully or clearly enough in one line, it is supported by means of the line that follows "so that the full meaning of the poem is still successfully conveyed." For example, "The fine rain – after the clouds – retreats/The mist – round the mountainsides – breaks up." (While this type of composition may seem common enough, it is much rarer in Chinese poetry, in which each line is usually a self-sufficient element.)

Strategy 9: "Through an inspired meeting of the world and one's emotions." The lines of poetry are produced by a sudden and spontaneous meeting between the emotion of the conscious mind (reacting as a sentient organ) and the realities of nature, which become clear through that catalyst. For example, "The seven strings sound clearly all around/And ten thousand trees purify this secret sound/Lo, the moon is whiter on the river/And its waters deeper." (The playing of the lute in the first line is supposed to evoke the emotion affecting the conscious mind and spreading out from it through the landscape; meanwhile the following lines describe how this whole landscape becomes sensitive to that emotion, is filled by it, and diffuses it.)

Strategy 10: "Through the implicit richness of the last line." According to one of the major precepts of Chinese poetry, the meaning must spread beyond the words instead of "being exhausted in them"; emotions must be evoked "in a pregnant way" and allusively, particularly when, after the penultimate line has suggested the poet's feelings, the last line rounds off the poem by evoking a landscape melting into those feelings. For example, "After drunkenness not another word/Fine rain over the whole landscape."

Strategy 11: "By expressing the meaning through combinations."
It is important that the feeling expressed by the poem should
emerge vividly from the text as a whole, so if one line is not fully
expressed, it must be assisted through a contrast in the line that
follows. For example, "The clouds pull back to the rocky cliffs –
and disappear/The moon illuminates the frosty forest: limpid"
(one line completes the other by expressing the opposite: on the
one hand the bad weather dissipates; on the other, luminosity
breaks through again and brightens).

Strategy 12: "By dividing a line in two." For example, "The sea is
pure, the moon is true." (In a way, this reverses the previous strategy: there, two lines were necessary for their combination to
express a single meaning, whereas here, a single line expresses two
relatively unconnected meanings, one after the other.)

Strategy 13: "Through a direct analogy in a single line." For example, "I think of you – the flow of the river." (This is remarkably
close to the famous French line, "Andromaque, je pense à vous! Ce
petit fleuve..." [Andromache, I think of you! This little river...].
However, the flow of the river in this case represents the thought
that links us constantly together.)

Strategy 14: "By [stressing] the cyclical course of things." "If you
evoke a feeling of affliction, then cut across it with an evocation
of destiny; if you describe society's taste for fame and favors, then
cut across that picture by appealing to the logic of nothingness"
(the second line stands in opposition to the preceding one and
lifts us to a more elevated view). No example is provided.

Strategy 15: "By penetrating the abstract meaning at the heart of
a landscape." Obviously, "a poem cannot continuously express

an abstract meaning," "so an abstract meaning should penetrate into the heart of the evocation of a landscape, to give it flavor." Abstract remarks evoking a state of mind must be concretely identified with a particular place and a particular visit there, and be harmoniously incorporated with them. For example, "Sometimes I become intoxicated by the woods and mountains/And drown in the meadows and the mulberry groves/The mists of the sophora plants gradually envelop the night/The moon — on the tower — is infinitely deep" (two lines of "abstract meaning" are followed by two evoking a complementary landscape).

Strategy 16: "By making the landscape penetrate to the heart of an abstract meaning." This case is the opposite of the previous one and complements it: a poem totally devoted to describing a landscape "would be equally insipid." Thus, after evoking a landscape, one should express the feeling it prompts, without either theme detracting from the other. For example, "The leaves of the mulberry tree fall upon the hamlets/The wild geese sing among the islets/When decline reaches its extreme point/Then I entrust myself to the supreme *Dao*." (Here, in contrast to the previous case, two lines evoking the landscape are followed by two expressing feeling.)

Strategy 17: "When the last line expresses an expectation." For example, "The flowers of the green cinnamon trees have not yet bloomed/In midriver, alone, I sound my lute." The poet provides his own commentary: at their flowering we shall meet again; today, with the flowers not yet in bloom, I am alone, waiting.

We need not dwell on the relative heterogeneity of this list. Some cases are accompanied by a commentary, others are not; some are illustrated by poems, one is not (although it would have been par-

ticularly interesting to have an example for it; see strategy 14).
It is less easy to accept the disparity between the various aspects
of poetic creation listed together here: the problem of the construction of a poem or a line, the question of imagery, reflections
on inspiration. Above all, a modern reader is surprised by the list's
incoherency.[14] It begins strategies 1–6 by addressing the first lines
of poems, and the final strategy (17) is devoted to the last line.
But already at strategy 10 the question of the last line has been
tackled, and the same problem of the "support" a line can provide for the preceding one seems to be tackled twice (strategies
8 and 11). Could such a list really reflect little more than desul-
tory, largely whimsical rumination?

The answer is by no means a foregone conclusion, for closer
inspection reveals discreet and subtle links beneath the apparent
disorder. Within the overall framework of the essential elements
linked in any poetic development, particularly the beginning and
the end, a logic of continuity leads us skillfully from one case to
the next: strategy 6 is conceived as a more metaphorical way to
introduce the subject than strategies 1–5; and strategy 7 is about
less transparent imagery than is strategy 6. Strategy 8 concerns
the advisability of a supporting line because it follows from strategy 7, which deals with a case whose explanation is deemed necessary; strategy 10 anticipates the way to end a poem, evoking the
subject from the perspective of the harmony between a landscape
and emotion, already considered in strategy 9. Then strategy 11
returns to the question of two complementary lines but with a
slightly different emphasis: now internal harmony is what counts,
a point to which the author returns in strategies 12–13 and even
in strategies 15 and 16.

It would be interesting to devote more time to analyzing this
modest exercise in establishing ramifications and implicit links,
the delicate art of moving from one point to another. But these

lists already demonstrate that we should recognize the existence of two different kinds of logic (one is reminded of the unusual "Chinese" lists "à la Borges" at the beginning of Foucault's *The Order of Things*). Chinese reasoning (for "reasoning" is certainly involved here, not incoherence and disorder) does not seem to proceed in the same way as "Western" reasoning ("Western" in the symbolic sense). The latter first seeks to adopt a commanding position that provides a theoretical perspective ordering all the material to be organized. This makes abstract thought about it possible, resulting in a vantage point from which one can usually derive some classificatory principle of homogeneity. Chinese reasoning, in contrast, seems to weave along horizontally, from one case to the next, via bridges and bifurcations, each case eventually leading to the next and merging into it. In contrast to Western logic, which is *panoramic*, Chinese logic is like that of a possible journey in stages that are linked together. The field of thought is not defined and contained a priori; it just unfolds progressively, from one stage to the next, becoming more fertile along the way. Furthermore, the path along which it unfolds does not exclude other possibilities – which may run alongside temporarily or intersect with it.[15] By the end of the journey, an experience has been lived through, a landscape has been sketched in. Not everything is visible and unequivocal, as in a Western picture; rather, the view unfolds like a Chinese scroll in which a path running up a mountainside (and thereby giving it consistency) appears at one point, then disappears around the hill, to reappear even further on.

So there is no evidence at all that the term *shi* is simply an empty label because it covers phenomena that, to us, seem far too disparate. Perhaps in reality we are still too bogged down in our own critical categories, too unaccustomed to considering poetic activity from this angle: that is, we are not prepared to take various "dispositions" as our point of departure or to think in terms of "propensity."

The Discursive Setup and Poetic "Depth"

Yet again, we are led to consider the poem as a setup. But now it is no longer simply a matter of a *semiotic* setup operating through symbolic concentration, as does a landscape in reduced scale. The general message conveyed by this list of seventeen *shi* is that the poetic text should be seen as a discursive setup not because of its spatial dimension, but its temporal and linear dimension. This stems from the various modes of development and internal linking used, and from the dynamic effects – of both contrast and harmony – that these produce, imparting life to the poem. The author of the list cited above frequently makes references to *shi* that support the above view. Jiaoran, writing on poetics a bit later, also makes such references. Admittedly, they are perhaps less explicit than we would deem necessary; however, we should remember that Chinese poetics relies on allusion rather than abstraction.

Jiaoran distinguishes between three different kinds of plagiarism:[16] "at the level of words," the kind most open to criticism (when one literally repeats an expression taken from an earlier poem); "at the level of meaning" (when one uses the same poetic theme, e.g., the first coolness to touch the autumn landscape, but varies the words), and "at the level of *shi*," the most delicate of the three (when one imitates a poetic theme for the sake of its internal disposition but changes its meaning). For example, taking as his model the famous couplet "The eye follows the wild geese / The hand strokes the five strings," one poet produced "The hand holds the carps / The eye follows the birds." The poetic management of the theme is similar (a contrast between the hand and the eye, between contact and vision, between proximity and dis-

Jiaoran
8th century

125

tance), but a different meaning is expressed. In the second poem, the misfortune of the captured carps is contrasted with the good fortune of the birds that are free, whereas in the first, the contemplation of the flight of the wild geese and the stroking of the strings bring the poet the same deep contentment. Similarly, the oldest Chinese anthology of poetry contains two poems whose opening lines run as follows:[17]

1. I gather, gather burdock
   But never fill even one basket.
2. Each morning I have gathered reeds
   But have not got even a handful.

The *shi* of these two couplets is identical, in each case contrasting the painstaking effort of gathering with the derisory result achieved. Yet, in the critic's opinion, the "inspiration" is different in that the emotional situations the two couplets refer to do not correspond.[e18] It is a subtle but pertinent distinction: the effect of the discursive setup can be dissociated from its symbolic meaning. As a result, *shi* becomes, *sui generis*, a separate factor in poetic textuality.[19]

However, for a deeper understanding of this particular concept of the nature of the poem, we should also consider certain influential features of the Chinese language. Chinese has particular characteristics due to its monosyllabic and isolating nature. It is an uninflected language (with neither conjugations nor declensions) and lacks derivatives. Chinese words stand like blocks of stone or posts, each uniformly independent, so that the meaning is determined by their paratactic relations (rather than by syntax); furthermore, their capacity for shorthand expression is peculiarly marked (somewhat like our own modern telegraphic style, to borrow Karlgren's comparison).[20] One must also consider the particular fact that the Chinese poetic tradition did not develop out of epic. This may account for its disinclination to expand into narrative or description, that is, to establish itself as discourse, as well as its bias against expansive, continuous sentences or phrases. Instead, its tendency is toward an opposite kind of effect produced by the briefest possible units (as we have already noted, a line of Chinese poetry in general forms a self-sufficient, end-stopped group of words, in the same way as a complete ideogram).

These features explain the importance that Chinese poetic writing logically places on the dispositional crafting of the text, that is, on the richness of the tension gradually linking all the various elements in the poem — from one line to the next, one couplet to the next, or even within a single line.

We can now understand why the Chinese critic Wang Changling considers that a great poet, one capable of "creating shi," must be up to "giving a new impetus to the feeling expressed by the poem"[f] in each line, or at least in each couplet. A poor poet, in contrast, is described as one producing a line that is "weaker" than the one it follows.[21] The art of calligraphy, to which Wang Changling refers, may serve as a model: just as the guiding principle of calligraphy is to create a combined relation of attraction and repulsion between the two complementary elements of a single ideogram (so that they both "turn to face each other" and "turn their backs on each other"), similarly the art of the poet is to introduce a relation of both affinity and contrast between two succeeding lines (which implies that these two poetic "elements" must be equally strong and consistent).[g] Consider the following well-known eight-line poem; it begins:[22]

Wang Changling

Du Fu
8th century

Long ago I heard of Lake Dongting,
Today I climb the tower of Yueyang.

Those two lines stand in opposition (long ago/now; the lake stretching out into the distance/the tower jutting into the sky), yet simultaneously collaborate (the tower of Yueyang stands on the edge of Lake Dongting: today the poet, from the top of the tower, contemplates the expanse of water of which he has been dreaming for so long). The same is true of the couplet that follows, one that more radically expresses the sense of the landscape:

> The lands of Wu and Chu — to the East and the South — are detached,
> Heaven and earth — day and night — floating.

The contrast between these two lines/elements is even richer: between horizontal and vertical, space and time, separation and reunion. At the same time the connections are even closer: the cardinal points in the first line, above and below in the second; dispersion in space in the one, synchrony in the other: the fundamental unity of the universe is conveyed. Even the next two lines of the poem, devoted to the evocation of "emotion" following the earlier evocation of "landscape," depend on the same effect:

> From family and friends not a single letter;
> Old and sick, a solitary skiff.

Separation creates one kind of tension — others/self, to have/to have not — that is offset by an opposite tension: the shared sense of overwhelming solitude. As one can see, the tension created by *shi* is here identified with effects of parallelism.[h23] But this is not just a rhetorical ornamentation of discourse. In Chinese poetry, Jiaoran it represents the actual process of creation.[24] The contradictory relation linking the adjacent elements of the poetic sequence is well conveyed by the following image: the startled wild goose flies away but twists its head back toward its companions.[25] There is both continuity and discontinuity here:[i] "At precisely the point where the next *shi* arises, the preceding *shi*, as it were, breaks off."[j] As is always the case in Chinese aesthetics and in China, it is in fact alternation (antagonism and correlation) that constitutes the principle according to which such a setup works. The following few lines, quoted out of context, are provided to illustrate this tension, so characteristic of the poetic *shi*:

> Floating or sinking, the *shi* are different:
> Our reunion, when will it take place?
> I long to lean on the southwest wind
> And journey afar — to enter your embrace.

Elsewhere, Jiaoran likens a discursive setup to a landscape contemplated from a mountaintop.[26] The relief contours mark out twists and turns, become entangled, and then stretch out, separately, one after another, always changing: now a solitary peak thrusts strongly upward, rock piled on rock, now a river flows peacefully for thousands of leagues, now follows the most uneven terrain imaginable. Images of the river's slow meander are followed by waterfalls: so many different dispositions, all interconnected, yet always in reaction to one another (and linked all the more firmly when reacting strongly). The poetic *shi* always consists in using these dispositions to impart the maximum energy and dynamism to the flow of the text.

The way the poem unfolds should not be considered as a secondary aspect of the creative process. It accompanies the movement of internal emotion and matches it, just as the poet's language matches his inspiration.[k][27] The flow of the text's linkages is, as it were, the perceptible manifestation of a hidden internal meaning, the source of poetry's foremost "profundities": "The fact that

Jiaoran

Jiaoran

129

a diffuse impression is everywhere present (like 'vapor' or 'condensation') is a result of the profundity arising from the way in which the text is set out."[28] Through the dynamism produced by this configuration, a wider meaning emerges from the theme and spreads like an aura, pervasive yet elusive. Or, one might say, it rises like a column of smoke – to infinity.[29] What both the Chinese and Westerners call the "poetic atmosphere" is for them created by *shi*.

Since a poem is based on the principle of alternation, it must be conceived all at once, from start to finish, as a continuous *variation*. It cannot be pieced together line by line ("like fish threaded on to a spit"). "A great poet is one whose *shi* is continually changing."[m30] In poetry, as in everything else, dynamism must be renewed, through internal contrasts and shifts from one pole to the other, in order to be continuous.

CHAPTER SEVEN

Dynamism Is Continuous

Common Evidence

A number of questions arise when we reflect on the arts in China. In terms of their basic underlying principle, to what extent can we really make distinctions between those "three jewels" of Chinese culture; calligraphy, painting, and poetry? (The difference in the media used in each is only relative, since they all resort to the intermediary of the brush.) Similarly, is there not, to a certain extent, a single common logic behind all these arts' creative techniques, a logic which makes possible the effect produced in each case? All three aim to express the unfathomable vitality of the Invisible (both inside and outside oneself) through the "actualization" of a perceptible "configuration" (either of painted marks or words). All three organize language according to the same principles of contrast and correlation. Furthermore, in each art the resulting dynamism stems from variation through alternation, and must be continuous. Is this due simply to a particular ideological attitude peculiar to the class of *literati*? The answer to that must be, no, for "Chinese boxing," a product of popular culture, expresses the same philosophy through the language of the body: its sole aim is to convey that same invisible breath through its gestures, and its continuity is construed as the uninterrupted and spiraling unfolding of contrasted movements. Only when there is a break in this circular continuity is one's opponent able to establish a hold and possibly emerge the winner. A single idea thus lies at the heart of each of these practices, the idea of an *energy* both fundamental and universal and based on a binary principle (the famous *yin* and *yang*) with seamless interaction between the terms (as in the great cosmic Process). This idea, logically enough, gives rise to the ultimate meaning of *shi* used as an aesthetic term: the power to promote the continuity of dynamism,[1] rendering it perceptible through that energy[a] and the semiotics of art.[b]

In fact it was this same concept that we found employed by theorists of military strategy at the beginning of this inquiry.[2] Since we cannot experience it on a day-to-day level, our external viewpoint helps us perceive the ubiquity of this coherence through our longer-term perspective and through the striking impact of cultural differences. Seen thus from outside, Chinese culture, despite its considerable historical mutations, gives an impression of unanimity (symbolized and idealized internally as the "Way" or the *Dao*). However, even as sinologists circle around this intuition of unanimity, they are forced continually to reconsider their evidence (always with the hunch that something even simpler, even more radical, continues to elude them). For although one is forcefully struck by this obvious coherence, as soon as one undertakes any "theoretical" commentary it turns out to be simultaneously too diffuse and too full of implications ever to be made totally explicit. As we read through this critical literature, its coherence is conveyed to us only through particular remarks of increasing subtlety that overlap from one domain to another, all reflecting one another across the different "arts," mirroring one another, supporting one another. So let us ponder those remarks again, with the goal of following them through to their fullest ramifications while remaining aware of the parallels between the various domains. Making the most of the perspectives provided by these tactics, we will perhaps succeed in illuminating the common underlying assumptions.

The Propensity for Linking: Calligraphy

The Chinese art of calligraphy provides a key example of dynamism *in operation*, as a coming-to-be, since its theoretical codification developed relatively early and since, above all, its linear nature made it an ideally direct and immediate means of registering the temporality of movement. (A calligrapher can never go back and touch up the lines already made by his brush.) Furthermore, writing exemplifies that dynamism at two levels: the level of the gestures creating the form as well as that of the form that thereby becomes legible on the paper. Just as an arrow released by a good archer is charged with a surplus of *shi*,[c] making it fly far and straight, so too, in the hands of a good calligrapher, the brush's movement is endowed with a surplus of *shi*, or potential, which enables it to continue onward in the most efficacious fashion.[3] The impulse deployed is communicated all the way through to the character, never faltering or grinding to a halt.[d4] Once the brush stroke is completed, that *dynamic continuity* remains forever active in the eyes of the beholder: each element anticipates the one that follows, and the latter is born in response to the former.[e5] The continuity is never strained, but always spontaneous. We know that, in Chinese boxing, the weight of the body should always be distributed unevenly between the two feet so that the body is constantly led, of its own accord, to carry through the execution of the necessary movement.[6] And in an ideogram painted by a calligrapher, a slight imbalance is similarly detectable in the brush stroke, so that the movement never comes to a complete halt, never becomes stiff or frozen, but always demands to

Zhang Huaiguan
7th century

133

be carried on: a horizontal bar is never exactly horizontal, especially if it is not the final element in the character; its slight upward curve or discreet downward flick betrays the tension expressed in the continuation of the stroke.

We have identified three important features: the brush stroke benefits from the spurt of energy leading up to it;[f7] the brush is impelled to move on; and a continuum is created through the apparent discontinuity of strokes and points. In all these ways a certain propensity is expressed by the art of writing, through the configuration of the calligraphic ideogram. For a better understanding of this, consider the art of writing at its most radical stage: "cursive" Chinese writing, which developed later than other styles, expresses this tendency toward dynamism in a particularly clear way in its firm emphasis on continuity — continuity not just between the successive elements in a single ideogram, but also between successive ideograms. Whereas "regular" writing, to which it is these days contrasted, generally uses the broken stroke produced by pausing slightly to lift the brush, cursive writing favors curves executed in a single movement.[8] The brush runs from the beginning of the page to the end, treating each ideogram elliptically and reducing its autonomy to the minimum. From beginning to end, there is barely time to lift the brush from the page, so great is the pull that leads it to continue the stroke. Cursive writing thus expresses par excellence the calligraphic *shi*. In regular writing, "once an ideogram is finished, the meaning that gives it life is completed," whereas in cursive writing, "even when the whole column of characters is completed, the impulse (*shi*) carries on beyond."[g9] This idea gave birth to the calligraphic tradition of "the single, continuous stroke," in which the power of *shi* is at its most developed:[h] "Even where the line is broken, the rhythmic surge is not cut off, and where the stroke is not interrupted at all, one and the same aspiration runs through

Jiang Kui
12th century

Zhang Huaiguan

from one column to the next."[10] The ideograms heading up the next column directly prolong those at the foot of the preceding one. The meaning and art of propensity could hardly be further developed.

However, we should not misunderstand the nature of this continuity. The occurrence of a sequence of several dozen words linked in an obvious, heavy-handed way could only be insipid, since it would be no more than a "threading together," devoid of all energy.[11] It is not so much the continuity of the brush stroke   Jiang Kui
that matters as the dynamism animating it. Here *alternation* comes in, since it is the driving force of this vitality. Ideograms linked in the surge of cursive writing symbolize so many different attitudes, a succession of contrasts: "like people who are here sitting down, there lying flat, there setting out on a trip; who now allow themselves to be carried along by the water's current, and now gallop along as fast as they can go; now pursue their lives gracefully to the sound of singing, and now beat their breasts and gesticulate in pain."[12] At one point the hand slows down, at another it speeds up, at one point the brush tip is "incisive," at another it is "blurred." This continual variation between opposites, one leading to another, each necessarily calling for the next to complement it, enables every successive stroke to attract in its wake the next line. Between two characters, where there is no dot or line in the writing, all that can be seen at the gap is "an attraction of lines"[i] (in modern Chinese, this technical term is also the imaginative designation for an electric current). In this way, "the dashes, the oblique strokes, the curves and the verticals, in all their twists and arabesques, are always determined by the propensity of the impulse of energy (*shi*)."[j][13] True calligraphic continuity is that of a line constantly acquiring new life as it oscillates between poles, in constant transformation.[14]

Bad imitations, whether of cursive or noncursive writing (imi-

Jiang Kui

tation of models was an essential part of the training of a calligrapher), confirm this idea. A poor pupil will reproduce the
external form of the characters from memory, but not the "rhythmic influx" running through them,[15] that is, the shared "pulse"
circulating through the elements of calligraphy just as it does
through the veins of our bodies and ensuring the continuous course
of the line by enabling the necessary metabolic exchanges. Without this "pulse," the various elements copied by the pupil are
inevitably isolated and "dispersed" – membra disjecta – lacking
anything to link them from within. The interdependence and correlation essential to the flowing line of genuine writing are absent.
What is lacking is the shi factor, the propensity of the particular
impulse that give the model its dynamic continuity and capacity
for renewal when combined with the calligrapher's flash of inspiration and the tonality of the text in calligraphy. Those qualities
continue to make all the features of the calligraphy vibrate in uni-
son before our eyes and to our infinite delight.

The Propensity for Linking: Painting

Shen Zongqian
18th century

Da Chongguang
17th century

Chinese painting lends itself to a similar analysis. As we have seen,
one of the foremost shi of calligraphy consists in making an initial movement in the opposite direction from that intended, thus
conferring greater vigor on the brush stroke (first moving the tip
upward if one wants it to travel downward or to the right if one
wants it then to move to the left). The same applies to painting:[16]
if one is about to move the brush upward on the paper, one should
begin by "creating shi" by moving it downward (and vice versa);[k]
similarly, if one is about to sketch a tenuous line, one should start
it off with a heavy stroke (and vice versa). If one wants the silhouette of the mountain to give the impression that it is turning
as it rises and falls, one must each time move "in the opposite
direction to the mountain's propensity,"[l] both in the hollows and

on the humps, and then it will begin to "turn."[17] This also applies
to the general composition: if it is to be dense and deep in one
place, let it be loose and dispersed in another; and if it is to be
flat and calm further on, it should begin abruptly and tensely.
Similarly, the full should be anticipated by the empty and vice
versa.[18] As in calligraphy, it is necessary to emphasize a contrast
so that one term prepares for the other: not simply so that the one
throws the other into greater relief but also so that the former
necessarily cries out for the latter to follow it all the more forcefully
precisely because the balance needs to be restored and a harmonious arrangement maintained through compensation. Even the
famous "line made by a single stroke," characteristic of cursive
writing at its fullest development, is also to be found in painting –
not literally, of course, as though it were a matter of covering the
entire space with a single stroke, but in spirit and internally, as
in good calligraphy. Thus, the *shi* emanating from the vital breath
manages to permeate[m] everything painted – mountains and rivers, trees, rocks, and houses – imparting life to them in a single
burst of inspiration.[19]

    It is therefore understandable that treatises on painting, like
those on calligraphy, should emphasize the common "pulse" permeating the composition. (They also emphasize how important
it is that this breath should be circulating freely through one's
body at the preparatory stage, before one begins to paint or set
down the characters in calligraphy.) It should be remembered
that, according to Chinese "physics," every element in the landscape, from the great mountain ridges to the individual tree or
rock, owe their creation solely to the accumulation of cosmic
energy and are constantly flooded by that same energy. In a painting, as in a real landscape, *shi* is responsible for the fact that every
diverse aspect and ceaseless mutation, all of them "governed by
that breath" and connected through it, "manifest" individually

Shen Zongqian

*Fang Xun
18th century*

Shen Zongqian

137

their own "tendency to become animated."[n20] The art of painting thus consists simply in managing to depict that "other propensity" seen at work everywhere outside oneself "in the actualization of things,"[o] and this is done through "the internal propensity that confers its energy upon the brush." It is a reciprocal relation: *shi* is produced by the brush that is "subject to the invisible energy," while the dynamism stemming from the Invisible is communicated via the visible figures "thanks to the *shi* that guides it." Just as the art of calligraphy is an art of uninterrupted metamorphosis, the art of a Chinese painter lies in depicting reality in its unceasing process.

The mounting of paintings on scrolls illustrates this most cogently. The scroll "opens" and "closes" just like the cyclical process of all reality (an expert in Chinese boxing likewise closes the sequence of positions that had previously been "opened" by returning to his original position). In the case of a scroll that unrolls vertically, the "opening" begins at the bottom, "creating an impression of inexhaustible vitality"; peaks and clouds, sandbanks, and distant islands "close" at the top, "leading the whole representation to completion – with nothing that spills over."[21] From the perspective of the unfolding of the year, the bottom of the scroll is considered to correspond to the spring, the time of "soaring," the middle section of the scroll corresponds to summer, the season of "plenitude," and the top of the scroll, finally, corresponds to autumn and winter, the seasons of "gathering and withdrawal." Not only does the painted scroll as a whole thus unfold "naturally," mirroring the progressive unfolding of the year, but at each stage and even in the most minute details of the depiction that same alternation of *opening* and *closing* imparts a vital rhythm. (This is always on the model of the temporal cycle, in which not only do the seasons alternate but equally, on an increasingly reduced scale, so do the full moon and the new moon, the

Shen Zongqian

138

day and the night, and the inhalation and exhalation of breath.)
Each separate aspect of the representation is part of a general pattern of appearance followed by disappearance and a passing phase
in the manifestation of becoming. The scroll thus lends itself to
a linear reading, as does calligraphy: every depiction "is executed
so as to accord with whatever precedes it" and is completed so
as "to leave room for whatever follows."p Everything is involved
in an unfolding *process* and is thoroughly permeated by the *tendency* toward renewal.

The whole art of painting stems from this, and it too can be
expressed in terms of *shi*: at each moment of surge and "opening" one must simultaneously think of completion and "closure," Shen Zongqian
which enables the entire representation "to be well constructed
in every part" without anything being "dispersed or left out."[22]
Conversely, at each point of completion and "closure," one must
also think of surge and "opening"; this will make it possible for the
picture "to be at each instant rich with extra meaning and vitality," so that "the dynamism of the Invisible is never exhausted."
A beginning is never simply a beginning, and an end is never truly
an end: in Chinese one speaks not of "beginning and ending" but
of "ending-beginning."[23] Everything both opens and closes at the
same time, everything interacts "logically" and acts as a dynamic
transition; the propensity of what is set down on the paper thus,
sponte sua, emphasizes the internal coherence of reality.q

The Propensity for Linking: Poetry

Liu Xie offers us a fine image for the dynamism at work in a
literary text: when one sets down the brush at the end of a para- Liu Xie
graph, it is like feathering an oar while rowing.[24] The boat con- 5th–6th centuries
tinues to drift forward just as, at the completion of a passage, the
text continues to progress. A "surplus of *shi*" carries it forward,
leading to the point where it will link up with its own continua-

tion. A text exists not only through its "order" and "coherence," but also through its "flow" and "unfolding."[r25]

The conditions for such fluidity are primarily ensured by the melodic and rhythmic crafting of the text. Such melodic and rhythmic aspects are particularly crucial in Chinese since the language is tonal (and tonal counterpoint constitutes an essential element of prosody). Rhythm tends to take the place of syntax and directly aids comprehension. Here we return to the strategic aspect of *shi*: "sonorities well adapted to one another" are like round stones that tend to roll down from the top of a slope.[s26] By encouraging the interaction of sounds and tones in their particular arrangement, one creates a dynamic propensity for continuity which the principle of alternation makes it possible to exploit. A fine text is above all one in which the melodic interdependence seems to flow as if from a spring when the text is read aloud, never encountering the slightest obstacle in the form of either monotony or disharmony.[t27] The same applies to rhythm, even in prose. Long and short rhythms must be interspersed within the text, filling it with dynamism.[28] In general, whether at the level of sounds, tones, or rhythms, repetition is to be avoided, for it destroys internal tension, which springs from contrast, and drains the text of vitality. *Variation*, in contrast, is an excellent means of renewing that vitality, since it is fueled by the interaction of polar opposites (a "flat" tone is complemented by an "oblique" one, expansiveness by brevity, etc.), which is inexhaustible: through it a text is drawn into whatever follows, encouraged to "flow on and down."

The theme of rounded objects disposed to roll down a slope is used in connection not only with the harmonious crafting of a literary text but also with its discursive composition. In an eight-line poem, for example, it is the job of the second couplet to set the opening theme in motion and get the poem started in its

Liu Xie

Bunkyô hifuron

Wang Shizhen
17th century

development.[29] These are transitional lines that both "harmonize" with the opening line and encourage the full development of the dynamism that will benefit the following lines; now the poem only needs the third couplet to "turn" and the fourth to bring the poem to completion as it "closes." The second couplet, then, on which the entire poem hinges, will logically be judged by the power of its *shi*.[u] As an example, Wang Shizhen quotes the famous lines cited earlier:

> Long ago I heard of Lake Dongting,
> Today I climb the tower of Yueyang.
> The lands of Wu and Chu — to the East and the South — are
> detached,
> Heaven and Earth — day and night — floating!

We have already read these lines in groups of two to consider the power of contrast and correlation provided by the parallelism within each couplet. Let us now read them again in sequence to see how the second couplet dramatizes the elements of tension introduced by the first and carries them to their climax. The tension introduced between the horizontality of the lake and the verticality of the tower culminates in the tension between Heaven and Earth; the tension between an individual's past and present is raised to the more general dimension of the passage of Time. The effects of contrast and correlation are themselves developed fully: the immensity of the expanse of water both separates and joins, establishing a great distance between the cardinal points yet simultaneously mirroring the totality of the World. Between the first couplet and the second, the poem attains its maximum momentum by picking up the initial theme and then transcending it. Thereafter it need only develop thematically, by tackling first the subject of personal solitude, then that of current misfortunes.

It is important for the poem to succeed in fully developing its potential, both to assure its dynamism and to form a logical and coherent whole.

In common with painters and calligraphers, writers on poetics unanimously cite the vitality of the "breath" as the source of poetic *shi*'s ability to make the poem unfold in this manner. However, we may also wonder precisely how such a factor interacts with and promotes the meaning of the poem. If a writer merely "positions" words here and there without the conscious mind truly expressing itself, the body of the poem "will resemble a sickly donkey laden with a heavy burden": it will stumble and lack the necessary *shi* to move forward.[v30] This is bound to happen if the inner feelings of the person composing the poem have not been truly engaged and he is simply opting for some subject or another in an artificial manner, and then decorating it with rhetorical figures (that is, with many "comparisons, sophisticated expressions, and historical allusions"). Such an exercise is like trying to cleave a block of oak with a blunt axe: splinters of wood fly on every side, but can one ever reach the wood's inner fiber?[31]

In contrast, a truly poetic perspective, one in which effective language is really created, must be based on whatever the inner emotions are inclined to express. Then the poetic *shi*, the *dispositional propensity* born of that emotion, will become the moving factor in whatever is expressed. Wang Fuzhi makes the point laconically: "Make the emotional will-to-tell the principal (factor) and the *shi* the next factor." Like the "overall movement" that gives a painting life, this "dispositional propensity" is defined as the "internal coherence" subtle and elusive which must direct the composition of the poem.[w] Let us be more precise (although, with this kind of ultra-allusive formula, glossing is such a delicate business!): propensity is the invariably subtle and particular logic implied in whatever emerges as the poetic meaning, the logic that

Wang Fuzhi
17th century

Wang Fuzhi

142

serves to articulate this meaning with dynamism. If the poet relies on and promotes this propensity, the urge toward meaning acquires the strength to develop into language and achieve total expression. Such is the *shi* we have already considered at work in the discursive development of the poem, operating from one line to the next and from one couplet to the next. For the poem as a whole, it is this *shi* that succeeds at expressing the "initial emotion" inspiring the work. To do so, it deploys all the necessary language, moving through "alternation and variation," "turns and detours," "expansions and retractions," to reach "the perfect expression of meaning."[x] This is an eminently fruitful intuition (which might merit further reflection, if we can establish it as the cardinal concept we so sorely lack), because it transcends the opposition between content and form – an abstract and sterile disjunction – and thereby (i.e., by not distinguishing them) accounts for the concrete creation of the poem. This creation stems from the propensity organically linking the poetic text in such a way that each new development reactivates its dynamism and, as it flows along, everything effectively propels it from one stage to the next.[32]

All this helps us understand why a cult of "pretty verses" was criticized in Chinese poetics. A "pretty verse" is like a "pretty move" in the game of *go*.[33] The effect it produces may seem sensational, yet good players are wary of such moves, preferring a game in which the moves are prepared in advance and thus more effective even if (or precisely because) they pass unnoticed at the time. In poetry too, the trouble with a pretty line is that it may disrupt the fabric of the poem, bringing profit only to itself instead of harmonizing with the text as a whole and promoting its continuity. For the same reasons, writers on poetics reacted against the increasingly common practice in schools of dividing a text into separate sections, since a change in the rhyming scheme does

Wang Fuzhi

143

not necessarily imply a new development at the level of meaning and a text may take a new turn without implying a break. The art of the poets of Antiquity, on the contrary, resided in their *refraining* from "changing the theme and the rhyming scheme at the same point." Continuity was managed in the most discreet and natural fashion without the need to forge links.[34] Like calligraphy and painting, a poem constitutes a global and unified whole, which communicates through a single surge of internal energy. It is not like "a melon," which can be "divided into slices"; its continuity is intrinsic[35] and proves that a true interaction is taking place (between "emotion" and "landscape," words and meaning) – in other words, that a true *process* is in operation. All true poetry is – to borrow Paul Eluard's expression – "uninterrupted."

The Propensity for Linking: The Novel

Chinese literary criticism is largely allusive, and frequently described as "impressionistic," but occasionally it undertakes an extremely detailed analysis of how a text functions. In particular, a commentary will sometimes grasp the source of the *propensity for dynamism* at work in a passage. Occasionally an initial line, rich in the power of imagination, is enough to impart its burst of energy to the entire poem.[y36] Sometimes, when one verse takes up another, the first gives rise to the dynamism of the second and paves the way for it.[z37] In some cases, a simple comparison between the title of the poem and the ensuing text is revealing in this respect.[38] For instance, one very long title (not uncommon in Chinese poetry) describes the situation about to be evoked: a letter has just arrived from the poet's brother, telling of floods caused by torrential rain and of the local officials' distress (among them the brother); the poet responds with compassion. However, the poem itself picks up these themes in a different order. First, it evokes the floods caused by the rains, then the officials' anxi-

Jin Shengtan
17th century

ety, then the brother's letter, and finally, in the envoi, the poet's sympathy. Through this poetic order, the poem is able "to ripple along in successive waves, alternating between emptiness and fullness." Otherwise, it would inevitably "lack *shi*." Jin Shengtan, one of the most sensitive critics in the Chinese tradition, invites us to look more closely still: as we travel against the poem's current, we can observe the poet's art in imparting dynamism to the text as it unfolds: the letter has yet to be mentioned by the second couplet, but the poem does begin by indicating that "it has been learned..." which introduces and lends importance to the as-yet unmentioned letter. In the first couplet there is no mention of the news of the river flooding, but the poem opens with a description of the landscape submerged by waves, which anticipates and highlights the theme of the flooding that follows. It is only after having evoked the distress of the local officials that "the tip of the brush," twisting slightly, as in the art of calligraphy, eventually mentions the letter received two days earlier. Jin Shengtan concludes by pointing out that, without such skillful variation, the poem would be nothing but a "smoothly spread drape," "fixed in rigidity." But through the "rippling" imparted by these successive folds that produce a varied rhythm through their alternation, the reader is able to inject his own breath onto the fabric of the poem as he recites it, and communicate with its vital rhythm.[39]

As might be expected, the longest poems pay the most attention to the various effects that contribute to the continuity of their dynamism.[40] Equally, in the romantic narratives, the "long" genre par excellence – especially in Chinese literature – this preoccupation is by no means incidental. For what is the art of narration if not to produce maximum tension between what comes first in the narrative and what follows? A reading of the famous *Water Margin* with its parallel commentary, again by Jin Shengtan,   Jin Shengtan

145

provides a number of examples. Jin Shengtan asks that we note, for instance, how the author succeeds in "creating *shi*" by engineering the following reversal:[41] two characters face each other with their weapons, each ready to launch an attack, when one of them believes he recognizes his opponent's voice and a recognition scene ensues. This twist in the tale brings into play both an opposition (between ardent aggression and friendship based on deep respect) and a correlation (since this scene echoes an earlier meeting and seals their friendship, the subsequent course of which is then tracked). The novelist thus uses two contradictory methods to confer dynamism on his account: on the one hand, he prepares the narrative in advance for the coming development "by introducing into it the *shi* of a drawn bow or a horse ready to leap forward."[aa42] On the other hand, he provokes surprise when "the *shi* of the brush is suddenly suspended," making possible the most abrupt break from the immediately preceding scene.[bb43]

Jin Shengtan

To strengthen the dynamic link between this episode and later developments, the novelist creates expectation through the effect (*shi*) of "the extreme sinuosity of the narrative thread"[cc44] or even through simple repetition.[dd45] For example, one of the heroes, who is penniless, enters an inn; trouble is clearly in the making. He orders wine, rice, and meat. And, as Jin Shengtan points out, the author makes sure to mention later on that the hero does indeed receive wine, rice, and meat. The effect of this discreet buildup gives the scene that follows extra dynamism (*shi*). A similar effect is produced when the novelist allows himself to interrupt the story at its most critical point with an "author's aside."[46] Conversely, to tighten the link between the present account and a previous episode, the novelist may set up an opposition between the two: a little phrase to underline the contrast is all that is necessary to set off the later development.[47] A whole series of diverse images, drawn from the Chinese tradition's rich catalog of metaphors, is used to express this *tension of imminence* (or suspense) made possible by the *shi* of a novel: "like a strange mountaintop floating up before us,"[48] "like a dish of marbles tossed into the air,"[49] "like rain that drives down from the mountain or wind that fills a tower,"[50] "like the heavens collapsing and the earth crumbling," "like the wind rising and the clouds massing,"[51] or, quite simply, "like a thoroughbred galloping downhill."[52] Suspense is heightened and the narrative is propelled forward.

Once again, variation through alternation is decisive, but in this context we see the art of reversal (or peripeteia), which ensures a renewal of dynamism. Most important, in the unfolding of the story the narrator's brush, like the calligrapher's, plays skillfully on continuity and discontinuity. A quarrel breaks out and the two involved are about to fight.[53] "First, let us drink," their host proposes, "and wait for the moon to rise." Goblets are passed around and the moon rises. At this point the host returns to the subject: "Well, gentlemen, what about this little fight?" A link, a pause, a return to the subject: as Jin Shengtan notes, "The *shi* of the brush rushes on in leaps and bounds." Throughout his narrative, the novelist is constantly either "reining it in" or "letting it go";[54] at one point the subject is treated more expansively, at another less so;[55] what is narrated first in one way is narrated later in the opposite fashion.[56] The story thus passes through a series of "highs and lows."[ee] Logically enough, it is when the novelist manages to make the thread of the story oscillate within a single scene that the tension linking everything is most taut — and the art of the narrative reaches its apex. For example, one of the heroes seeks revenge on his sister-in-law, who has caused the death of her husband after committing adultery. But, in the presence of all the terrified neighbors, he has also cast at his feet the old go-between who played a part in the deception. He seizes his sister-in-law to reproach her for her crime, but begins by insulting the old woman. Jin Shengtan notes that this "enjambment" between the two women produces an "extra measure of *shi*," which "gives the brush its drive."[57] The more successful the construction of the scene, the more the momentum is discreetly implanted in the slightest details as the text unfolds.

In general, regardless of the *œuvre* under consideration, the novelist's ability to "give rise to a certain momentum [i.e., more *shi*], which enhances the development that follows,"[ff] constitutes "an essential technique of composition."[58] In their general reflection on this art, Chinese theorists of the novel have always recognized two complementary rules. The first is the rule of "the clouds which cut across the chain of mountains, and the bridge that crosses the torrent."[59] In other words, the text of a novel must be both continuous and discontinuous: continuous (the bridge) so that the same inspiration can pass through it from beginning to end and discontinuous (the clouds) to avoid an excessively boring text. Just as in the manipulation of the series of hexagrams in divination, the text's *shi* will then have the capacity to transform the text by fully exploiting the potential of "the same" and "the other" through the technique of "inversion or reversal."[gg] The second rule is that of "the ripples that come after the waves, the light rain that follows a downpour."[60] Through the extra *shi* endowing the end of an episode, the effect carries over into the following one, "put into play," "reflected," and "carried along" by *shi*.

The rules of continuity and discontinuity are important in the novel for other reasons. For one, Chinese literary criticism of the novel discovered the problems peculiar to lengthy literary genres, above all that of retaining the reader's interest. For another, the Chinese novel, which developed later than other genres and, as elsewhere, was composed in the vernacular, only gained recognition from the *literati* by acquiescing to their critical theo-

Mao Zonggang
18th century

ries. It is no surprise, then, that the Chinese theory of the novel insisted on the importance of dynamic continuity: such continuity was reckoned to elevate the novel over historical narratives (which from the beginning comprised distinctly separate parts). It was also this continuity, thanks to the unifying drive of its inspiration (breath), that rescued the novel from the "obscenity" sometimes encountered in it, according to the prudish *literati*. The unfolding of the novel's story, even over many volumes, was to be conceived according to an intimate sequence of links comparable to those in an eight-line poem. Of course, it all came down to the idea of a common "pulse" and its "rhythmic influx," which was so important in calligraphy and painting. A single inspiration runs through the novel from beginning to end, so that "100 chapters are like one chapter" or "like one page."[61]

Even an art form developing so late (relative to the long history of Chinese civilization) and whose origins were so different (they are admittedly obscure but were certainly oral, popular, and connected with the spread of Buddhism) did not elude the common vision developed and imposed by an entire culture – the vision of a continuous process, linked together by rhythmic undulations. This very vision was already reflected in China's earliest imaginary representations, the symbol of the dragon.

CHAPTER EIGHT

Conclusion II: The Dragon Motif

The body of the dragon concentrates energy in its sinuous curves, and coils and uncoils to move along more quickly. It is a symbol of all the potential with which form can be charged, a potential that never ceases to be actualized. The dragon now lurks in watery depths, now streaks aloft to the highest heavens, and its very gait is a continuous undulation. It presents an image of energy constantly recharged through oscillation from one pole to the other. The dragon is a constantly evolving creature with no fixed form; it can never be immobilized or penned in, never grasped. It symbolizes a dynamism never visible in concrete form and thus unfathomable. Finally, merging with the clouds and the mists, the dragon's impetus makes the surrounding world vibrate: it is the very image of an energy that diffuses itself through space, intensifying its environment and enriching itself by that aura.

The dragon is one of China's richest symbols, and many of its most essential meanings have served to illustrate the importance attributed to *shi* in the creative process. Tension at the heart of a configuration, variation through alternation, inexhaustible transformation and animating power: all are aspects embodied by the dragon as it surges forward, and all are features of the method at work in Chinese aesthetic creation.

The Potential Invested in Form

Even before it comes to serve as a model for works of art, the dragon's weaving body surrounds us everywhere. It is the dragon we
see as we contemplate the continuous folds in the land and the
endless relief of the mountains.[a1] The undulations of this infinite
body are the "lifelines" (*shi*) in which cosmic energy never ceases
circulating, like breath coursing through its veins.[b] In the bends
of this body, where a downward slope curves upward, the geomancer perceives an accumulation of vitality, a point where beneficent influences are richest and from which they can best spread
out and prosper.

Guo Pu
4th century A.D.

The Chinese painter, anxious to tap into these cosmic influxes
by stressing the expression of the dynamism present in the landscape he depicts, also favors the theme of a sinuous mountain
ridge. Gu Kaizhi asks us to see how, under the effect of *shi*, the
ridge "curves and stretches out," rising from among the rocks
"like a dragon."[c2] He likewise expresses this tension at the heart
of his painting through the twisting trunk of a lone pine tree
which stretches toward the heavens: with its carapace of ancient
bark covered in lichen, it rears up its "dragon body" "in a convo-
luted movement," rising from the immensity of the void "to reach
the Milky Way."[d3] Two mistakes, then, are best avoided by anyone
wishing to render the proud energy of these trees: either concentrating solely on the interplay of curves, for this would reproduce
nothing but a tangle of sinuous bends totally lacking in energy,
or painting overly stiff lines that fail to undulate sufficiently, for
they would not convey an impression of animation.[4] But if the
curve of the tree condenses the latent energy of the uncoiling
to come, and the hint of a movement in one direction suggests
another movement in the opposite direction, then the sinuous
line of the tree trunk will thrust upward, as vigorous as a dragon's
body.[5] For the shape of a dragon, the simplest of all shapes, can

Gu Kaizhi
4th century A.D.

Jing Hao
10th century

Han Zhuo
12th century

be reduced to the line made by energy in movement. If the composition of a painting captures that line in a tree or landscape relief, it will quite naturally achieve maximum intensity.

Variation through Alternation

The dragon is at once *yin* within *yang* and *yang* within *yin*. Its body is constantly transformed but never exhausted: a finer embodiment of alternation as the driving force of continuity could not be imagined. It is thus no surprise that the capacity for uninterrupted energy that characterizes cursive writing is commonly contrasted with the balanced structure of regular writing and likened, in its *shi*, to the mobile body of the dragon. Its undulating line continues endlessly, highly charged and powerful. In a perpetual "to and fro,"[e6] it alternately brings into play the big and the small, the slow and the quick: "The *shi* of the shape set down has the air of a serpentine dragon: everything is seamlessly linked, first thrusting up, then sloping down, now rising, now falling."[f7] As with the dragon, only oscillation makes progress possible; energy is renewed through change. A "flat," "even" course would be contrary to this spontaneous reactivation of energy and would inevitably lead to discontinuity: "uniformity" is always "deadly."

Wang Xizhi
3rd century A.D.

As we have seen, the same goes for the writing of a story: only variation through alternation can guarantee its propensity to link everything together. For example, Jin Shengtan, commenting on the following passage, remarks that "the *shi* of the brush is marvelously sinuous and undulating" and compares it to "a dragon advancing in fury."[8] A dissolute monk descends from his monastery to the valley. As he goes along, he hears the ringing sound of metal being beaten. Famished and thirsty, he comes to the forge that is the source of the sounds of hammering. The door of the house alongside displays a sign for an inn. These few lines introduce a

Jin Shengtan
17th century

twofold development: the monk orders himself some weapons, then starts to get drunk. Jin Shengtan notes how the narrator begins by concentrating on the theme of the monk's gluttony, then "in a first switch," abandons that theme to introduce the forge from which the sound of hammering has already been heard; but before fully developing this second subject, he drops it and, in a second switch, reminds us incidentally of our protagonist's searing desire for a good meal. By coming together, the two themes mutually provoke and stimulate each other: each is "planted in advance," like seed "the fruits of which will need simply to be harvested later." By oscillating from one theme to the other, by transforming one theme into the other, these few opening lines enhance the narrative's forward impulse. This fact is borne out more generally by many forms of interjection and parenthesis in the fabric of the story.[9] They are introduced to prevent the narrative from becoming stiff and uniform and to help it to remain supple and animated. They are used to convey dynamism.

It was sometimes simpler to represent this dynamism of alternation symbolized in the shifting shape of the dragon by using the form of two dragons coupling. The theme of two dragons intertwined or shown head to tail is common in ancient Chinese iconography and here, as Jean-Pierre Diény points out, "collaboration," not "conflict," is most important in the symbolic relationship.[10] Jin Shengtan's meticulous commentary on the passage cited below illustrates this well.[11] After many misadventures, two friends are reunited, and the greeting of one of the heroes which recalls their respective circumstances after the moment of their separation, is fueled by a continuous equilibrium:

Brother, from the day that I left you after buying the saber, / I have not ceased to think sadly of your suffering (1). / When you were sentenced, / I had no means of coming to your aid (2). / I learned that

Jin Shengtan

you had been banished to Cangzhou / but I could find you nowhere in the neighborhood of that prefecture (3).

Five more sequences follow in which the theme of "the other" continues to be complemented by the theme of "self": "The *shi* of narrative," as used in literary composition, "is that of two intertwined dragons."[g] And when the two friends *are* reunited, it is as though "the two dragons suddenly become fused." The account unfolds under *proprio motu* through these two intertwined, oscillating bodies, with the dynamism constantly redirected from one moment to the next through alternation between the two poles. The reunion concluding the story was prepared for in advance; directed by that undulating force, the whole passage is forcefully self-propelled toward its *dénouement*.

Endless Transformation Results in Unseizability

Since it is constantly changing, a dragon has no fixed form and can never materialize in a permanent, definitive shape. Now you see it, now you don't, now it unfolds, now it coils up again: "As for its appearance, no one can control its variations,"[12] and it is therefore regarded as a divine being. As one ancient saying has it, the dragon is honored "because it cannot be taken alive":[13] Grasping it once and for all is as impossible as grasping the Way or *Dao* itself. Emerging from his memorable meeting with the old Daoist master Laozi, Confucius supposedly told his disciples: "Of the bird, what I know is that it can fly; of the fish, that it can swim; of the quadruped, that it can walk. An animal that walks can be caught in a net; one that swims can be caught with a line; one that flies can be caught with an arrow attached to a wire. But of the dragon, I can know nothing: supported by the wind and the clouds, it rises into the sky.... Today I have seen Laozi: he is like a dragon!"[14]

As we have seen, this ideal is precisely that of the military strategist. He constantly redeploys the army at his disposal, making it "now a dragon, now a snake" and "never using a fixed formation."[15] This makes it possible for him never to be where expected, never to lose the upper hand or be pinned down. Not only can the enemy never reach him, but it feels increasingly bewildered by the impact of this dynamism that constantly springs anew. It is likewise the ideal of the painter. When he depicts pine trees, "their *shi* is so varied that the aspect of all these transformations becomes unfathomable":[h16] in this dragonlike tree, the artist represents the infinite fertility of life. The same applies in poetry, especially long poems (which are relatively rare in classical Chinese poetry). As it undulates along, the poem unfolds in a process of constant variation that defies any prosaic interpretation by the reader, refuses reduction to a single, static theme, and remains elusive, as can be seen from the following example (more than 100 lines total) in which Du Fu retraces "the long march northward" that brought him back to his family after the great troubles that had just occurred in China:[17]

Han Zhuo

Du Fu
8th century

> From the top of the slope, I gaze at Fuzhou:
> The hills and valleys now emerge, now fall away.
> I have already reached the river bank
> While my servant is still above the treeline.
> The owls hoot in the paling mulberry trees,
> The shrews gesture from the edges of their burrows.
> At dead of night we cross a battlefield:
> The cold moon shines on whitened bones:
> Thousands of soldiers in Tongguan
> Wiped out – everything collapsed at a single blow!

The essence of Chinese poetry, and one of the ways it differs most from our own classical tradition, is that it is neither descriptive nor narrative. In the above example, only a subjective reaction is retained from what purports to be "an account of a return." What is registered is a continuous oscillation: the variation through alternation that is first glimpsed shaping the landscape, with its sequence of hills and valleys stretching as far as the eye can see, is repeated in the endlessly undulating themes: the transition from one man's impatience to another's slowness, from the natural serenity to human anguish, from the description of the landscape the poet passes through to the emotions it arouses in him, from the personal destiny represented by this solitary journey to the collective tragedy illustrated by the battlefield. The poem weaves its way between all these contrasts, but none ever arrests its course. According to Jin Shengtan, the poet remains ill at ease once home among his dear ones. Those "whitened bones" come to his mind again, reminding him in turn of the recent military disasters, and "as soon as this great political theme arises, the personal, family question is dropped altogether," only to reemerge later, of course. Jin Shengtan adds: "To see the *shi* of the brush weaving in this way, first in one direction, then in another, you would truly think it a dragon, in its supple and sinuous progress: impossible to lay your hand on it!"[i]

Jin Shengtan

This reflection, slipped between the lines, warrants further examination. For critics, the idea of a dragon poem contains a rich intuition about Chinese poetry. Since it never adopts a fixed form, the dragon remains forever fascinating and strange, always elusive, always the symbol of a limitless Beyond. The same goes for a poem that, as it unfolds, reacts constantly to its own words, never remains uniform, never settles down. A poem never limits itself to a single theme, so as soon as the reader's attention begins to attach itself to one theme, it is turned aside and led further afield. In this way, the language of the poem eschews heaviness, avoids losing the reader's attention, and maintains its vigorous

157

impact by being constantly unpredictable. By these means, it achieves a flexibility that is adept at capturing and directing the constantly renewed rhythm of our emotional responses, thanks to its poetic twists and turns. Poetic discourse thus reveals itself as an ongoing process of transformation with the potential to reach constantly beyond itself. One might even define a poem as an instrument or means *to reach beyond*: through all the zigzags of its weaving course, each a passing streak of lightning, the poem eventually opens on to the ineffable, the formless, the infinite.

This effect of elusiveness is also important in the narrative of *The Water Margin*   a novel. Here is an example, again from *The Water Margin*: The outlaw band is heading for the marshes of the Liang Mountains. On their way, they are joined by new troops, with their arms and baggage. But as they are about to resume the journey together, their leader suddenly cries, "Halt! We cannot go off like this!" Jin Shengtan   The commentary then runs as follows:[18] "The *shi* of the text relating this journey is like a dragon plunging into the sea: at this point the author suddenly changes tack as he goes along, so the reader no longer knows where that scaly carapace is hidden." Elsewhere, as in the poem, Jin Shengtan comments: "The *shi* of the brush constantly takes possession, keeping us in a state of uncertainty."[19] In other words, at every turn the story takes off on its own. Its ability to undulate, arising from the reversals and restarts of its peripatetic course, is irrepressible. Swept along by such to-and-fro movement, the novel's narrative endlessly metamorphoses. Through this device, it gains new life at unexpected moments, constantly cheating all expectations. It always carries the reader along forcefully, since he is hooked to the thread of the story, bewitched by it, eyes glued to the ever-changing course of events carrying him from page to page, through every twist and turn, as it forges its path to adventure.

Dragon and Clouds: The Power of Animation

The Beyond of poetry and the magic of the novel permeate these works with their atmosphere. Similarly, in Chinese iconography, the dragon's body is frequently represented as emerging from the clouds, enveloped in mist. As the Legalists pointed out, with the prince's position in mind, it is because of those clouds' support that the dragon is able to soar up into the sky, in contrast to the miserable worm slithering along the ground. Conversely, when the dragon stirs, "shining clouds rise and congregate." The dragon can be fleetingly glimpsed through these cloud banks, its body shrouded in mystery. Through a single dynamic impulse, it animates the entire cosmic space with the inimitable tension of life.

When we examine cursive writing, the strong connection uniting the whole page with its undulating, urgent movement is something we experience almost physically and in its full intensity. Poems that celebrate this kind of calligraphy frequently combine clouds and dragons:

Jiaoran

> Around Mount Langfeng countless clouds arise,
> Startled dragons are galloping, rising only to fall![20]

Because it proceeds from a continuous inspiration, the line traced by the brush gives life to the entire space in which it is deployed, and constantly reactivates it. And the space itself cooperates in its deployment. In Chinese aesthetics, space is never limited a priori; there is no such thing as a "piece" or "corner" of space. Invariably "space" means cosmic space in its entirety: it actualizes itself from the depths of the void and so opens out onto infinity. This interaction is essential and detectable if we pay close attention: the theme of clouds drawn from every horizon to enfold the body of the dragon is designed to evoke that intensification of the space traversed by the flow of cursive writ-

159

ing. Meanwhile, the vaporous clouds intermingle with the tension of the forceful lines, fill the composition with air, and allow it to exhale its vitality.

The creation of *poetic space* may be similarly described, for it involves no more or less than opening up language to its full potential. According to Wang Fuzhi's already-cited theory, whoever "can attain *shi*" will be able, "through a continuous to and fro and contraction and expansion," to express every innermost aspiration without a single superfluous word: "The poem is like a vigorous dragon, always undulating, with whirling clouds surrounding it. The impression given is that of a live dragon, not a painted one."[21] The effect of the poem's ceaseless oscillation as it develops is the condensing of an aura, which makes the poem all the more striking, since this condensation allows its impact to radiate. The lines of the poem echo in the emptiness around them; the tension of the words increases as it liberates a whole host of imaginary representations and is, as it were, carried along by them. Through this constant striving for what lies beyond, for what is unsayable, the effect of the composition of the text is to produce a poetic "world."[22]

Wang Fuzhi
17th century

The "Void" and the "Beyond" Are Implied by the Tension in the Setup

As the reference to the dragon helps to show, the Chinese concept of effectiveness in the aesthetic domain is a far cry from that of a rigid, mechanical, and stereotyped operation. As in the field of strategy, it is dominated by ideas of efficacy and variability (i.e., efficacy through variation), and as in the domain of politics, it stresses the spontaneous nature of the effect produced as well as its inexhaustibility. In this way it can account for both the objective elements materially conditioning the process as well as the experience of "reaching further" that is involved and communicated. In a single process, it combines a meticulous technique and a dimension of ecstasy. For, as we have by now discovered, this accession to the Beyond can be brought about purely through the potential, or force of propensity, which the work derives from its organization.

The "infinite," "spiritual," and "divine" elements in all this are not tacked on by some idealist metaphysics of mind in reaction to the reductive perspective of an analysis of forms and procedures. Nor are those elements invoked to offer rhetorical support to vague and inflated rhapsodies on art or poetry. On the contrary, they are engendered by the internal tension within the work of art itself, just as they are integral to the cosmic dynamism. References to the Void or the Invisible are not introduced as spiritual compensation or even as lyrical effusion. On the contrary, they constitute a natural dimension of any aesthetic phenomenon, just as they do in every other process. Art does not "imitate" nature (as an object). Rather, by exploiting the actualizing relationship between the visible and the invisible, the empty and the full, it simply conveys the logic behind nature.

Oscillation through alternation, symbolized by the dragon, is the great regulatory principle of this dynamism. It is thus a constant motif not only in the aesthetic thought of the Chinese but indeed in all their thinking. Accordingly, the theme resurfaces in how the Chinese examine historical origins and, more generally, in their concept of the natural propensity of reality.

畫山起手法
山之輪廓先定然後皴之。今人從碎處積為大山。
最是病處古人運大軸只三四分合所以成章雖
其中細碎處甚多與皴法不一。要之取勢為主元
人論米高三家先得吾心。
古人云有筆有墨筆墨二字人多
不曉畫豈無筆墨哉但有輪廓而
無皴法。即謂之無筆有皴法而無
輕重向背即謂之無墨然輕重向
背卻又不在皴滿。而在輪廓初定
之下。如橫屋者欲施皴梢必先梭
梁棟梯如立即有巧公輸不能以
根柄異其承拱矣。

是之謂嶂蓋期脈絡連接左右
顧盼。即加至千重萬重不外此法。

FIGURE 1. To achieve *shi* as a principle in painting: to render a mountain, one should proceed not by piling one rock on another, progressively filling the whole space, but by first grasping the overall movement of the composition. (⬇ indicates the vertical column in which the word *shi* appears; • indicates the phrase in which the word *shi* appears).

Left panel (Figure 2):

畫石下筆法及層景取勢法

余所謂一字金針曰活者尤須
於三面未分一筆初下具有稜
落輝壯氣概一筆須有數頓使
之橋若游龍先用淡墨頻千
石萬石不外參伍其法參伍中
又有大小開小之別畫成
則墨宜精淡以分陰陽向背干
則右宜精淡如左既勾框再
以焦墨破之石廓如左勾廓
法不一石體固地而施諸家破
家之中一尺幅之內或齊卉於山或
帶於水甚夥其形總不外此一
二法則他無論此山乃全是
勾之中來畫勾廓者然於不
勾之中未嘗勾廓不具此法於層
層烘染處道出甚森嚴也

聚一
聚二
聚三
聚四
聚五

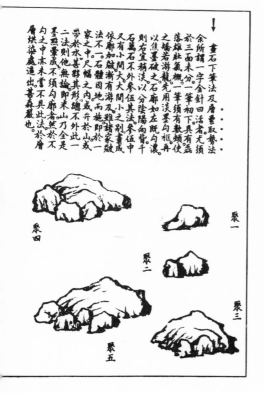

Right panel (Figure 3):

畫石起手當分三面法

觀人者必曰氣骨氣乃
地之骨而氣亦寓焉故謂
之曰雲根無氣之石則為
頑石。猶無氣之骨則為
朽骨。石之氣由文理而施於
人領士筆下乎是畫無氣
之石固不可。而畫有氣之
石即覓氣於無可提摹之
中。尤難乎其難非胸中練
有媧皇指上立有顯未未
可從事。而我今以萬無難
也。蓋石三面者即
地凹深凸淺条合陰陽
石之凹深凸淺以及
步伍高下務疊厚薄
勢以生氣。亦隨此雖
勢以生。請以及
一字金針相告。

FIGURE 2. *(left)* The art of achieving *shi* in a dynamic configuration by combining rocks (from one to five).

FIGURE 3. *(right)* Even in the painting of rocks, the vital energy emanates from and is expressed by the tension in the painted lines (*shi*).

163

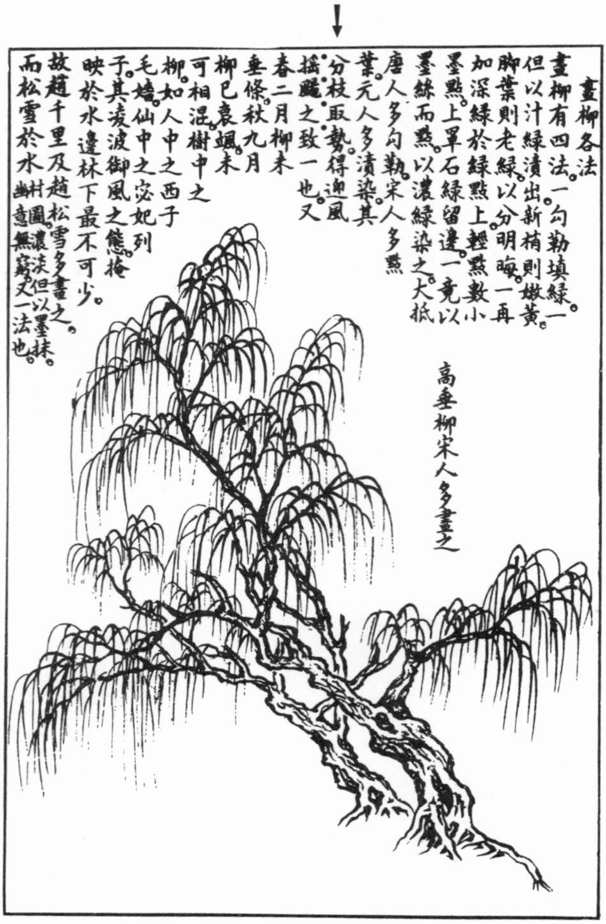
畫柳各法
畫柳有四法。一勾勒填綠。一但以汁綠漬出。新梢則嫩黃。脚葉則老綠。以分明晦。一再加深綠於綠點上。輕點數小墨點。上罩石綠留邊。一竟以墨綠而點。以濃綠染之。大抵唐人多勾勒。宋人多點葉。元人多漬染。其分枝取勢。得迎風搖颺之致一也。又春二月柳未垂條。秋九月柳已衰颯。未可相混。樹中之柳。如人中之西子毛嬙。仙中之宓妃列子。其凌波御風之態。掩映於水邊林下最不可少。故趙千里及趙松雪多畫之。而松雪於水村圖。濃淡但以墨抹。幽意無窮。又一法也。
高垂柳宋人多畫之

FIGURE 4. To achieve *shi* in the painting of willow trees, one need only separate the delicate branches waving in the wind to animate the composition.

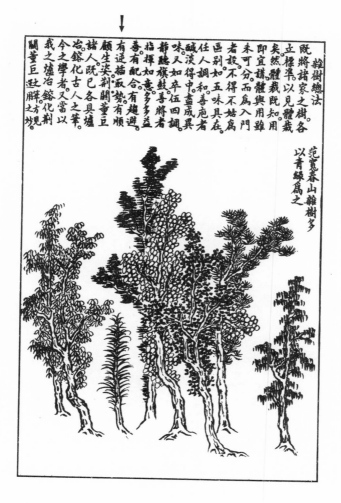

FIGURE 5. To achieve *shi* the painter Fan Kuan combines different species of trees in a copse. The tension in the configuration is a result of the irregularities and contrasts.

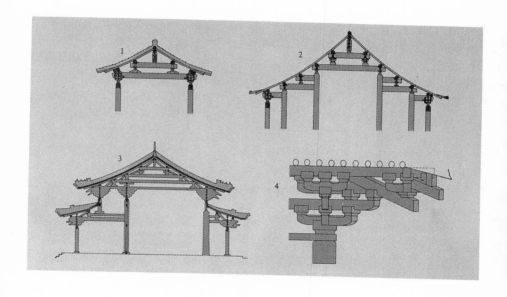

FIGURES 6 AND 7. In the traditional configuration (*shi*) of Far Eastern architecture, tension is expressed by the curve of a roof. Such a curve is not predetermined; rather it results from a particular calculation based on a number of variables in the particular building.

167

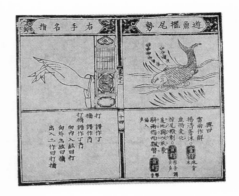

FIGURES 8 AND 9. These two plates from the *Great Treatise on Supreme Sound* illustrate the various "efficacious dispositions" (*shi*) of a hand on the strings of a lute. The sketches on the upper left represent each movement/position, with the commentary appearing below. The sketches on the upper right refer to the animal world, representing the instinctive perfection of the gesture. The short poems below allegorically express the desired state of mind. *Top:* the nonchalant flick of a carp's tail. *Bottom:* a white butterfly hovering at flower level.

開嶂鉤鎖法

凡人百骸未具鼻準先生。初下一筆
所謂正面山之鼻準是也偏體搆視。
更重顴骨。此處起伏爲一山之主。而
顴骨是也。此處起伏爲一山之主。而
氣脉連絡齊爲通幅之一樹一石皆
奉爲主。又有君相存焉故郭熙爲主
山欲聳拔欲偃蹇欲軒豁欲渾厚欲
雄豪而精神欲顧盼而嚴重上有蓋
下有承前有揖後有倚其法盡之矣。

脉
絡

正
面

FIGURE 10. The "lifelines" of the relief constitute a network of veins that
vitalize the cosmic pulse.

169

FIGURE 11. The dragon symbolizes tension within a configuration. "The pines of Li Yingqiu rise up with sinuous movements reminiscent of the coiling body of the dragon (or the flight of the phoenix)."

170

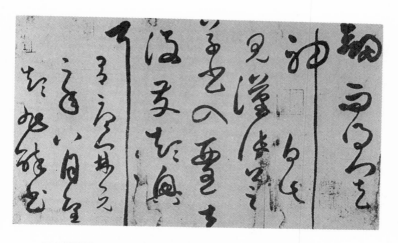

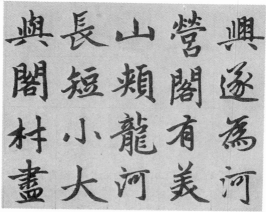

FIGURES 12 AND 13. A rich surge of energy guarantees the continuity of the dynamism characterizing cursive calligraphy (*top*, Zhang Xu's *Ziyantie*), in contrast to the more stable — and discontinuous — structure of regular writing (*bottom*, calligraphy by Zhao Mengfu).

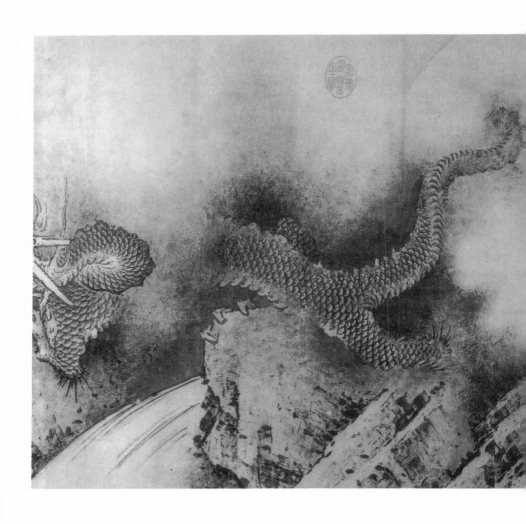

172

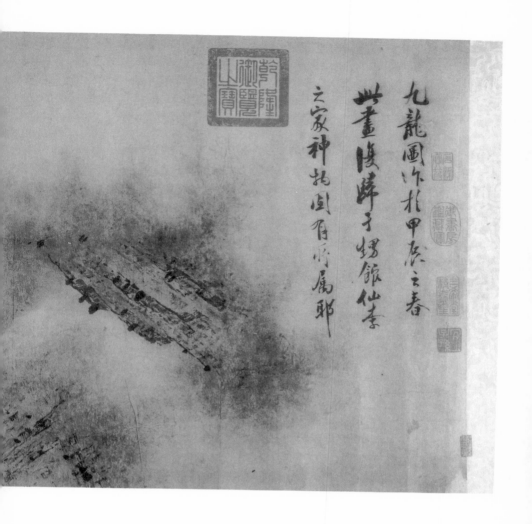

FIGURE 14. How Chinese aesthetics work through tension and atmosphere: The dragon's body appears fleetingly through the clouds, thus creating a more intense and animated space (whether calligraphic, poetic, etc.). Chen Rong, *The Nine Dragons*, 1244.

FIGURE 15. How Chinese aesthetics work: In the distance, the mountains are sketched in; in the foreground, a few roofs appear between the trees, and a fisherman's boat floats on the water. The tension created by the correlation between the lines and the washes, the visible and the invisible, fullness and emptiness, endows the landscape with a power to suggest more than the merely visible and opens it up to the life of the spirit. *Evening Light over a Fishing Village*, attributed to Muqi.

Part Three

CHAPTER NINE

Situation and Tendency in History

What Is a Historical Situation?

What is a historical situation and how can it be analyzed? This is the same fundamental problem we have been treating all along, but now transferred into the social domain. Our goal remains to conceive reality better, to move beyond the antinomy between stasis and movement, between an established state and a process of becoming. In other words, to reconcile somehow the immobilizing perspective promoted by any synchronic vision with a dynamic perspective that can accommodate the ongoing evolution and flow of events. While circumstances of a situation constitute a unique whole, they are all simultaneously undergoing change. We need to think of the system as an evolving one; then the process of history can also be seen, at every instant, as a setup with potential. In this context *shi* signifies both a particular situation and the tendency expressed through it and orienting it.[1]

Every situation constitutes in itself a direction. The Chinese thinkers of Antiquity, and in particular the theorists of authoritarianism, stressed the dual nature of this inherent tendency from the point of view of its *shi*. On the one hand, a historical situation — seen as a set of factors operating in a particular way — can be used to determine events objectively, since it allows one to constrain the initiative of individuals; on the other hand, every such situation is new and unprecedented in character, one particular moment in an evolving process. As such, it cannot be reduced to previous models; it leads the course of things constantly to take new turns and, arguably, favors modernity.

Anything that appears as a result of *circumstance* in the course of history acts as a *force* and is endowed with efficacy. And yet all forces in history depend on a particular disposition and cannot be abstracted from this. A simple example illustrates this distinction. Consider the strongest man in the land: he cannot revolt through his own efforts, not because he lacks the strength but because the "situation" (*shi*) does not allow him to use this strength.[a2] In general, objective conditions matter the most, since they are the determining factor in the process.[3] A politician should thus base this moves on those conditions,[b4] just like a general who knows how to exploit the advantages of the "terrain." Otherwise, he will be obliged to alter those conditions radically in order to render them favorable to his own actions. (Authoritarian Legalists favor just such reforms.) Just as cowardice and bravery in warfare depend solely on the potential born of the situation, public morality stems entirely from the historical conditions of the era: if, because of a totalitarian regime, the situation is such that it is no longer possible to behave badly, even the worst brigands will become trustworthy. But if the situation is reversed, everyone's morality, even that of paragons of virtue, will be suspect.[c5] The historical situation of its own accord either leads to order or, instead, to disorder.[d6] Similarly, in a power relationship that sets each principality in opposition to the rest, only a particular kind of situation will make it possible for one to win complete sovereignty (e.g., if there are few powerful principalities), whereas the opposite situation will make hegemony the only possibility.[7] What counts is not the

Xunzi
4th–3rd
centuries B.C.

Shang Yang
4th century B.C.

Guanzi
3rd century B.C.

178

individual's moral caliber, but the age in which he lives.

However, among the ancient Chinese schools, a number of different theories on the evolution of society were in competition, and these produced a heightened sense of the human process of *becoming.* In the moralists' view, civilization is the achievement of the Sages, who, out of concern for the common good, taught human beings first to find territory, then to provide for their material needs, and finally to develop their moral inclinations.[8] The naturalist perspective (that of the Daoists) is directly opposed to this. It claims that the ongoing deterioration in social relationships is due to the misguided intervention of the "Sages." Because of their intervention, spontaneous harmony was gradually destroyed, wars broke out, and the Golden Age came to an end. Robber Zhi openly accuses Confucius of being the last representative of that line of malefactors.[9] The "realists," partisans of authoritarian policies designed to end the rivalries tearing China apart, drew the conclusion that humanity has passed through a number of different stages and that the painstaking interventions of one period will inevitably appear as a mockery to the following generations.[10] Furthermore, new factors such as demographic pressure intervene, altering the old balance and radically changing people's way of life. Thus, an atemporal model is impossible. Only existing conditions matter; only they can create an element of urgency. It would be a bad idea for a man who one day had the good fortune of seeing a rabbit break its neck in his field to abandon his hoe forever, lying in wait in the hope of being as fortunate a second time. For, like Johnny Lackland, the rabbit in this story never passes the same way twice; every moment produces a different situation, and one should neither lag behind one's own age, placing faith in outworn policies, nor become bogged down in circumstances, clinging blindly to the present.[e11] One should evaluate the present by realizing that time moves forward; the

Han Fei
3rd century B.C.

179

newness of each successive moment must be appreciated. At the same time, however, one can also assess the precise logical nature of the situation and exploit the historical opportunity it offers by stepping back to acquire an abstract perspective.[f]

Consider, as an example of historical opportunity, how Chinese Antiquity came to an end. In the course of two centuries the Qin principality, a relative latecomer among the existing powers, gradually managed to overcome its rivals through its authoritarian policies, destroying the other principalities one by one and eventually founding the empire (in 221 B.C.). But less than two decades later it was overthrown by revolts, and the dynasty collapsed. The reason for its collapse was that, when one does not behave morally "the situation-tendency (*shi*) that makes it possible to conquer is different from that which makes it possible to preserve."[g12] The lesson here is twofold: the regular rise of the Qin illustrates the ineluctable nature of the tendency, and the sudden collapse of the Qin at the zenith of its power illustrates the equally ineluctable logic of reversal.

Jia Yi
2nd century B.C.

The Historical Necessity of Transformation
(from Feudalism to Bureaucracy)

The first emperor not only unified China politically, he also proudly transformed it by replacing the earlier system of fiefdoms with a system of administrative areas — commanderies and prefectures — that would remain predominant. This important change provided Chinese civilization with most of its unique character, for it replaced the common and widespread ancient hereditary privileges with a bureaucratic structure composed of appointed officials who were both registered and dismissible. Writing more than a millennium later, in the last century of the Tang dynasty, Liu Zongyuan tried to explain this change by considering it in relation to the general evolution from which it stemmed, conceptualizing the inevitable nature of the transformation with the term *shi*.[13]

To understand the inevitability of this evolution, it is necessary to return to its origin: the old system of fiefdoms itself had not been introduced by any "creative intention" or "idea" on the part of the sage-kings. Rather, it was the product of "a tendency that stemmed from the situation"[h] (*shi*) that, as a *propensity*, ran through early history without interruption. According to Liu Zongyuan, returning to the origin of this historical process logically brings us to the very beginning of humanity (even letting us infer by induction that there *was* a historical beginning to humanity). It is "the progressive development of that tendency"[i] that has brought man from the state of nature to a more highly developed social organization. Human beings, initially at a disadvantage compared to animals, needed material resources, which inevitably became a source of rivalry. To resolve their differences, they required some kind of intervening authority to act as arbiter and assume the power to punish. Accordingly, human beings came together in groups, forming the first communities. But the more this took place, the more rivalries developed, resulting in wars and each time requiring the intervention of a higher authority with the power to end these dissensions. At first, arbitration was sought from the earliest village chiefs, then from the heads of districts, then from the heads of principalities, then from the leaders of confederations, and finally from the Son of Heaven. The establishment of a hierarchical structure simply corresponded to the expanding scale of society. But once such a structure becomes established throughout space, it tends to become fixed in time, with hereditary titles passed down from father to son. As a result of a sequence of necessarily linked developments, a feudal system is thus created.

The progressive dislocation of this system during the final cen-

Liu Zongyuan
8th–9th centuries

Liu Zongyuan   turies of Antiquity also stemmed from a chain of developments: the central authority grew weak, the old fiefdoms became independent, new principalities were formed, and eventually the royal power was usurped. A new order emerged — the empire. Those nostalgic for the past now declared that the feudal system established by the old sovereigns had been vastly preferable to the administrative system that followed, because the great sovereigns of the past, so respected for their wisdom, had never renounced it. However, as Liu Zongyuan explains, this view is illusory. The sovereigns of Antiquity did not renounce the feudal system because "they could not": they had obtained their power through the support of the other lords and, once they had acquired it, they found themselves obliged to reward their allies by allotting them fiefdoms. They did this not out of generosity and magnanimity but to safeguard their own security and that of their lineage. Contrary to moral idealism, which claimed that humanity needed the work of the Sages to survive,[14] history is clearly a process unfolding of its own accord through internal necessity. Liu Zongyuan uses the same argument against the false justifications of the provincial governors who are tempted at this time to behave as new feudal lords, as always occurred in China when the central authority weakened. He points out that the superiority of the administrative system has become a definitive fact and the process is irreversible.

Nearly 1,000 years later, this analysis of the major transformation in Chinese history was emended by the important philosophical development of "Neo-Confucianism":[15] the *tendency stemming*

Wang Fuzhi   *from a situation* (*shi*) is ineluctable because "that to which it tends"
17th century   is eminently "*logical.*" In early civilization, there was a "*logic*"[j] to the feudal system. The exercise of power benefited from its hereditary nature, for political thinking had not yet developed and all that mattered was the acquired experience handed down from

father to son. Similarly, the bureaucratic system that took over contained its own logic. Since its officials were appointed and could be fired, the people suffered less from their demands: as time passed, more light was shed on the art of politics and, as a result, it became accessible to everyone who possessed the necessary abilities. Given this general tendency, we need to explain next how this transition took place. The development of the crisis inevitably provoked by change is itself perfectly intelligible as it proceeded from one stage to the next. In the beginning, only princes held hereditary positions, but later great officials also wanted to pass on their responsibilities to their sons: hence the source of the "excess" to which "the tendency inevitably led."[k] But as soon as all posts became hereditary, a glaring disparity developed between the responsibilities themselves and the abilities of those who took charge of them; "stupid minds" can be found in noble families, just as "brilliant people" are to be found among the peasants. The latter, unable to tolerate their lowly condition, will attempt to rise: "The tendency stemming from the situation leads inevitably to an exacerbation of tensions and to the unleashing of their effects."[l] This situation brought about the historical change that rescinded the principle of heredity: the exacerbation and release of tensions were followed by a new, more coherent state of affairs. Under the pressure exerted by the tendency, the pattern (or "logic") itself underwent a change.[m]

Wang Fuzhi explains that such an important transformation was not brought about solely through the initiative of the first emperor, or solely through his ability, even if the emperor believed he was satisfying his own private ambitions by establishing the bureaucratic machine. In truth, it was the natural course of things: "Heaven," in all its fathomless dimensions, made use of the emperor's personal interests, with a view to catering to the general interest. From the perspective of the emperor's individ-

Wang Fuzhi

ual benefit, dynastic longevity suffered more than it gained by depriving the emperor of the support afforded by the whole pyramid of vassals (later imperial dynasties never lasted as long as the ancient feudal ones). This proves that the change was decided by the order of things and that "not even a sage-king could have stood in its way."

The change from feudalism to bureaucracy, decided in authoritarian fashion by the first emperor, may appear to have brought about a sudden revolution. Nevertheless, beneath the surprises and reversals of history, a Chinese philosopher will not fail to perceive a more gradual and regular evolution confirming the natural logic of the tendencies producing the transformation. For one thing, the change was discernible even before the emperor's decision; in the last years of Antiquity, many territories that had lost their overlords had already switched to an administrative form of government.[16] The new system already existed before the emperor's decision, which did no more than bring it into widespread use. Second, no sooner had that first dynasty disappeared than the restorers of the empire, less than twenty years later, returned to the system of fiefdoms. Besides the bad memories left by the first emperor, the promoter of the reform, the ancient feudal system was still in fact very much a part of Chinese custom and popular thought; thus, the tendency directing the course of history could not sustain such a sudden change.[n17] However, there could be no question of a return to the past: those who feared at the time that the new masters of the empire, by distributing great fiefdoms to their supporters, might diminish their own power (and return China to an earlier age of rivalries between principalities) "lamented pointlessly," for they did not understand how logical and inexorable evolution is, once in motion. Clearly, once the Han dynasty's power was consolidated, the revolts of feudal princelings throughout the first century of the dynasty were destined

Wang Fuzhi

Gu Yanwu
17th century

Wang Fuzhi

by their very nature to cease and constituted no more than "the last flicker of a lamp on the point of going out." Faced with the accumulated pressure exerted by the tendency toward centralization, the great fiefdoms were bound to disintegrate in the end, and the opponents of centralization fell on their own.[o18] The granting of those fiefdoms had represented "the last waves" of a world coming to an end, and their quasi abolition constituted the "prelude" to the periods to come. In history, restorations are always impossible. Wang Fuzhi thus concludes that historical tendency is necessarily both *gradual* and *irreversible*.

This transformation was all the less reversible since it was part of a much more general evolution, the tendency toward unification. We are told that the Chinese realm was originally just a mosaic of small domains and many chiefdoms, each with its own jurisdiction and customs. This world only gradually became more homogeneous through the recognition of an overlord and the formation of larger fiefdoms, until a common culture emerged.[19] The establishment of the feudal system already constituted in itself an important step in this process of unification, and the adoption of the bureaucratic system not only ended the system of fiefdoms but was also in line with the same logical tendency toward uniformity that had characterized feudalism in its day. Thus, the measure adopted by the first emperor was simply the conclusion of an evolution that had been taking place over a full millennium.[p] It was furthermore justified by the *overall* nature of this mutation: not only did the transition from fiefdoms to prefectures offer administrative and political advantages, it also affected the life of the people as a whole, especially their material condition. As has already been shown, once the imperial unification had enabled public expenditure to be spread equally throughout the empire, such expenditure could be considerably reduced; taxation thus became lighter and rationality entered

Wang Fuzhi
Gu Yanwu

Wang Fuzhi

185

economics.[20] The historical tendency, seen as the propensity peculiar to the existing situation, represented progress, and the strongest obstacle to a return to feudalism was simply that "the strength of the people could not tolerate it."[q] In this sense, even domains seemingly affected the least by that change, such as the educational system and the mode of selection, were in fact an important part of it.[21] All the institutions of a particular era are part of the same system and are "mutually supportive." In the age of administrative constituencies, for us to seek inspiration from the system of recommendations operating in feudal days would demonstrate that we simply have not understood the overall unity of each of those ages, nor, consequently, the break that occurred between them and the radical nature of that change.

There is a *before* and an *after*, and the two are incompatible. Wang Fuzhi explains, by way of an example, that there was no distinction in Antiquity between the military and the civil sectors, but once the empire was established, it proved necessary to separate them: "The state of things evolves in accordance with the tendency, and institutions must be adapted accordingly."[r22] The tendency at work must be considered in light of the differences between one period and another, with a long-term view.[s] Nothing comes about in a single day, yet from day to day everything is changing. History is made up of precisely such "in-depth shifts" and "silent transformations."[23]

Wang Fuzhi

The Tendency toward Alternation
The transition from feudalism to bureaucracy constituted relative progress, thus contradicting the myth of a Golden Age.[24] Chinese reformers, in response to those who praised the past, now commonly remarked that, if the human race had done nothing but degenerate, "we should by now have become no better than devils!" And while it is as difficult without evidence and docu-

mentation to speculate on origins as it is on ultimate ends, we
can see how far man has gradually risen, Wang Fuzhi tells us, sim-   Wang Fuzhi
ply by considering those times (in Chinese history) where historical evidence does exist, first the stage of barbarity, then that of
civilization. The earliest Chinese lived like animals, and the reason
the first sovereigns are so honored by tradition is precisely because
they succeeded in leading man to evolve from that original animality. "It is clearly easier to govern the people today than it was
in the time of the ancient kings." But does that mean that progress dominates the world and serves as its law? For Wang Fuzhi,
certain catastrophic periods in Chinese history, for example the
third to fourth centuries (after the collapse of the Han), when
the political world seemed to totter on the brink of savagery, are
a constant reminder that regression is equally possible:[25] prehis-
toric man, "the animal that stands erect," the one that "grunts
when hungry and throws away any food that remains, as soon as
he is satisfied," is not only behind us but may also lurk ahead.
The power of evolution, a challenge to all dogmas on human
nature, should be recognized to operate in both directions. Once
man acquires civilization, his way of life changes, his practices
evolve, and his "organic nature itself is altered"; yet at this point
he is ready to return to brutish animality, and civilization is ready
to plunge back into chaos. Then everything associated with his
rise, down to the smallest trace, would be wiped out.

Thus, it is not progress that rules the world but rather alternation; alternation in both space and time.[26] To Wang Fuzhi, there   Wang Fuzhi
is no evidence that when the Chinese were still living in a savage
state there was not some other place "under the sun" already
experiencing civilization (an unusual instance of a Chinese writer
not limiting the "world" to China!). But it is hard for the Chinese
to be certain of this, since at that time they were themselves as
yet uncivilized, and other civilizations must gradually have degen-

erated since then and been wiped out. However, for Wang Fuzhi, such alternation can be demonstrated from the last two millennia of Chinese history on. In Antiquity the North constituted the cradle of Chinese civilization, which then shifted slowly southward while the North relapsed little by little into obscurity. Under the Song dynasty (eleventh to thirteenth centuries), the people of the South were still despised but, since the Ming dynasty (from the fourteenth century to the present), culture has clearly been concentrated near the Great River, while the plains of the North have become the source of all scourges; and it is the extreme South – Guangzhou and Yunnan – that is now being progressively touched by beneficent influences. As time passes, the "cosmic influxes" shift, but the balance (between civilization and barbarity) remains constant.

In this form, this concept of a tendency toward alternation (*shi*),[t] an upward surge followed by a decline, is shared by all the Chinese theorists of history[27] and constitutes their dominant perspective. It is even something they assume to be self-evident. But for Wang Fuzhi, it is also important to establish clearly what is meant by the two terms *tendency* and *alternation*. In contrast to the moralist view initially inherited from Antiquity,[28] he believes it crucial to understand that the phases of upward surging are not simply brought about by great sovereigns but are inherent tendencies in the regularity of historical processes. In this view, history loses in creative heroism but gains in internal necessity. In contrast to all those who later subscribed to the imperial ideology, Wang Fuzhi deems it important to show the extent to which the very principle of alternation implies rupture and difference between one age and another, and thus should never be regarded as simply a "prop" for superimposed continuity. In such a case, the reverse of the earlier one, the negative tendency would no longer have any substance to it and would seem to be reabsorbed

Wang Fuzhi

into itself: regularity would be so codified as to become artificial.

The second of those mistakes in particular deserves denunciation, since it nurtures an illusion that is not innocent. The establishment of the empire led to the construction of an integrated general conception of history, beginning with the ancient royal dynasties. New imperial dynasties could profit from that integration by being able to present themselves as the legitimate outcome of the historical process. To that end, ingenious attempts were made to present historical alternation systematically as following the model of the cycle of nature, which was traditionally construed on the basis of the interaction of the "five phases." Sometimes the schema was sometimes conceived with an antagonistic bias: *wood* is overcome by metal, *metal* by fire, *fire* by water, *water* by earth, *earth* by wood, and so on; sometimes it simply implied a mutual production: *wood* (which is also the spring, the East, birth) engenders fire, *fire* (which is also the summer, the South, growth) engenders earth, *earth* (at the center of the process, controlling all the seasons and representing both the center and full maturity) engenders metal (which is also the autumn, the West, the harvest), and *metal* engenders water (which is also the winter, the North, the storing of the harvest).[u29] This schema is sometimes further complicated by correlations with "colors" and "virtues." But it always entails a closed and repetitive cycle in which alternation operates simply as a factor aiding transmission, and makes the cycle start all over again. Projecting such schemata onto the course of history (with each successive dynasty corresponding to some cyclical phase, virtue, and color) makes the course of history seem homogeneous and regular, as though it were simply an uninterrupted chain of "reigns"[v]: all of these are imagined as harmonious, united totalities, with one dynasty spontaneously giving way to the next and the successor taking over in all equity. Wang Fuzhi considers this repre-

Zou Yan
3rd century B.C.

Dong Zhongshu
2nd century B.C.

189

Wang Fuzhi

sentation to be all the more reprehensible because it has been deliberately used throughout Chinese history to mask the worst usurpations. The integrating function of official historiography has been so formalized that it has wound up integrating anything and everything: a sinister bandit needed only pompously attribute to himself a particular phase, color, and virtue (as did the barbarians who laid claim to the empire in the third to fourth centuries) or even dignify himself with the name of the preceding dynasty (as Li Miau did in the tenth century), and he could officially claim to be inaugurating a new era and guaranteeing the continuity of legitimacy.[30]

Wang Fuzhi

Wang Fuzhi's view is that this falsely comforting attitude toward history, which promotes a uniform view of it, rests on artificial bases that should be denounced. In between two great dynasties (the Han and the Tang) were periods (in the third and the tenth centuries) of confusion and anarchy; these constituted, as it were, gaping holes in the fabric of so-called continuity. It is necessary to understand that order "is not to be found in the continuation of disorder, even if it does replace it";[w] political unity "is not produced" by fragmentation, even if it does succeed it. A tendency only exerts itself and becomes dominant within a particular historical situation to the detriment of the opposite tendency. Order or disorder, unity or fragmentation: these are rival factors that, Wang Fuzhi tells us, impart dynamism to history through their opposition. A *tendency* is truly a *tension* through which history is innovative. Such tension has accounted for the great mutations of Chinese history: political unification (at the end of Antiquity), fragmentation (in the third century, after the Han), reunification (under the Sui and the Tang, in the seventh to ninth centuries), and foreign occupation (from the Song onward, in the eleventh century, again in the thirteenth century, and yet again under the Manchu, in the seventeenth century). Thus even a sage cannot foresee the next mutation.[31] One only knows that, by thus oscillating under the tension of alternation, history moves forward: it neither follows a continuous line of progress nor turns in circles.

According to Wang Fuzhi, we can appreciate the reality of this alternation in history even more when we consider the particular and independent principle by which, as one period succeeds another, the negative tendency is reconstituted. This tendency leads to usurpation, schism, and invasion.[32] To start with, often an episode judged to be of secondary importance sets off the tendency (such as the brief interregnum of Wang Mang at the beginning of the first century). This marked the point of departure of a tendency toward usurpation, which then continued with Cao Pi, at the beginning of the third century (among others). No sooner has such a tendency surfaced than its impulse spontaneously grows, making it develop more and more until it is exhausted. (One example is the tendency toward schism arising in the third century and continuing sporadically until the tenth century; another is the tendency toward invasion that replaced it and recurred in China from the time of the Song on.) The starting point of a tendency may be almost undetectable, but it determines the future, for it introduces a new inclination in history and can follow this downward slope to new depths. Historical tendency possesses a great potential force; a seemingly insignificant precedent may alter the course of history for several centuries. Once a certain groove is followed it later becomes nearly impossible "to change the line or get out of the rut." Hence the extreme caution constantly required of all who play a role in the course of history (and the caution required of us too, with regard to the moral deviations deep within us):[x33] the first, false step is so simple to take, and, as time passes, it becomes difficult to correct that waywardness.

Wang Fuzhi

Wang Fuzhi   Wang Fuzhi tells us that the founders of the Tang dynasty, who established a new age of peace and prosperity at the beginning of the seventh century, prove this. However concerned for justice they were, however well-intentioned, when they took power they were unable to disengage themselves from the old tendency toward usurpation that had long since entered political behavior in China. Moreover, no matter how conscious they were of the dangers involved, they could not totally dispense with the support of "barbarian" forces in their military operations along the frontier regions, if only to avoid attack by these same barbarians. By acting in this way, they were willy-nilly moving toward the new negative tendency, the tendency toward invasion, that would dominate the entire following millennium. The Tang sovereigns subsequently appealed to the Uighurs for help against the rebels threatening the dynasty (An Lushan in the mid-eighth century), and then to the Shatuo to crush the revolts that eventually brought the dynasty down (Huang Chao, at the end of the ninth century). Subsequently the Shatuo themselves depended on other barbarian peoples (the Kitan), as they tried to plant themselves in China. The situation became even graver under the Song, for they appealed first to the Jürchen to combat the Liao, then to the Mongols to combat the Jürchen, only to be themselves eventually submerged by the Mongols, their latest "allies." Like a "plant run wild" or a "arrow let fly," the rot proceeded further and further until it became unstoppable.

The most general definition of the "tendency that stems from a situation" (*shi* in history) is "that which, once set off, cannot be arrested."[y34] The peasant revolts at the end of the Tang dynasty (in the second half of the ninth century) are cited as an example: one revolt has barely died off when another erupts (the revolt of Pang Xun followed fast on that of Qiu Fu); the tendency unfolds *sponte sua* and cannot be countered.[z35] Of its own accord, it

192

becomes progressively more pronounced. Another example is found in the empresses' tendency to interfere in state affairs.[36] A remedial ruling of the third century categorically forbade such interference. After a limited recurrence under the Tang, this evil began again with renewed vigor under the Song, when a (never truly justified) regency sparked its reemergence at the time of the minority of Renzong, in the eleventh century. This situation continued to dominate during following reigns, when it was not even considered necessary to find pretexts to justify it. Once the rut is there, the tendency transforms itself into a sluggish force that blocks any subsequent attempts to remedy the situation. It becomes increasingly difficult to reverse gears[aa] or shake free of it.

It is thus possible to follow the gradual decline of dynasties (a matter that particularly engaged Wang Fuzhi's attention, during his life at the end of the Ming dynasty in the seventeenth century). Past a certain point of no return, the dynasty's fall becomes inevitable.[37] At this stage, it is pointless to blame the invincibility of the enemy or some faulty political decision or operation of doubtful merit (e.g., under the Song, the power given to the Jürchen or the disastrous alliance concluded with the Jin). Decline is in fact always an overall phenomenon, as is any other historical transformation.[38] It is not produced by individual events but stems from a general degeneration: "The prince no longer resembles a true prince," nor is his "prime minister anything like what a prime minister ought to be"; mores have degenerated and the indispensable moral cohesion is lost. Everything is warped, crumbling; not a single factor is going the same way. The disintegration is total.[bb] Only a vast, general upheaval, which would deal the cards anew, could remedy the situation.

The Logic of Reversal

In Wang Fuzhi's opinion, the course of history is always decided by a twofold logic. On the one hand, every tendency, once born, is naturally inclined to grow; on the other hand, any tendency carried to its ultimate limit becomes exhausted and cries out for reversal.[cc39] This principle is absolutely general and constitutes the justification for alternation. Nevertheless, one can distinguish between two forms of negative tendencies and, on that basis, two modes of reversal. A negative tendency may lead to progressive *deviation*; it becomes increasingly difficult to backtrack, so that, unless the tendency exhausts itself, only an overall transformation can resolve the situation; alternatively, it will lead instead to an *imbalance*. In this case, the imbalance itself will generate a reaction, and the greater the imbalance, the stronger the reaction will be.[40] In the first of these two situations all one can do is passively recognize that one is increasingly becoming stuck in this groove. In contrast, in the second, which involves opposite poles, a dynamic force creating equilibrium is present. Different strategies should accordingly be adopted in the two situations: in the former, it is essential to foresee the difficulty as soon as possible; in the second, one can also count on the effects of a reversal and rely on time to do its work.

When a tendency leads to imbalance, the more accentuated this imbalance becomes, the more fragile it becomes. The more it "leans" to one side, the "lighter" and "easier to reverse" it becomes on the other.[dd41] This "logic" of reversal is inherent in the regular unfolding of every process (i.e., in "Heaven").[ee] In politics, for instance, any extreme pressure is later bound to relax. As an example, we are shown the great emperor of the Han dynasty (Wudi, in the second to first century B.C.), who initially launched into extremely authoritarian, ambitious, expansionist, and costly policies, which were impossible to oppose. But from excess itself,

Wang Fuzhi

Wang Fuzhi

194

weakness results; "the more one becomes committed to an impracticable path," the more "inevitable is the distress that follows." Resentment increased all the time and, in his heart, even the emperor was worried. For this reason, he desisted in his final years from his military expeditions and softened his internal policies "without it being necessary for anyone else to badger him to do so." He did so simply "because his own views had already been modified." Wang Fuzhi tells us that a similar episode occurred under the Song, when the political ambitions of a new emperor (Shenzang, in the eleventh century) played into the hands of his prime minister (Wang Anshi), who seized power for himself. Solely supported by his own clique and reducing all others to silence, he embarked on a series of reforms as radical as they were utopian. But under the following reign these measures were inevitably abandoned, as ineluctably as "withered leaves fall in the autumn." Every revolution brings a reaction in its wake and whatever is forced destroys itself spontaneously.

This logic of reversal is modeled explicitly on the shape of the hexagrams of the ancient *Book of Changes*. Based on two types of lines, antithetical yet complementary (the continuous and the discontinuous, — and – –), these provided the basis for the Chinese concept of becoming. Consider, for example, hexagrams 11 and 12, *tai* and *pi*, ☰☷ and ☷☰.[ff] The bottom part of the former is composed of three continuous lines (symbolizing the principle of initiative and perseverance, or Heaven), while the upper part consists of three discontinuous lines (symbolizing the principle of obedience and fulfillment, or Earth). Heaven, from below, tends toward what is above, and Earth, from above, tends downward, which means that their beneficent influences cross, and the above and the below communicate harmoniously. From this perfect interaction stem prosperity and concord among existing beings; the diagram serves to evoke a positive surge. In contrast, the second hexagram is composed of the three discontinuous lines below that symbolize the Earth, and the three continuous lines above that symbolize Heaven. Heaven above and Earth below move farther and farther apart, withdrawing into themselves. There is no longer a beneficial interaction; their potentialities enter into a phase of stagnation. It is a time of decline. These two opposite patterns alternate, each proceeding out of the other purely through reversal. Between them, the two account for all alternation: one is attached to the first month of the Chinese year (February–March), when the forces of renewal well up with the beginning of spring; the other is connected with the seventh month (August–September), when, following the culminating point of summer, the subsequent atrophy begins.

The interior of each hexagram illuminates still more about this process of transition and inversion. For while the opposite principles (*yin* and *yang*, rise and decline) are categorically exclusive and mutually repulsive, at the same time they condition one another, each implying the existence of the other. An open conflict and a tacit entente: whichever principle is actualized, it always latently contains its opposite. At every moment the progress of one implies the regression of the other, but simultaneously the progress of either principle necessarily leads to its own future regression. The future is already at work in the present, and the expanding present will soon pass away. Becoming is gradual; only transition actually exists. Thus, at the stage of the first of those two hexagrams, the stage of prosperity, the third line (i.e., the

Book of Changes third up in the bottom half) is already warning us that "there is no going without a return," "no flat terrain that is not followed by a slope"; at the sixth line, at the top of the hexagram, the message runs: "The wall returns to the moat." This is the pattern of the *breakdown*.[42] The change announced in the middle of the hexagram now enters its phase of actualization. The city wall collapses into the moat from which it was built, the positive factors are exhausted, and the only thing to be done is to confront the "downside" phase cautiously and firmly. In contrast, at the stage represented by the other hexagram, that of decline, the factors of negativity are gradually contained and defeated, and they withdraw. By the end of this hexagram (at the sixth line), the expected reversal takes place, and a new period of well-being can begin. The rise spontaneously became a fall, and the decline is itself the start of a new surge upward.[43]

It is this logic of reversal, defined already in Antiquity, that Wang Fuzhi finds to be currently at work in history. Exactly like the process of nature, the historical process operates regularly through the restoration of equilibration and compensation: "That which contracts may once again unfold: this is the tendency that stems from the situation (*shi*)."[gg][44] The same clearly applies between rival powers: in ancient China, the principality of Jin gradually achieved hegemony (under Prince Jing), then inevitably declined;[45] what we regard as destiny in this process is nothing but the inexorability of a perfectly natural process.[hh] Similarly (for such is Heaven), in the earlier example of Shenzong and Wang Anshi of the Song, excessively authoritarian political pressure relaxed of its own accord, with no need for human intervention.[ii][46] The reason the Song emperor launched into such ambitiously restrictive policies was his own reaction to the long preceding reign of Renzong (1022–63), when pacifism had been carried to the point of passivity. One excess leads to another: détente calls forth tension, then tension is followed by more détente.[jj][47] The slightest political event can be interpreted according to this dynamic of alternation and of "a continuous tendency toward change."[kk] How else, for example, can one understand the harmful edict of one of the Han emperors (Yuandi, in the first century B.C.) who, by laying down moral criteria for the hierarchi-

Wang Fuzhi

zation of officials, led them into baseness and caused them to lose the moral integrity a state badly needs?[48] Such a measure can only be explained as a reaction against the preceding situation: anarchy had previously reigned among the *literati* officials, and, denied the official recognition that would have ensured them a stable position, they attempted to impose their own authority at all costs, even to the point of offending the emperor. Hence, "through a tendency toward reversal," the emperor decided to reorganize their ranks and force them into docility. The conclusion to be drawn here is, "The course that is followed is to be feared, its reversal even more so."

Moral Strategy: The Historical Situation as a Setup to Be Manipulated

"Tension-détente," "deployment-withdrawal" — or "order-disorder," "rise-decline": all history inexorably passes through "highs and lows,"[ll49] not as a result of any metaphysical principle projected onto the passage of time but through the inherent necessity of every process; the factors at work, both positive and negative, necessarily become exhausted and are replaced by compensatory factors. A regulatory dynamic is thus inherent (even if in no more than a discreet or even inchoate fashion) within every stage of becoming, turning every historical situation into a setup that can be manipulated. In this respect, the tactic to employ could not be more simple, yet it is so constantly applicable that it serves as a Moral Way for mankind: Learn how to make the most of the tendency at work in the course of things; allow the setup represented by the situation simply to develop according to its tendency. Every historical situation, even the most unfavorable, is always rich in the possibility of change, since a positive development over the more-or-less long term is always a possibility: if not now, then later. One only has to count on the one factor that is the most influential: the factor of time.

According to Wang Fuzhi, two general principles suffice for successful management of the temporal logic of alternation: first, even before the change occurs, refrain from excess so as to avoid the contrary excess that might follow in reaction; next, at the point when the change occurs, remain firm within yourself and simultaneously go along willingly with the change.[50] Nothing could be more stupid and destructive than attempting to block the change once it can be seen as necessary.[51] Whatever his personal qualities, whoever obstinately tries to maintain the status quo out of loyalty will achieve nothing but his own ruin, without improving the situation in any way. True skill lies in being able to *ride* the change (and always derive the greatest profit from it). In particular, if a chance reversal of misfortune into good fortune occurs simply through the logic of alternation that rules every process, it is up to us to exploit all the possibilities and to help it reach full fruition: "Heaven helps man," but it particularly helps those who help themselves.

Wisdom thus logically amounts to a zero degree of human intervention, and this has the potential to be richly effective. It means "knowing how to wait." We are told that a wise man is one who knows that any process that leads to imbalance becomes fragile of itself as it becomes more pronounced and that the tendency impelling it in one direction ineluctably leads to a reversal. He accordingly *knows* precisely how to *wait* for the objective process to reach the stage most likely to lead to a reversal, that is, to wait until it exhausts all its negative factors and is consequently inclined to move in a positive direction. At this point, the wise man, with minimum personal intervention, can reorientate everything in the right direction and recuperate the situation.[52] The course of things then naturally meets us halfway, and we profit from the dynamism inherent in the situation at the height of its

Wang Fuzhi

Wang Fuzhi

intensity. It is insane to try to "struggle against Heaven," that is, to take action when the natural course of the process runs in the opposite direction; but it is equally dangerous, although more difficult to discern, to intervene before the natural course of the process has completely ended at the desired result. Even though our action in this case operates in the direction "logically" entailed by the process, it nevertheless forces that process, impelling it to go further than it would have under natural circumstances. It will thereafter be even more difficult to restore balance to the process in a stable and lasting fashion. Not only does such rash behavior expose us pointlessly to conflict, it may also deprive us of our opportunity just as it was about to occur — with dangerous results. To be impatient is the worst of all mistakes. In contrast, the wisdom of the ancient dynasty founders lay in their ability to recognize the moment when the tyranny of decadent kings had peaked and the pendulum swung back into their hands. Having held out until then, patiently waiting, they only had to "calmly rise up" and effortlessly implement their salutary plans, as their fellow men desired.[mm]

Wang Fuzhi   The earlier examples of an excessively authoritarian and constraining power provides the same lesson: those immediately rebelling against it were broken by it; but those who, "depending on the progressive tendency toward decline,"[nn] had waited until "that which is impracticable should fall apart of its own accord" could eventually regain control of the situation and calm things down (e.g., Huo Guang under Wudi and Zaodi of the Han, and Sima Guang under the Song).[53] In this sense, chance and "fathomless Heaven" are no less than a "logic" that itself is "nothing but pure conformity with the tendency that stems from the situation"[oo] (i.e., the historical *shi*). On the basis of an analysis of a given situation, it is rationally possible to foresee and anticipate the ineluctable turn events will take. They are implied by the tendency already underway, and as it is reaching its climax, its reversal has already begun.[pp54] However, "rare indeed are those who can see this," and for this reason we need "wisdom." Another example is provided by the growing power of the eunuchs under the later Han (first to second centuries): here too, everyone who clashed head-on with that power lost their lives (including the most important dignitaries: Dou Wu in 168, and, similarly, He Jin some twenty-one years later). All that was necessary was to see that this tyranny, by becoming excessive, had aroused too many kinds of resentment, all silently accumulating to seal the tyranny's inevitable doom. One fine day "a single gust of wind would be enough to extinguish the lamp that was on the point of going out"; "the swiftness and ease of that reversal are already assured in advance." One perspicacious general (Cao Cao) just laughed about it from the sidelines, declaring "a simple jailer will be enough to rid us of this scourge!" In the end, he was indeed the one who managed to impose his own authority.

A proof *a contrario* is provided by a subtle analysis of the case of a famous Song general (Yue Fei, in the twelfth century). When the Song abandoned the whole northern half of the country to invaders, Yue Fei wasted no time in relaunching the offensive and taking revenge. But the court was weary not only of wars but also of turbulence among its own generals, and tended at that time toward pacifism. As a result, his zeal, once so extolled, soon became an embarrassment and made him seem suspect. The upshot was that he wound up in prison and was then executed in the prime of life. If he had instead been willing to control his desire for glory at all costs and had managed to sacrifice somewhat his own personal myth of implacable valor, he could have waited for his principal political opponent (Qin Kui) to die, for the invaders to encounter difficulties, and for the court's morale finally to be "reinflated," all of which indeed eventually came to pass.[55]

Then he would have been able to set off again at the head of his troops, with a far greater chance of success. For "possibilities which cannot exist simultaneously," because exclusive, eventually take place "by the substitution of one element for another" later on.⁹⁹ One who can "pull back" when the tendency is running against him and resume the initiative when the tendency becomes favorable again is never "under pressure" and eventually "obtains everything." In a bad situation, what is essential is to ensure one's own safety in order to manipulate chance better later. Thus, those who showered so much praise on this "heroic" general for refusing to surrender were applauding the very quality in him that would lead to his downfall and death. In this respect, the inexhaustible dance of history reveals itself to be more "deadly" than the worst slanders.

Wang Fuzhi All this leads to the construction of a hierarchy of values: moral "constancy" is a greater factor in success than intellectual "perspicacity."⁵⁶ The latter, since it is purely mental perception, operates only fleetingly; the former, which draws on the fortitude of the soul, depends on duration and is thus coextensive with the totality of reality as it unfolds. Moral constancy is "nature," intellectual "perspicacity" only a "function." Eventually perspicacity, as a result of being required at every moment, is bound to fail; whereas constancy, which consists in holding firm by espousing the course of time, is fundamentally inexhaustible. In this respect it resembles Heaven, the virtue of which is its ability "always to persevere." Constancy rests on a superior understanding of process because it is open to the longer-term view in which success is only temporary and no reversal is definitive. If the logical and necessary character of tendencies is recognized,ʳʳ one will be able to remain prudent in times of victory and confident in the moment of defeat. Such is the interpretation of the famous struggle between two claimants to the empire at the end of the

second century B.C. (Xiang Yu and Liu Bang). One showed perspicacity over the long run but, when defeated and forced to
flee, cut his throat, out of disappointment. The other, in contrast, was at the point of defeat several times and barely managed
to survive, but thereafter he immediately made the most of the
troubled times, built up his forces again, and returned to the
attack. In the end it was he who emerged victorious, and it was
only just that he should.[57]

However thoroughly self-determined the setup of history as
conceived in China may initially seem, through its own logic it
nevertheless leaves plenty of room for human initiative. In the
first place, the process of history always possesses within it a cer-   Wang Fuzhi
tain measure of play exceeding the inevitability of tendencies:[ss][58]
there is a residual element of chance (or destiny). For while every
tendency, once begun, is necessarily inclined in a particular direction, nevertheless, even at the embryonic stage when the tendency
is just beginning, when everything is decided by infinitesimal
proportions,[tt] there is still a certain element of unexpectedness,
an unpredictability stemming from the unfathomable dimension
of "Heaven." (This element restores to Heaven a transcendent
aspect that the pure rationality of tendency had seemed to deny
it.) In the course of nature as in the course of history, Heaven is
at once a principle of *constancy* and a factor of *circumstance*:[59] on
the larger scale, an ineluctable regulatory process is in operation
(through the alternation of things coming to be and then disap-
pearing, rising and declining), even if from up close, the process
sometimes appears to us as a purely contingent operation. But
Heaven is a unity, and a sage, in his wisdom, can reconcile both
aspects. He can understand the regulatory logic behind the circumstances as well as perceive an opportunity as it begins to arise,
thanks to his understanding of the processes. Second, while "a
tendency is always predetermined," it also remains within human

power to manage it skillfully. The sage knows in advance and as a matter of principle one cannot hope in a state of weakness "to achieve a sudden expansion of force"; but he also knows that no power is ever definitive, so one must "manage to wait for the opposite power to weaken."[60] Within any power relation, the tendency to decline is thus never inexorable, and responsibility for one's own misfortunes always rests with oneself.

Wang Fuzhi

Evidence of this is provided by one of the most dramatic collapses in Chinese history: the fall of the Song dynasty and the Mongol invasion that followed. Wang Fuzhi tells us that this invasion was not inevitable: between the first, partial invasion of the North by the Jin (in the twelfth century) and the definitive invasion of the Mongols a century and a half later, the situation had changed several times as the tendency oscillated.[61] Plenty of trump cards remained to be played against the Mongols, and so the struggle against them could have lasted much longer had the Chinese pulled back to the South. In the end they would have blocked the enemy's advance and retained possession of many important positions. For anyone "who could correctly evaluate the tendency of the particular moment," a solution always remained possible. The defeat was thus the fault of the Chinese leaders (Emperor Lizong and his two successive prime ministers). Incidentally, by referring to the end of the Song dynasty in this way four centuries later, Wang Fuzhi was no doubt also justifying his own failure to lay down his arms when faced with the Manchu invasions.[62] Far from leading us to resignation, basing our behavior on the determinism of tendency should encourage resistance in us.

Illustration: The Tendency toward Renewal in Literature

The role played by *shi* also affects more particular forms of history with other kinds of processes. Since every situation is given its direction by the tendency that presides over its evolution, all history can be conceived according to the same schema. This is particularly true of literary history, which was so important in China. Literary history should thus provide us with a convenient way to verify two crucial points. First, an examination of the tendencies at work in literature will allow us to demonstrate the necessity of mutations and support the argument for the modernists' party (corroborating our point of departure by returning to the arguments of Legalist reformers). Second, it will justify the basic concepts of literary history, which are founded on alternation and thus correspond to the concepts we have just been considering: rise, decline, and renewal.

In the Chinese concept of literature one early idea was that "a particular tendency follows its course" (*shi*, the tendency of taste or fashion) and that return is never possible.[uu63] Another early idea held that, since "contexts (*shi*) differ" from one another, imitation becomes impossible.[vv64] But these ideas became particularly important at the end of the Ming period, from the sixteenth century on — for one, because contemporary theories of imitation were excessively rigid (only the prose of Antiquity and the Han dynasty and the poetry of the Tang period were to be imitated). As a result, a chasm was developing between living literary creation (novels, theater, poetic prose) and the ossified judgments of the critics; a reaction against the stranglehold of dogma and immobilism was becoming urgent. The change also became necessary due to the emergence of intuitionist philosophy, which emphasized the artless workings of consciousness and spontaneity.[65] According to this philosophy, only ingenuousness is authentic; but the perceptions of our senses and their logical reasoning combine to dispossess us of it. Our knowledge increases and our "taste" is formed, but this cultivation, fortified by reading and study, shields our early naïveté, and our words no longer come

Li Zhi
16th century

205

from deep within us but are "borrowed." However successful they may seem, such words are cut off from our inner selves and become worthless, submerged in artificiality, distancing us from the only "truly successful" literature: the kind born "in our child-like hearts." It would hardly be possible to carry further an insistence on *naturalness*. This insistence led literature to undergo a change; it was the only way for it to move away from the genres and forms that repeatedly threatened to be imposed on it, blocking its naive source and turning it into something "borrowed." Literature must be constantly innovative to remain faithful to that insistence on authenticity. *Its propensity to evolve* was the condition of its existence.

Hence the attitude of the modernists, those able to understand the tendency of their period: because of the time factor, they claimed, literature cannot fail to evolve from the past to the present;[66] there must be a break between one age and the next. To plagiarize the writings of the Ancients in order to pass oneself off as an "Ancient" is like dressing in light clothing of raffia in midwinter. Like all human productions (from clothes to institutions), literature has evolved from the greatest "complexity" to the greatest "simplicity" and from the greatest "obscurity" to the greatest "clarity"; or, from "disorder" to "order," from "what is difficult" to what "flows from the source" and is "carried along."[67] Literature thus tends naturally toward viability. The fact that "the past cannot serve the present" is a result of *shi*[ww] and evolution is inevitable. The characteristics of modernity are incompatible with those of Antiquity. One cannot issue a political proclamation today in the same terms as those used 2,000 years ago; nor, similarly, can our love songs borrow anything from times past. Times have changed and literature has changed with them: "The fact that today one does not have to imitate the past is also a result of *shi*." In this context *shi* acquires the force

Yuan Hongdao
16th century

of an argument and is even used as an ultimate explanation.

Literature is thus only comprehensible in a historical perspective. Indeed, its very nature is historical — not because of any external conditioning it may reflect, but through internal necessity. The poetry of each age "cannot *not*" be led to "make way as it declines" for the poetry of the following age. "The *Shijing* [The Classic of Poetry] (the first poetic anthology in China, compiled in the twelfth to seventh centuries B.C.) could not fail to decline and to be followed by *The Songs of Chu* at the end of Antiquity; nor could *The Songs of Chu* do anything other than decline, to be followed by the poetry of the Han and the Wei dynasties; the poetry of the Han and Wei dynasties was likewise bound to decline, to be followed by that of the Six Dynasties (third to sixth centuries); the poetry of the Six Dynasties was bound to decline, to be followed by the poetry of the Tang dynasty (seventh to ninth centuries): such is *shi*,"[68] seen as a propensity for evolution. The genre becomes identified with that evolution, while this metamorphosis from one age to the next constitutes the law that rules the genre. Renewal is ineluctable, since if I imitate the poetry of the past the imitation is either a failure, so that I "lose that through which there was poetry," or a success, in which case "it is that through which there is me" that is lost. The solution to the dilemma lies in the ideal (embodied by the greatest poets, Li Bo and Du Fu) according to which "it (poetry) never fails to resemble, yet without ever resembling": the identity of everything poetic is all the stronger when one manages to innovate. Or, to put it another way, it is only by ceasing to become other that poetry maintains *itself*. Such a statement is paradoxical, but it brings us back to the following primary — and most general — intuition: nothing can persist except through transformation.

The modernist party thus ends up with a balanced view of literary history. Midway between a progressive view of literature

Gu Yanwu
17th century

207

(developing in stages, generally in step with civilization) and the opposite view of decadence (according to which, apart from the canonical texts that represent the ultimate perfection, all subsequent literature is doomed to degeneration),[69] the idea of periodic renewal offers the desired rule. Each age inherits the preceding one but is simultaneously itself creative.[70] There is both a "break" and a "tradition" (a "turning point" and an "affiliation"). Rather than divide up ages, seeing them as so many temporal, separate, isolated blocks, Chinese ideas concerning literary history emphasize the continuous nature of literary evolution: every "font" gives rise to a "stream"; from the "trunk" one moves on to the "branches." The factors of change become part of the regularity of the process; the dynamic of alternation is inexhaustible. Like any other history, the history of literature passes along an uninterrupted chain of phases, rising and declining, which does not necessarily mean that "what comes first is necessarily a time of rising and what follows is a time of decline," for every decline itself leads to a new rise. Once again, the "tendency" for change, perceived as "inexhaustible,"[xx] is part of the "order of things" and is justified by reason.

Ye Xie
17th century

The Chinese Concept of History Foresees No End and Does Not Consist in an Account of Events

The analysis of history in China thus implies "starting from the individuality of the moment" to "evaluate its *shi*."[71] The concept of a "tendency stemming from the situation" ultimately serves as a bridge between history and logic: that is, as an intermediary between the successive ages that constitute the course of lived history on the one hand and the internal logic discoverable through them and which justifies this evolution, on the other. This intermediary makes it possible to pass from one to the other, and to link becoming with reason: Historical tendency bestows

Wang Fuzhi

a necessary direction and a logical end upon all evolution. And this direction, this result, always stems anew from the play of factors making up the relations of force at a given moment. "If the moments differ, the tendencies which result from them (*shi*) also differ, and if those tendencies differ, the logics which govern the processes also differ";[yy][72] "the tendency depends on the opportunity of the moment just as the internal logic depends on the tendency."[73] One cannot deliberate generally and hence abstractly on the course of things: "One must appraise the moment in such a way as to detect its tendency and, consequently, seek to conform with its coherence."[zz][74] Once a historical moment is perceived as a particular setup to be exploited, every individual situation becomes intelligible; and it is from its tendency – and from it alone – that one can deduce what we are today accustomed to call "the meaning of history."

There is undeniably a certain objective analogy between this Chinese concept of rationality in the historical setup together with the idea of its evolution, on the one hand, and the Hegelian view of history conceived as the realization of reason on the other; both are founded on the idea of the ineluctable nature of the unfolding process (cf. Hegel: "The study of universal history itself must show that everything in it has happened rationally, that it has constituted the rational, necessary advance of the universal spirit").[75] In both cases, negativity is seen as merely temporary, only a necessary moment in the process of change; it is possible to understand and transcend it in the context of the more general evolution taking place. We are invited not to lament the misfortunes of history but rather to acquire a "conciliatory understanding"[76] of this process of becoming. In similar fashion, the course of history exploits human passions and private interests to bring about, eventually, what in effect corresponds to the general interest. From the Chinese perspective, we could apply what Hegel said of Caesar to the first emperor of China: he unified the world politically and imposed a new administrative regime on it. "The outcome of his initially *negative* plan" (after all, his ambition was to be "the only master of the world") was itself a necessary and influential event in history, whether Chinese or global. "It was not only personal gain that played a role here, but an instinct that fulfilled what the times themselves called for."[77] The secret "instinct" (of reason) is what the Chinese call "Heaven," the fathomless source of all regulation.[78] Even the unhappy destinies of these great men, "whose vocation was to manage the genius of the universe," as Hegel put it, was, logically enough, similar. Caesar was assassinated; before long, the dynasty of the first emperor was overthrown and dynastic longevity thus reduced forever:[79] the "bale soon fell to earth, emptied of its grain."

But that analogy itself makes the difference between these two concepts of history all the more striking and reveals the wide divergence between each discourse. Hegel conceives of reason in history as a relation between a "means" and an "end": everything that comes to pass over time, including the actions of great men, is only the means through which the "end of the universe" is realized, namely, man's accession to an awareness of liberty. For Hegel, who was an heir to the Judeo-Christian tradition, universal history should be regarded as a progress, the fulfillment of which constitutes from the beginning its rightful destination, even though it may no longer be conceived in a purely religious mode (as in *The City of God*). Now, as we have already noted, the concept of *shi*, right from its initial formation in connection with strategy, never dealt with any such relation between means and end, however natural that relation may seem to us. If Heaven can make use of the individual interests of great men within the framework of history, it is purely through the internal determination of a process that will unfailingly manifest its eminently regulatory role when conceived in its global dimensions. But no providence, no concerted plan, is involved here. The Chinese view of history is not theological, since it involves no revelation, nor does it detect any purposeful design. It involves no eschatology, for no final cause directs it. It is justified by no *telos*; rather, its own "economy"[80] is immanent. In the final analysis, this difference can be largely explained by the Chinese concept of time: Although Chinese tradition is clearly familiar with the notion of an immediate future — the future that is already hinted at in the present moment and that the current evolving process cannot fail to bring about — it seems to have no place for any idea of a pure, abstract future. The time in which the process unfolds is infinite. Its logic, since it is self-regulating, implies no end. An end to history is unthinkable.

In these circumstances, the divergence between the two traditions is bound to become ever more marked. Certain definitions may seem to us absolutely general and inescapable; for example, "History is the account of true events (or facts) in which man is the actor." (Recent concepts of history have taught us that a past not constructed around the concept of the event is simply "historicity of which we have not yet become fully aware.")[81] However, such a definition is not as pertinent to the Chinese tradition as it has been, over twenty-five centuries, to our own. In China, history as a genre focuses its attention not so much on events or facts but rather on change. It is never presented as a continuous narrative (whether an annalist record or a compilation of documentation). Instead, facts and/or events figure more as reference points in the evolving process. Perhaps such perceptions, prompted by considering a different culture, may stimulate us to reconsider our own position: if, in our tradition, history as a genre concentrates on events or facts, that "choice" in the selective editing of reality surely reflects our own metaphysical prioritizing of individual entities (*ens individuum*, from the atom to God). The Chinese tradition, in contrast, gives priority to relations. Similarly, our formulation of history is, from start to finish, narrative in character primarily because our historical genre stems from epic narrative. China, meanwhile, is the only great civilization that produced neither a cosmography nor an epic. Finally, the difference between the two traditions is affected by the very concept of the historian's task. In the West, history is explained on the basis of causality; but, as we have seen, the Chinese tradition concentrates mainly on an interpretation based on tendencies.

In the West we are familiar with the logic of causal explanation in history. This logic rests on more than just a matter of selection (first settling on the "effect" to be considered, then identifying and picking out the most satisfactory antecedents). A fictional procedure is also involved here, since imaginary evolutions are used to gauge the efficacy of causes: What would have happened "if," i.e., in the absence of this or that antecedent?[82] We engage in a retrospective evaluation of probability (a "backward" kind of prediction or a "retrodiction"),[83] which, of course, is never exhaustive, since each fact and/or event is situated at an intersection with countless others, each of which could be traced back *ad infinitum*. All this returns us, via a different route, to the perspective of probability that we recognized at the outset of this work as stamping the strategic concepts of the West — a point of view that sharply contrasts with the automaticity characterizing Chinese strategy. For instead of constructing a hypothetical chain of causality, the Chinese favor an interpretation in terms of "tendencies" from which they simply deduce the "ineluctable" (and, since it does not follow from any retrospective illusion, whatever is "ineluctable" is also logical). As we have seen, the process can only evolve from one stage to the next in one direction or another (either via an accentuation or a reversal of the tendency through a process of rebalancing and compensation). In consequence, when we consider events "which do not come about in a single day," it is necessary to "return to the starting point of the whole evolution" which, through continuous change, has resulted in things as they are. (Hence the traditional interest in Chinese thought in a long-term view and the "silent transformations" of time, whereas Western thought focuses much more on the shorter term).[84] But this revelation of tendencies at work is itself only possible through a twofold theoretical operation which the Chinese tradition, for its part, seems to take more or less for granted. In the first place, historical evolution must be considered as an overall process that constitutes a system in isolation (in contrast to the causal explanation that remains open and, in accounting for what comes about, accepts the fact that new data must constantly be introduced).[85] Second, reality must be organized in a bipolar fashion in which what counts are relations of opposition and complementarity (from which it is possible for equilibrium to stem, e.g., from tension and détente, impetus and decline, etc.). Chinese civilization is particularly suited to such an attitude. Since it takes account only of its own tradition and considers it invariably from a unitary perspective (such being the strength of its ethnocentrism), it tends to consider its history as unfolding in isolation. Meanwhile, on the level of Chinese philosophy, the incidence of duality that at every turn serves to structure the way that history develops corresponds to the very principle of all reality, namely, the correlation of the *yin* and the *yang*. The Chinese civilization was thus culturally predisposed to account for human history according to a logic based on tendencies.

Causal Explanation and Interpretation Based on Tendencies

However, Western historical thought has not been totally unaware of the notion of tendencies as the basis for interpretations. A theme as classic as the "greatness and decline of the Romans" comfortably accommodated it. For example, when Montesquieu draws a parallel between Carthage and Rome on the bipolar model dear to the Chinese, he is fully aware of the internal logic through which success is followed by its opposite: "It was the very conquests of Hannibal that began to change the fortune of this war." Because he was unfailingly victorious, Hannibal received no more reinforcements; having conquered too many territories, he could not retain them. More generally, the notion of "corruption" which lies at the heart of Montesquieu's work is made to account for the structural necessity of reversal at least when it manages to shed its moral implications, which are too ideological to serve as a satisfactory historical explanation (were the Romans really corrupted by the influence of Epicureanism?).[86] Thus, although Montesquieu remains attached to causal explanations, he is simultaneously tempted to look beyond them:

> It is not chance that rules the world. Ask the Romans, who had a continuous sequence of successes when they were guided by a certain plan, and an uninterrupted sequence of reverses when they followed another. There are general causes, moral and physical, which act in every monarchy, elevating it, maintaining it, or hurling it to the ground. All accidents are controlled by these causes. And if the chance of one battle – that is, a particular cause – has brought a state to ruin, some general cause made it necessary for that state to perish from a single battle. In a word, the main trend draws with it all the particular accidents.[87]

The notion of a "general cause" or, as Montesquieu hastens to amend, a "principal trend," is close to the idea of a tendency. Montesquieu does have an intuition of *shi*: "The mistakes of statesmen are not always voluntary. Often they are the necessary consequences of the situation in which they find themselves, with difficulties giving rise to still more difficulties."[88]

Montesquieu's intuition was possible because the West, in the eighteenth century, was leaving behind the providential view of history that had culminated with Jacques-Bénique Bossuet. Nor had the secular version of that view been imposed yet, according to which the development of science was seen as the law governing the destined progress of the human race; this view would not be adopted as a general law until the nineteenth century. Similarly, at the beginning of the twentieth century, when people again distanced themselves from the idea of progress, they were forced to resort to an interpretation based on tendencies, such as rise and decline. We can see this in the works of Oswald Spengler and Arnold Toynbee, who tried to elaborate a morphology of civilizations based on their phases of growth and disintegration. But, as Raymond Aron has noted, the problem now was, "What could that old idea of cycles mean for us, in the twentieth century?"[89]

The theoretical difficulty raised by Toynbee's work stems partly from the fact that he was obliged to isolate each civilization within its own closed process (as the Chinese themselves isolated their civilization). But more crucially, it is caused by the absence of any model – above and beyond generalization through comparison – that could structure a formulation of the process of becoming. The cyclical formulae of Western Antiquity did not pose any problem to him since they were based on a cosmogonical view linking, as a matter of principle, the life of man and the destiny of the world. However, when those cosmogonical hypotheses fall out of favor (and by the Renaissance only vestiges of them remain, even in the work of Giambattista Vico), the only possible bases for cyclical ideas that can no longer be astronomical are either zoological or botanical: civilization is compared to an animal or plant species. Each has its period of blossoming, reaches maturity, and then sinks into decline (on the model of Aristotle's *De generatione et corruptione*). In Spengler, the biological view remains unadulterated. However, Toynbee is all too aware that, in the last analysis, this is no more than an analogy: "Every human being, as a living organism, is bound to die at the end of a more or less long time but...I, for my part, do not see why the creations of a mortal organism need themselves be mortal as a matter of theoretical necessity, even if many certainly do die."[90] Hence the *aporia* to which the cyclical schema ultimately leads in Toynbee's work, and hence his return to a progressivist view, ultimately converted into theology. All this may help us to appreciate the value of the contribution made to the Chinese tradition by the famous *Book of Changes* (the most important of the Chinese canonical texts since Antiquity). On the sole basis of an alternation between continuous and discontinuous lines and the sixty-four hexagrams derived from this, it provides a single formula for change independent of all other references. The interpretation is systematic yet valid in all circumstances. Becoming is itself interpreted and ordered in accordance with its own principle. The Chinese theory of history was thus, in every period, provided with a ready-made mold.

We should accordingly pursue even further our analysis of the difference between the Chinese and Western views of history and try to trace the origins of that difference even deeper. We need to understand why Greek thought was so concerned with extricating "being" from becoming, whereas in China the only reality is change itself. It is, of course, not as though the Greeks were any less aware of the ephemeral, as is shown by their earliest cosmogonies, in which successive generations of gods take over from one another. But within this list of gods, the Greeks already showed more interest in identifying and fixing the characteristics of each deity than in exploring the fashion in which they followed each other: it is not so much the series of stages that is important but instead the clearly defined aspects that the gods of each stage acquire.[91] Greek thought little by little ordered the obscure process of becoming that emerged from chaos through establishing one transcendent law, namely, the necessity of destiny. The continuous flow of things was given consistency by a theoretical framework providing it with numbers, shapes, and elements: the coherence of becoming stems from the mathematical or logical formula fixing the immutability of different types within it. As is well known, such dissociation reaches its apex in Platonism: on the one hand there is "being," which is eternal and perfect and the object of knowledge; on the other, "becoming" (the order of *genesis*), that which is born and dies but never "is." Under the Platonic reign of the "same," the rebellious nature of the "other" is revealed; becoming is in itself a principle of irregularity, disorder, evil. The lower one descends in the hierarchy of beings, the greater the proportion of becoming to being, and only by "participation" in the immutable ideas can the mutable be given order. Aristotelian realism, although presented as a doctrine of becoming, changes nothing in the above vision. Even if forms and becoming are no longer separable, eternal forms nevertheless retain their sway, and it is only through them that becoming can be determined.[92] Anything eluding their control is the residue that belongs to the irrational — accident, fortune, monstrosity, or any other unintelligible manifestation of necessity. Becoming is once and for all identified with "matter" and there is no escape from this fixing of essences.[93]

Thus, the essential difference is that Greek thought introduced order into becoming from the outside (on the basis of numbers, ideas, forms), whereas in Chinese thought order is conceived as lying within becoming; it is what makes becoming a process.

One could say — metaphorically, at least — that Greek thought was marked by the idea, at once tragic and beautiful, of "measure" attempting to impose itself on chaos. In contrast, Chinese thought became sensitive early on to the regular, spontaneous fecundity stemming simply from the alternation of the seasons. But the theoretical stakes in this difference are important. Because Western thought projects order from the outside, it most values the causal explanation (according to which an antecedent and a consequence, A and B, are extrinsically related to one another). Because Chinese thought considers order to be internal to the process, it emphasizes above all the interpretation based on tendencies (the antecedent and the consequence are successive stages in the same process, A and A', and each phase spontaneously changes into the next one). Clearly, the concept of history as a setup that can be used to one's advantage is itself only intelligible through that opposition. Now, moving on from the level of history to that of foundational philosophy, let us consider how each way of proceeding is justified both in its underlying principles and as a general theory.

CHAPTER TEN

Propensity at Work in Reality

Chinese Tradition's Scant Interest in Causal Explanation

"We never reckon that we understand a thing till we can give an account of its 'how and why,' that is, of its first cause"; "We consider that we have unqualified knowledge of anything [as contrasted with accidental knowledge] when we believe that we know that the cause from which the fact results is the cause of that fact"; "Wisdom is concerned with the primary causes and principles."[1] These pronouncements of Aristotle are as valid in the field of physical nature, which is given over to becoming, generation, and corruption, as they are in first philosophy, the philosophy of Being qua being (metaphysics), in which "the primary cause peculiar to the thing" comes down to the absolutely first cause and ultimately refers to God. In the Western world, the formula *rerun cognoscere causas* has served as a motto for our philosophical apprenticeship, for it is by going back into the causes of things that we apprehend reality and its underlying principles: this formula has shaped our investigations and determined the progress of our thought.

It does not seem possible, for us in the Western tradition, to question the absolute validity of this understanding of causality, for its legitimacy is treated as self-evident and serves as the logical basis for the tradition. Kant tells us that causality is a general law of understanding that must be established a priori. Chinese thought, in contrast, seems almost never to rely on such a principle, even in its interpretation of nature. Of course, it cannot totally ignore the causal relationship, but it resorts to it only within the framework of experiences taking place in front of us, where its impact is immediate. It never extrapolates it in imagined series of causes and effects extending all the way back to the hidden reason for things or even to the principle underlying reality as a whole.

One indication of the Chinese tradition's scant interest in causal explanation is provided by its lack of enthusiasm for myths. The importance ascribed to the etiological function of myth within Western civilization is well known, whether this function intervenes at the so-called prescientific stage of the development of thought or remains vibrant in providing answers for all the questions that continue to defy positivist understanding. In China, the few mythological elements one can trace in "folklore" were never advanced by theoretical speculation to provide answers for the bewilderment human beings feel in the face of enigma and mystery. However, we can detect the beginnings of another style of reasoning at the dawn of Chinese civilization, in the striking development of a minutely precise practice of divination, that is, in the analyses of divinatory diagrams: The configuration of the cracks that appear on a tortoise shell heated over a fire, following a series of extremely elaborate manipulations, is never interpreted as the result of a relation of cause and effect but as some *particular disposition* which is highly revelatory. Léon Vandermeersch writes as follows: "From one event to another, the relation revealed by the science of divination is not presented as a chain of intermediate causes and effects, but as a change in a diagrammatic configuration. This is the sign of an overall change in the state of the universe, which has to occur for any new event to take place, however infinitesimal that event may be."[2] The divinatory diagram takes it on itself to convey the overall interplay of the event's cosmic implications, for they "stretch far beyond the causal links and entirely control them": the configuration should be interpreted as an insight, momentary yet simultaneously global, into all the relations involved. This insight strongly contrasts with a deductive sequence of cause and effect.

The Chinese interpretation of reality in any realm, and even where most generally speculative, thus appears to proceed through the understanding of the disposition of things. One starts by identifying a particular configuration (disposition, arrangement), which is then seen as a system according to which things function: instead of the explanation of causes, we have the implication of tendencies. In the former, one must always find an external element as an antecedent, and reasoning can be described as regressive and hypothetical. In the latter, the sequence of changes taking place stems entirely from the power relations inherent in the initial situation, thereby constituting a closed system: in this case we are dealing not with the hypothetical but with the ineluctable. In the context of natural phenomena and in first philosophy, this *ineluctability* of *tendency* can be expressed by the term *shi*, translated as either "tendency" or "propensity" depending on the word chosen by the first Western interpreters of Chinese thought as they tried to convey its originality. Thus Leibnitz, attempting to refute Nicolò Longobardi's arguments, declares: "The Chinese, far from being at fault, deserve praise for their view that things come about through their natural propensities."[3] But then the question is: What is nature in relation to this "propensity"?

The Meaning of Natural Propensity

Book of Changes

To the Chinese, the principal "disposition" (or arrangement of things) concerns the relation between Heaven and Earth. Heaven is above and Earth beneath; one is round, the other square. Because of the Earth's situation — it is beneath Heaven yet also matches it — its "propensity," *shi*, always leads it to "conform with and obey" the initiative emanating from Heaven.[a4] Earth and Heaven, through their "disposition," embody the antithetical and complementary principles presiding over everything that happens. They constitute on the one hand the "initiator," on the other the "receiver," the Father and the Mother. It is from the configuration of this primary pair that the entire process of reality stems.

Propensity thus provides the key to the actualization of things. We already find this idea at the end of Chinese Antiquity, when the theme of endless renewal began to be envisaged in a theoret-

Laozi

ical and global fashion:

> The *Dao* [the Way] engenders them,
> Virtue nurtures them,
> Material reality confers physical form on them
> And propensity brings them to full fruition.[b5]

In this extremely general perspective, the actualizing "virtue" inherent in the process is the ever-renewed dynamism stemming from the original duality of Heaven and Earth, *yin* and *yang*; and the *Dao* or "Way" is the unifying principle in the never-ending deployment. At the end of the whole chain of connections which accounts for the great process in which the world is engaged, the term "propensity" designates both the particular circumstances characterizing the various stages in the process and the particular tendency produced in each case. It is just such a "propensity" that brings the slightest potential for existence to concrete frui-

tion at the first hint. At the most embryonic stage, the tendency *Guiguzi*
toward the fullness of actualization is already latent.[e6] It is this
tendency that one must examine attentively from the very beginning, from the first hint of its existence, for it gives us certain
information regarding the evolution of things and provides us with
a dependable basis for success.[d7]

Attempting to act upon the physical or social world without
going along with the tendency objectively implied in it and governing its development would be vain and therefore absurd, as
would seeking to aid the unfolding of reality rather than acting
in conformity with the logic of the propensity that always stems
from the given situation. This perspective is particularly high-
lighted by those trying to retain "Daoism" as the state doctrine
at the beginning of the Empire.[8] No matter how obvious the following formula they used may seem, it contains a lesson in wis- *Huainanzi*
dom: "It spontaneously follows from the propensity of things"[e] 2nd century B.C.
that "a boat floats on the water and a cart rolls along the ground."[9]
Things tend of their own accord toward similar things that "correspond in their propensity."[f10] Possibility or impossibility results
from the particular "disposition" (situation) produced by their
coming together. For everything there is a proper place and a
proper time, which can be neither altered nor transgressed:[11] the *Huainanzi*
great Yu succeeded in making the whole territory of China healthy
by getting its rivers to flow eastward through exploiting the natural inclination of the land levels; then Ji proceeded to the necessary land clearance and succeeded in spreading agriculture; but
he could not have gotten plants to grow in the winter.[12] It is
impossible to go against the propensity inherent in the regular
unfolding of processes.[g] This does not, of course, mean that one
should completely desist from action; instead, one should simply
understand how to put aside all "activism" and disregard one's
own desire to take the initiative. Having done so, one should go

223

along with the flow of the phenomena, profit from their dynamism, and induce them to cooperate.[13]

This type of reasoning about the use of the disposition of
things is itself indissociable from the adoption of a particular
strategy relating to nature. One sees that the causal explanation
for phenomena can be replaced by an interpretation based on
tendencies:

> If two pieces of wood are rubbed together, fire results,
> If fire and metal come into contact, fusion results;
> It is normal for whatever is round to turn,
> Whatever is hollow in principle floats:
> That is the natural propensity.[14]

Just as each reality in the world has its own particular nature
("birds fly by beating the air with their wings, quadrupeds move
by stepping on the earth"), similarly, an ineluctable change occurs with every appropriate conjunction of elements (wood with
metal, metal with fire, round things with the ground, hollow
things with water) because it stems from those particular dispositions. The relationships are seen as a downstream movement
from one stage to the next,[15] in the sense of an unfolding process. One does not move upstream to explore a series of phenomena envisaged as a chain of causality.

The natural thus merges with *spontaneity*, and this concept of
propensity led to an explicit critique of finalist causality.[16] It was
not as a result of a cause, or intentionality,[17] that Earth and Heaven
engendered man, but "out of the union of their breaths, it so happened that man was spontaneously born," just as a child is spontaneously born from the union of *qi* (energy) between spouses.
It is not because, at that moment, those spouses desire to engender a child; rather, "from the movement of their desires this union

Wang Chong
1st century A.D.

224

has resulted, out of which the engendering proceeds." Likewise, Heaven makes grains and flax grow not to provide for the needs of man (no more than calamities damaging the harvests occur to punish him). This "spontaneous" development stands in opposition to the model of human fabrication planned.[18] Heaven proceeds without causes, through its interaction with Earth, simply through their mutual dispositions: it is not a "creator."

The Demystification of Religion and Interpretation Based on Tendencies

One of the most striking peculiarities of Chinese civilization is that it moved at an early date away from religious feeling toward a sense of universal regulation. As early as the second millennium B.C., initial belief in the gods faded away. Sacrifice was replaced by divinatory procedures designed to detect the regular forces at work, and this encouraged cosmological speculation. The earlier animism, which culminated in the notion of a "Lord above" in command of nature in its entirety and imposing his own will on men, gave way before an idea of a "Heaven" that tended to be liberated from anthropomorphic representations and whose physical functioning alone was considered to incorporate the whole of divine omnipotence. At the same time, the many ancient chthonic powers were dissolved into a single, cosmic entity, namely, Earth, seen as physically symmetrical to Heaven and as working in synchrony with it. The whole universe was "functionalized" – or ritualized – and it was by virtue of the perfection and universality of the norms it embodied that Heaven was transcendent.[19] A sense of mystery based on the fear of an arbitrary deity no longer characterized the supernatural. Instead, this mystery became fused with a feeling for "nature" itself, that unfathomable fount of spontaneity, stemming ceaselessly from the inexhaustible potential in the disposition of reality.

As the various schools of thought of late Antiquity flour-
ished, a major philosophical development ("Concerning Heaven")
emerged. Replacing the religious idea of a caretaking deity, it
tended to separate the function of Heaven from human destiny.
Xunzi The functioning of Heaven was characterized by its constancy: it
3rd century B.C. could never vary in response to the alternation of order and disorder experienced by human society; nor could it pay any attention to human feelings and "put an end to winter because man
has a horror of the cold."[20] An entire tradition of Chinese thought
continued to develop such ideas, particularly the Neo-Legalist
groups under the Tang, at the turn of the eighth and ninth centuries. These radical reformers were attempting to work against the
political and social crises then shaking the empire. Did their "elementary materialism" really go hand in hand with their plans for
reform, as Chinese historians of philosophy today maintain? What
is certain at any rate is that their position was based on the prin-
Liu Zongyuan ciple that it is absurd to believe in a Heaven dispensing retribu-
8th–9th centuries tion and justice – to complain to Heaven and plead with it for
pity is even more absurd: as if Heaven could respond in any way
or was anything but a "fat melon"![21]

Faced with the idea of some all-seeing sovereign mind that
Liu Yuxi "secretly determines the destiny of men," the "naturalist" per-
8th–9th centuries spective thus defended the idea of two independent "capacities"
developing on separate, parallel levels: Heaven's work is to make
things grow and is manifested in physical force. Man's work is to
organize and is manifested in social values.[22] When order reigns
in society and its values are universally recognized, merit automatically is rewarded and misbehavior justly punished: at such
times, nobody would dream of calling for Heaven's intervention in
any way. But if order "relaxes" in the slightest, if values become
even a bit confused and society's retribution is no longer fulfilled in regular fashion, although people continue to explain

everything functioning well by "the reason of things," their only recourse with regard to anything considered unjustifiable is to pray to Heaven. And if the social order breaks down completely and nothing goes as it should, then everything is laid at the door of, not men, but the authority of Heaven alone. In this way, Liu Yuxi explains, religion owes its existence solely to the unsatisfactory state of society: only when the social order is failing do people – mistakenly – begin to confuse one level with the other and Heaven's powers of regulation with man's happiness. Under good sovereigns it is impossible "to hoodwink the people with the supernatural"; but when political mores degenerate, Heaven is invoked "to keep people in line."[23]

The same applies in man's relations with nature: he only starts to believe that Heaven is in charge when he can no longer under- Liu Yuxi stand what is happening to him. But such mystery is invariably no more than relative. One who sets off in a boat on a small waterway feels himself to be totally in command, whereas on a large river or at sea one is much more inclined to appeal to Heaven. Even though the same exercise is involved, the difference in proportions makes the rational explanation of phenomena in the one case clearer, in the other more obscure. Even in an extreme case, where two boats are traveling together under the same conditions of wind and currents, the fact that the one remains afloat while the other sinks is no grounds for suggesting that Heaven has played a part, for it can be adequately explained in terms of *shi* or propensity.[24] The water and the boat are both "material realities" and, once the one becomes involved with the other, a certain objective (and numerical) "relationship" is established; further, once that relationship is determined in a certain way, a particular "tendency" orientating the process in one direction or another ineluctably appears (either a tendency to remain afloat or a tendency to sink).[h] Each case conforms with its particular configuration and takes up the resulting propensity:[i] this propensity is produced as indissociably as are "shadows or echoes." Depending on the form of the phenomena, the reason for that propensity may be detectable or undetectable, but in either case the same logic is at work.

Thus, even more clearly than before, the expected causal explanation comes to be supplanted by an interpretation based on tendencies, which here serves as the ultimate and strongest possible argument for the demystification of religious illusion. The matter is posed explicitly in terms whose full metaphysical impact we would do well to gauge. If everything in reality is governed Liu Yuxi by a certain propensity systematically stemming from the objectively measurable relations between things, "is not Heaven itself limited (and constrained) by this ineluctability of tendencies"?[j] Heaven, in its operation, is indeed subjected to the determination imposed by the measurements of the hours and the seasons. Once it "has become high and large" it cannot on its own return to being "low and small"; once it has set itself in motion, "it cannot halt on its own for a single moment." Thus, Heaven too is subjected to the inviolability of tendency, whose reign is absolutely universal.

The Setup of Reality and Its Manipulation

The sway of tendency is not only universal, but also logical. With the development of Neo-Confucianism from the ninth century on, Chinese thinkers become exceedingly inclined to emphasize the principle of internal coherence that accounts for the processes of reality. Although they react against the influence of Buddhism (in their view, it has perverted their modes of thought), they are nevertheless obliged to consider the metaphysical necessity brought to their attention by this new tradition, and so they return to the sources of Chinese thinking. The idea of a *principle* and *reason for things* (*li*) thus comes to the fore and serves as the basis of their view of the world. This idea gives reality a new structure, which is described at three levels:[25] at the level of "principle" is "duality-correlativity"; at the level of "tendency" (*shi*) is "mutual attraction between the two poles" ("they seek each other out");[k] finally, at the level of "relationship" and its numerical determination is a constant "flux" that is in perpetual metamorphosis. At the starting point thus remain two factors standing in opposition and interrelation; from this "disposition" stems a reciprocal interaction which constitutes their propensity; from that dynamic relationship proceeds the actualization of phenomenal manifestations in a perpetual state of variation. In this chain, tendency is the intermediate term linking the principle to the coming-to-be of what is concrete, and it constitutes the creative and regulatory tension coextensive with reality in its entirety.

Liu Yin
13th century

Within the Chinese tradition, there is general agreement over this understanding of the way that things are disposed. Disagreement only arises over its correct use. Reacting to the worsening political situation with increasingly rigid moral intransigency, the Confucian *literati*, concerned for the "people" and the "State," were tempted to accuse their opponents of fraudulently exploiting tendency out of private ambition. Does not the Daoist sage (in the manner of *Laozi*) advise one to abase oneself humbly, even to "empty oneself of one's 'self'"? Does he not recommend as models the "piece of uncarved wood" and the "newborn babe"? But he does so because he knows full well that opposites are necessarily mutually attractive and interchangeable, and that the compensatory function of tendency must then operate to his advantage (not in some hypothetical Beyond, of course, but within the highly imminent future). He humbles himself to be in a better position to rise; if he withdraws, he does so to be all the more certainly pulled forward; if he ostensibly drains away his "self,"

Liu Yin

he does so to impose that "self" all the more imperiously in the future. For he knows very well that, conversely, "the propensity of that which is dazzling is to grow ineluctably dimmer";[1] "the propensity of that which is full is to eventually spill over" and "the propensity of that which is sharply pointed is to come to be broken."[26]

The *literati* argued that this false humility thus cloaks an extremely strict art of manipulation. Not only are others taken in by these appearances, but, above all, the tendency propelling us forward cannot be imputed to ourselves, for it proceeds simply from the objective situation. It is not I, myself, on my own, who seeks to push myself forward; rather, I find myself carried forward, as if in spite of myself, by the ineluctable logic of reality. From a tactical perspective, since an individual always looks ahead to later developments and puts himself in a position from which he can profit, the good manipulator is already ahead of the game: "No sooner is he on the point of beginning than he is already anticipating the end, and no sooner has he entered than he is already preparing his exit."[27] He is never at a loss, just like the great process of the world itself, and he becomes as "unfathomable" as that process. As we have seen earlier, under the influence of ancient Daoism, the Chinese tradition defined wisdom as relying on the tendency objectively at work at the heart of phenomena in order to allow oneself to be carried along and succeed in one's undertakings. But now we find a perverse use of that same procedure as well. In this world that has rejected sovereign arbitration on the part of the deity, the sage merges with the manipulator in this art of exploiting the disposition of things. The two become identified because they share a sense of effectiveness. Of course, their intentions differ, but can one truly distinguish them by that criterion?

Liu Yin

The Concept of "Logical Tendency" and the Interpretation of the Phenomena of Nature

The idea that propensity contains a rationality eventually led to the new concept of "logical tendency,"[m] which was used over the later centuries of Chinese thought to clarify the view that Chinese civilization evolved of nature and the world. "Logical tendency" incorporates two ideas that Chinese thought cannot dissociate: first, the notion that in reality everything always comes about immanently as a result of an internal development, with no need to invoke any external causality; second, the idea that this spontaneous process is itself a supremely regulatory force and that the norm it expresses constitutes the basis for transcending reality. In the last analysis, this is the Chinese "Heaven": its "natural" course also constitutes an absolute "morality."

Once again, although here at the level of the whole of reality, alternation stems from the disposition of things; it constitutes the general mode by which everything functions. The course of the world is simply an uninterrupted succession of opposed but complementary phases of "latency" and "actualization." Given that at the harmonious stage of latency the bipolar duality (of *yin* and *yang*) is already at work behind a "logical tendency," this tendency "ineluctably" leads to the process that develops spontaneously when the opposing principles are reciprocally put into motion.[n28] From this actual phenomena come into being, with no external intervention. But subsequently this actualization, through an equally spontaneous "logical tendency," reverts to the stage of latency and become dissolved in the undifferentiated "Great Void."[29] The entire universe follows a rhythm created by the invariable correlation between the concentration and dispersion of the two cosmic energies, through the endless chain of the life and death of everything.[o30] For phases of flowing as of ebbing, any change in tempo is impossible. Faced with the ineluctable nature

Wang Fuzhi
17th century

231

Wang Fuzhi

of this "logical tendency," the sage's only possible attitude is that of "calmly awaiting his destiny." This general concept has been given a much more precise physical interpretation. Of the two sources of energy fueling the actualization of reality, the nature of one (*yin*) is to "congeal" and "concentrate itself," while that of the other (*yang*) is to "rise up" and "disperse itself." Whatever the one condenses, the other ineluctably dissipates, and "the two then tend equally [with the same *shi*] to become dispersed."[31] However, two possible outcomes should be kept in mind: either this dispersion takes place harmoniously, producing the normal phenomena of frost, snow, rain, and dew (each corresponding to its own particular season: frost to autumn, snow to winter, rain to spring, and dew to summer), or, alternatively, the dispersion does not take place harmoniously and we then find violent whirlwinds darkening the whole sky. This disharmony results because the *yang* has tended to disperse in too hasty a fashion while the *yin*, for its part, has become more and more solid. To be sure, the ineluctability of the tendency means the *yin* will be unable to remain in this condition for long, but before the dispersion eventually takes place, a certain amount of violence is unleashed.[32] This provides a perfect analogy for the social turmoil and clashes that can suddenly succeed a period of gradual and uninterrupted historical transformation, if a period's inherent contradictions have been exacerbated (at this point, it is worth recalling in particular Wang Fuzhi's analysis of the transition from feudalism to bureaucracy; see p. 186). Nevertheless, in both instances, even if the tendency has produced some sudden eruptions, it never ceases to be the fruit of a perfectly rational necessity. If we simply analyze this phenomenon of propensity "minutely," Wang Fuzhi tells us, this apparent discontinuity becomes reabsorbed.[p33] Even crises and storms are "logical."

The Inseparability of Tendency and Logic

It would be a crude mistake to believe that "when the world is well governed" it obeys only "logic" (or the "pattern," *li*), whereas "when it is badly governed," it obeys only "tendency" (*shi*),[34] for in both cases logic and tendency are indissociable; the philosopher's job is to prove it. To borrow the alternative suggested by *Mencius*, whether the less deserving is subjected to the more deserving or the weaker is subjected to the stronger, we see a relation of "dependence" bound to operate in the form of a *tendency*. And since the operation of the tendency in either case implies that "it could not do otherwise," then such a tendency is justified whatever the circumstances; thus, it always possesses a logic of its own.

The first case could not be clearer: the fact that "the less deserving is subjected to the more deserving" corresponds quite simply to "how it ought to be"; in that case the logic (conformity to the principle) makes the tendency (the relation of submission) come about.[q] Each side, both the rulers and the ruled, receives its due: "respect" for the former, "peace" for the rest. A hierarchy based on merit automatically imposes itself.

But the opposite situation, when hierarchical superiority is established not through greater wisdom or virtue but rests solely on a power relation, is problematic. It must be recognized that in this case the tendency that makes the weaker submit to the stronger is not "intrinsically" logical (since it does not correspond to "how it ought to be" in moral terms). Yet neither is it illogical, we are told. To see why, one merely must proceed *a contrario* and imagine the weaker party (without differentiating him from the stronger on the basis of merit) refusing to submit and seeking to challenge the stronger: such insane ambition will lead inevitably to his doom. If he happens to be responsible for a small kingdom (as *Mencius* envisages), he will drag the whole country

Wang Fuzhi

233

into ruin; that is "absurd." Since it leads to self-destruction, the refusal to submit is assuredly worse than agreeing to submit, even from the perspective of the weaker party. Although it does not correspond to the logic of how it ought to be, this last solution is nevertheless justified by the fact that it is unavoidable. More precisely, "one cannot claim that the submission of the weaker is not a possible outlet for the workings of the reason of things." If not ideal, this justification nevertheless stems from necessity.[r] The force of things is substituted for the reason of things, and the "tendency" thus serves as a "logic."[s]

Wang Fuzhi

We are told that the moral preconception that dissociates tendency and logic on the basis of whether the world is governed "according to the Way" rests on a metaphysical preconception: the separation within the notion of Heaven of *the energy that fuels actualization* (the *qi*) on the one hand and *the principle that rules that process (the li)* on the other.[t] Heaven, as it proceeds along its course, is both of those; it is what the actualizing energy cease-lessly becomes, under the influence of the regulating principle.[u] No actualization, whether desirable or undesirable, is possible without the energy that fuels the actualization; conversely, both good and bad times depend on an eminently logical process of evolution. Bad times are not due to an absence of regulation but to the negative fashion in which regulation is currently operating, making for disorder — as is proved by the experience of illness, in which a regulating force is certainly at work, albeit unfavorably. Each series of hexagrams in the *Book of Changes* possesses its own particular "virtue," not excluding those that symbolize reverses and stagnation.

Wang Fuzhi

Thus, it is only in exceptional circumstances that actualizing energy can be deployed without being subjected to a regulating principle: in nature, when whirlwinds and squalls suddenly spring up; in history, during periods of total disorder in which "every-

234

thing that begins to take shape forthwith disintegrates" and when no authority, good or bad, manages to impose itself (such as in fourth-century China, at the time of the Liu Yuan and the Shi Le). But storms do not undermine the regularity of the seasons, and total anarchy could not last for long without provoking its own annihilation. Hence the following necessary conclusion: since the actualizing energy and its regulating principle cannot be dissociated, "the tendency at work in things depends, for its fulfillment, not only on the actualizing energy but equally on the regulating principle." It is, moreover, through the relation between those two terms that, in the last analysis, "tendency" can best be defined. For how could it be conceived — in the most abstract fashion, even outside this philosophical context — other than as *energy* spontaneously *oriented* in a particular direction?

Critique of Metaphysical Idealism and the Ideology of Order

What is so striking about this reasoning, which is borrowed from one of the most profound Chinese thinkers of the seventeenth century, is its systematic and radical character. However, it could have only been elaborated across several contexts that themselves imply a number of different levels of thought. Its clearest line of reasoning is its rigorous critique of metaphysics. By refusing to allow the regulating principle at work to be dissociated from the actualizing energy, or the domain of principles from that of phenomena, or the ideal abstraction from the concrete facts, it also rejects the idealist separation — and does so deliberately. (It is, after all, in reaction against the influence of Buddhism, which the author claims has penetrated even the *literati* tradition.) This does not mean those terms were not carefully distinguished, but, as Jacques Gernet has shown clearly, the distinction never led to separation.[35] Although the concept of a possible dualism between them is abstractly entertained, it is seen as a correlation of con-

235

traries, the precise opposite of dualism: as we have seen, in the
Chinese theory of deployment, Heaven and Earth operate in conjunction and the "here and now" cannot be separated from some
"Beyond." Moreover, since the illusion of moralism comes hand
in hand with a metaphysical split that sets up a categorical opposition between happiness and misfortune, and relies on Heaven
when anything goes wrong, the Chinese thinkers deliberately
rejected that illusion too. (Moralism in fact found its starting
point in metaphysics.) Contemporary Chinese commentators frequently compare this to Hegel's famous reversibility of the "real"
and the "rational" (as he puts it: "All that is real is rational and all
that is rational is real"), which Western philosophy only achieved
by pushing the idealist position to its ultimate conclusion. In
China, by contrast, the implication flows naturally and fundamentally from the philosophy of propensity.

On the other hand, the status which this line of reasoning attributes to negativity is more ambiguous. When it justifies the logical character of a process that evolves negatively, is it simply
attempting to show that even deregulation involves modes of regulation, as in sickness, or does it consider that this negative phase
contains its own positive side, which leads to the negative phase
eventually being discarded, such as with winter's preparation for
the renewal of spring (to borrow the favorite example in the Chinese tradition, particularly in the *Book of Changes*)? This ambiguity (to us, at least) is connected with what has always constituted
the basis of the Chinese perspective in contrast to the Western
tradition, namely, its lack of interest in the ontological status of
evil and its preference for the idea of "functioning" (in which
"evil" is generally considered as nothing more than a kind of
disfunctioning). But here we must recognize that a purely philosophical interpretation is inadequate: it must be complemented
by a more anthropological interpretation of the different modes

of understanding found in the world, so far as a typology of the possibilities or "major options" is concerned.

A third, ideological, mode of interpretation is also needed here. The trouble with the notion of disorder in this line of reasoning is not so much its ambiguity as the effect of confusion it exploits (in connection, of course, with the question of hierarchy and power). Both *bad* order and an *absence* of order are opposed to "good order." Under the cloak of a measure of confusion, every effort is made here to promote the first alternative at the cost of the second. Behind that effort lurks the Chinese civilization's congenital horror of anarchy; even the worst tyrant is better than a vacuum of authority.

From the start, the whole line of argument rests on the notion that it is logical that the weaker should submit to the stronger "if his virtue and wisdom are different from those of his superior." But what about the case (here passed over in silence) in which the one placed in the inferior position is nevertheless more deserving, through his "virtue" or "wisdom," than the one in the dominant position? Surely revolt is conceivable, a revolt that would make power (once again?) correspond to merit. This would mean that, rather than content oneself with a makeshift "logic" contrary to ideal principles, whose sole justification is that it stems from the power relation — in other words, rather than accept that the "force of things" can serve as a sufficient "reason" — it might perhaps be better to reject categorically the all-too-convenient reversibility of the two terms involved (i.e., to reject the idea that the situation is just as acceptable *the other way around*). That is, it might be better to *decide* always to act so that the reason of things defeats the force of things and to *fight* (despite the power relation, and to the point of self-sacrifice) for the domination of the ideal.

But this course of action would necessarily lead to reestablish-

237

ing the metaphysical split, according to which the ideal is sacred and an absolute good exists, making it the basis for such moral heroism. Now we seem to have returned to "Western" thinking.

It is only parenthetically at the conclusion of this line of thought that Wang Fuzhi (without specifying whether the weaker party in this instance has the greater merit) envisages the possibility of the weaker being able to change a logic of disorder into a logic of good order. He then immediately observes that, until the actor achieved his aim, he would be rushing to his doom. As we have already noticed, general ideas of how the world is disposed and of universal regulation so colored political thinking in China at a very early date that it promoted a totalitarian and absolutist theory of power. Cosmological and social ritualism clearly accompanied each other. The eruption of "disorder" can be considered only in the interstices of regulation and in such a way that it is logically integrated at that point. "Storms" and "crisis" are not unthinkable – but revolution is.

Concrete Tendency Reveals the Regulating Principle: The Reversibility of the Relation between the Two

In this critique of metaphysical idealism, the idea of a tendency (shi) is the key because it provides a connection between the two aspects of reality.[36] One is the regulating principle that, qua principle, is never "something" that can come about concretely and is never exhausted, whatever its orientation. Hence it stems from the "intangible." (We are told that we must be careful not to allow the idea of it as a principle to be "materialized" by confusing it with one of its particular forms, even when dealing with its extreme manifestation, the Dao, or Way, which is central to political or moral thought.) The other is the energy that enables actualization, energy that never ceases to transform (itself) and whose "ordered" and "harmonious" character constitutes the

Wang Fuzhi

perceptible manifestation of that invisible principle. "The regulating principle can only be perceived in the inevitability of the tendency."[v] Since the tendency orienting the course of reality stems spontaneously from its setup, its task precisely is to *reveal* the guiding principle always at work within the perceptible actualization.

Once again – but this time at the level of reality as a whole – the propensity stemming from the disposition of things serves to mediate between the visible and that which is beyond the visible. In this connection, it is worth remembering the Chinese aesthetics of landscape painting, in which it was the tension emanating from the configuration of brush strokes that opened the dimension of the void and disposed the viewer toward a spiritual experience. We could also invoke the Chinese theory of history, in which the tendency inherent in the concrete situation allowed a passage from the immediate moment to the hidden logic behind the course of events. Through the objective workings of propensity the Chinese come face to face with the invisible and thus have no need for the "incarnation" of a mediator or for any "metaphysical postulates." Things make sense *naturally*.

The best proof of the impossibility of any idealist split between "principles" and the concrete is provided (as we are now beginning to see) by the reversibility of their relation. But let us try to formulate that relation more clearly by moving from the concept of disposition to the corresponding one of praxis. Inevitably we are again presented with two complementary perspectives, but here they give rise in every case to an alternative (because they each correspond to a moral choice): on the one hand, "conformity" or "nonconformity" toward the principle of order that determines the path to follow (at the level of the moral ideal, the *Dao*); on the other, the "possibility" or "impossibility" of the actual situation that produces the tendency (in the sense of the effective

Wang Fuzhi

orientation of the course of things).[37] Whether one conforms to the principle of order and encourages the arrival of the concrete possibility or whether one renders the situation impossible by opposing the principle, it is still the "principle" that brings about the "tendency."[w] However, there is also another way of envisaging the relation: an ideal order results from doing what is, in effect, possible, whereas a principle of disorder results from setting up something impossible. In this case, the tendency (within the concrete situation) "makes the principle come about."[x]

Wang Fuzhi   Let us take as an example the question of how a state should organize taxation – an issue in which politics, economics, and social theory all overlap. With good management, taxation is levied when the people have a surplus, even if the state has no pressing need; under bad management taxes would be levied whenever the state needed them, regardless of the people's situation. According to this example, levying the people's surplus for the benefit of their superiors satisfies everybody and corresponds to equity. Such is, in this case, conformity with "the principle of order." On the other hand, taxing only the surplus and operating so that one is never short of funds (reserves are built up for difficult times) amounts to "effective possibility at the level of the concrete situation." Within this framework, we can see how a good policy is conceived (always, of course, according to the Chinese model of harmonious regulation): it consists in acting so that *conformity with the principle* has the effect of *making the tendency viable.* Now let us imagine the opposite (of course, we need not "imagine it," since Chinese history provides plenty of examples): if the state tries to pressure the people without forewarning or regard for their poverty because it needs funds, the only result will be to exhaust the people and damage itself even more – an example of effective impossibility at the level of a concrete situation. In this case again it is the *tendency* that, under the pressure of circumstances, brings about the *principle*, but *negatively* – as a "principle of disorder."ʸ The constraint of the situation consists in having to levy emergency taxes from the people because the state has a pressing need for them. But the situation in itself is not possible (since the people cannot pay). Thus, the combination of these two factors results in discord between those who govern and those who are governed, between the "high" and the "low," which destroys harmony. In the first case, conforming with the principle meant that everything went well (as regards the concrete situation), but in the second, the impracticable character of the attempt leads to a logical contradiction.

Idealist philosophy has always stressed that "principles" and "reason" should determine what happens in a concrete situation. Chinese thought, in contrast, opposes the idealist position and reveals its bias by maintaining instead that an effective tendency, depending on whether or not it is viable, reacts according to principles and gives rise to a logic of regulation or its opposite. The logic of transcendence rests on a one-way relation (of the *logos* to becoming, of the intelligible to the empirical, of whatever is celestial to whatever is human). In contrast, the kind of thinking that founds a functionalist system on a duality of poles and focuses on the disposition of things puts value on interaction and reciprocity, even in the context of *a hierarchical relationship*: Heaven is superior to Earth but could not exist without it. Not only does the principle of order inform the world, it also depends on the course of things and is brought about through it.

Critique of Political "Realism": The Indissociability of Principle and Tendency

The model of the disposition of things is universal, as is the praxis that accompanies it, a point illustrated in the above example. Whether the world or human behavior is at issue, understanding the regulation of things means thinking in terms of the intimate and reversible harmony uniting principle and propensity and implies rejecting the two contrary positions: not only metaphysical idealism, as above, which tends to divorce the principle from the concrete propensity, but also political realism, which tends on the contrary to favor propensity at the cost of principle. In the case of politics, the "principle" is the ideal that enables society to function harmoniously and that reflects the immutable order of morality, while the "propensity" (*shi*) is the favorable tendency emanating from the power relations in a given historical situation and on which one can productively rely. In politics as well, it would be a mistake to think that these two aspects can be separated or that ideal and efficacy are not necessarily combined.[38] Wang Fuzhi tells us that the error of political "realism" lies in its attitude toward reality itself when, through opportunism or cynicism, it considers only relations of power. This error should be criticized not in the name of some ahistorical moral a priori but from the perspective of *objective* efficacy and from *within* the course of history. As a more rigorous analysis will necessarily show, only respect for principles can engender a truly favorable tendency, since it is only to the extent that it is in "conformity with the way things are regulated that a tendency can be dependable and lasting."[z]

Wang Fuzhi

One might, for example, think that in the name of "realism" a distinction should be made between a situation in which one seizes power and the condition for holding on to it;[aa] power can only be won by relying on the favorable tendency (*shi*) that comes from the relation of force, but to preserve the prestige of one's authority, one should demonstrate one's morality and respect for "principles." But in truth one can win power, that is, "truly subjugate others," only if one is already in a position to preserve it; similarly, one can preserve one's power, that is, "truly enlist the

Wang Fuzhi

support of others," only if one is still in a position to win it (again). Of course, one must have already won power to be in a position to preserve it, but only the ability to preserve it makes a complete and stable victory that does not run into opposition possible in the first place. The seizure of power thus does not represent the critical moment, as one all too often naively imagines, but is itself only conceivable if one has in mind the model of preserving it. *To preserve power* is "to enlist the support of all and make order reign," which boils down to "relying on the ideal nature of the principle to bring about the effective propensity [i.e., the propensity favorable to one's power]";[bb] *to win power* is "to obtain the submission of all by conforming with moral exigency," which amounts to "following the effective propensity favorable to one's power, in such a way as to conform with the regulating principle."[cc] The conclusion, then, is that the *principle* of morality necessary for the preservation of power must also be respected at the stage of winning power and that the *propensity* necessary for winning power must also be present at the stage of its preservation.[dd] Even if these two stages stand in opposition to the extent that, between them, they punctuate through alternation the course of political life and history, winning and preserving power are perfectly homogeneous; both depend on "the same regulating principle" and call for "the same type of propensity."

Despite this alternation of winning and preserving power to which history is subjected, history constitutes a uniform and continuous course in which *principle* and *propensity* must always go hand in hand. For this reason any seizure of power that fails to obey the ideal principle but relies solely on the favorable tendency generated by the relation of force is doomed in advance. Even if the historical situation seems initially favorable, it will inevitably evolve in the opposite direction. Thus, one cannot count on the future tendency,[ee] since it will operate against one in the end. In fact, while history proceeds constantly from the play of forces, even they cannot elude the logic of balance. For this reason the Chinese never imagined a final judgment that would transcend human history: in the last analysis, only that which is just can succeed, so history is completely legitimated by its very self.

Wang Fuzhi   The history of the great dynasty founders in ancient China is considered exemplary proof. Because they showed respect for morality when they seized power, their dynasties reigned for centuries (e.g., Tang, the founder of the Shang, and Wen, the founder of the Zhou). In the first place, the source of their motivation was not personal ambition but the fact that the reigning lineage had become totally degenerate and the situation demanded that it be replaced. Furthermore, Wang Fuzhi says, even in their behavior toward corrupt sovereigns they strove to conduct themselves as faithful subjects and postponed for as long as possible the task of banishing or punishing them. On the other hand, however, they hastened to exterminate pitilessly the vassals who had been supporting these bad princes, even though, from the perspective of a positive evaluation of the situation, their faults might seem "to weigh less heavily against them" than those of their sovereign. From a moral perspective their faults in fact weighed more heavily, since respect should always be shown to one's sovereign. The dynastic founders, isolating the sovereign, depriving him of all support, and extending their own ascendancy among the population, gradually managed to reverse the relation of power in their own favor, without ever having to confront the sovereign directly and so violate the principle of hierarchy. It was not so much a matter of seizing power; rather, power eventually slipped of its own accord into their hands and settled there all the more firmly because they did not acquire it illegitimately.

By contrast, if a vassal begins by seeking open confrontation

244

with his sovereign (as in the case of King Wu on the plain of Mu),
he cannot gain ascendency through virtue, no matter how degenerate the sovereign or how just his own cause. Instead, his lack of
respect for the hierarchical moral principle objectively increases
the fragility of the power he seeks. It was in vain that King Wu
proclaimed "the end of the war" and made a demonstration of
his peaceful intentions to prove his good will to everyone. Revolts
soon broke out again anyway, making punitive expeditions necessary. If the vassal claiming power lacks the respect due to his
sovereign, his own vassals will certainly later lack respect for him,
and consequently there will be no stable order or assured power.
This provides an example of someone seeking to "win power"
(relying on the relation of force) without simultaneously doing
what is necessary to "preserve" it (i.e., respecting legitimacy).
Ultimately, even from the perspective of positive force, he is never
really able to win power.

The effects of these ideas on politics and history are not hard
to gauge. Instead of attributing to revolutions the virtue of lending dynamism to the development of history, the Chinese strove
to associate power and legitimacy as closely as possible. They
conceptualized potential efficacy only within the framework of
a continuous process of transmission, reducing to the utmost all
forms of rebellion and discontinuity. Instead they favored an eternal *transition*. The only chance any form of opposition has for success is in not wearing itself out in a conflictual relationship.
Rather, it should assume the form of a regenerative alternative
within the framework of a regulatory logic of alternation, simply
a link in the chain of successive developments.

It is equally easy to gauge the philosophical effect of these
ideas. They lead to an explicit critique of metaphysical idealism
(which separates the principle of order from the actualizing course
of things) as well as of the moralism that accompanies it (which

245

contrasts periods in which "only principle reigns to periods in which only tendency reigns"). But at the same time, this link between ideal principle and effective propensity has a repercussion: the foundation, *in the name of realism itself* (and even in the domain of politics), of a moral idealism whose *ideal* nature is all the more marked in that it does not rest on any ontological or religious basis. Indeed, this seems to me to be one of the most influential ideas in Chinese thought. The following formulation fully sums it up: "There is no principle of order separate from concrete reality nor any tendency at work that is separate from the principle of order."[ff] On the one hand the Chinese refuse to hypostatize a principle of order that is a metaphysical Being; on the other, they consider that nothing can be brought about without the application of that regulatory principle. There is no norm that transcends reality (which is seen as truth); instead, normativity is constantly at work, which is what eternally controls the whole "flow" of reality. Not only is success assured if man truly conforms with this principle, but, by going along with the disposition of things, he "fulfills" his nature and can "understand" Heaven and be a part of it.

Wang Fuzhi

The Chinese Concept Is neither Mechanistic nor Finalistic

To account for the source of reality, Western philosophy early on produced two rival theories. The "mechanistic" or "determinist" explanation (the precursors for which were thinkers such as Empedocles and Democritus) treats this process as a necessary genesis followed by a necessary chain of consequences. The "finalist" and teleological explanation (first adumbrated by Anaxagoras and Diogenes of Apollonia, developed by Plato in *Timaeus* and *Laws*, and sanctioned by Aristotle)[39] understands the processes of reality in terms of their final, optimum, and logical end. The contradiction between these two options has provided the dynamic for the development of Western thought. One theory asks, "from what?"; the other queries, "to what end"?[40] The Chinese idea of a functioning configuration of things and a propensity stemming spontaneously from it seems in a way to overlap with both Western alternatives; in the final analysis, it corresponds to neither. Despite their opposition, both Western alternatives are based on a *common notion* of causality, a notion that Chinese tradition does not seem to share.

As in the determinist option, the Chinese concept of the disposition of things stresses the idea of an ineluctable unfolding given shape by propensity, and accounts for their generation purely on the basis of physical qualities ("hard," "soft," etc.); these qualities are regarded as phenomena produced by energy.[41] But in the Greek theory, this ineluctable necessity is simply the other side of chance, and the adaptation of nature cannot be a principle immanent in that nature. (According to Empedocles, whom Aristotle criticized on this point, nature simply proceeds as the result of a series of happy coincidences and through the elimination of everything unviable.) In contrast, the idea of regulation is at the root of Chinese thinking on the whole process; instead of some blind mechanism, the propensity that conducts the process is, as we have seen, conceived to be eminently logical.

Hence the connivance sometimes detected between the Chinese tradition and the opposite Aristotelian tradition, which approaches reality from the angle of "what always or usually happens." Both stress functional regularities, such as the regularity of the cycle of the seasons;[42] both have a sense of an organizing dynamism at work in the whole universe (the *ouranos*). But in the Greek theory, the regularity of the process is justified by what it achieves, which corresponds to the fulfillment of nature seen as a form (*eidos*) and serving as the "end" to the process (*telos*). Fulfillment is stressed over the material means employed. As we have seen, whether in strategy, history, or first philosophy, the Chinese logic of propensity is not conceived in terms of finality: hence the essential divergence in the two cultures' concepts of nature. Even if Aristotle criticizes the idea of cosmogony and the "demiurge" that still inspired Plato in the *Timaeus*, he himself still imagines the transformations of nature through an "analogy" with technical craftsmanship:[43] "According to how one makes a thing, so it happens in nature," and, in his view, "if the art of building boats was inherent in wood, it would act just like nature." The fundamental difference between the two cases is simply whether the "principle of movement" is or is not in the thing itself. As in art, nature operates with a view to the end, and the series of antecedents to that end is determined by the form ultimately to be realized, since the parts are determined by the whole (monstrosities of nature are themselves simply "errors of finality"). Thus, order, within the process of becoming, proceeds not from the becoming itself, from its own internal logic, but from the final cause to which the process of becoming leads. The Chinese, in contrast, never conceptualized the birth of the world and the transformations of nature according to a model of divine creation or even according to a demythified model of human fabrication. Thus, they never needed to extract (or abstract) from the notion of a regular process the notion of a *Good*, seen as a *goal*:[44] the idea of autoregulation was sufficient.

In Aristotle's *Physics*, the relation of means to end overlaps with the relation between *matter* and *form*. Just as the Chinese made no attempt to set up forms as the ends of processes, so too it is difficult to match their concept of the energy that fuels actualization with the idea of matter-as-means. The question that, for us, goes back to the discovery of China (through Father Longobardi, Father de Sainte-Marie, and Father Leibnitz) is the following: Are the Chinese "materialists" or not? However, it is not hard to see that this question is too heavily stamped by our own preconceptions to understand truly the other culture and provide an answer; consequently it has remained unresolved. For us to recognize an "anti-idealism" in the Chinese position (in reaction to the insistence on metaphysics imported into China via Buddhism) does not mean we should consider it as positively materialist, as though it had developed out of the identification of some kind of matter providing its logic.[45]

A methodological problem consequently arises if we are to press on with the comparison of the two cultures. If we are to escape from a quid pro quo situation and sterile debate, the only solution is surely to try to retrace further the process that established our own conceptual frameworks, to identify where the split began and how it developed. Such an investigation will only be possible if we can establish a point of true agreement before the split, a point from which we can see how the difference emerged and the basis on which to reconstruct it. I am not, of course, suggesting a realistic, historical perspective, but a theoretical *genealogy*.

The Absence of Any Theory of Causality: No Subject and No Mover

This *point of agreement* between Greek physics and the Chinese concept of a process, before any divergence, can certainly be found in both traditions' conceptualization of change in terms of contraries. According to Aristotle, all the thinkers who preceded him agreed on this, despite appearances to the contrary and despite their "lack of reason," "as if truth itself forced them to be."[46] Not only are contraries seen as the principles of change (in its most general sense, *metabolē*, which incorporates at once generation and corruption, movement and alteration), but furthermore their contrariety must be unique (since "there is a unique contrariety in a single *genus*" and "substance is a single *genus*"). The Chinese tradition was also united in its agreement on this point, for the opposite principles of *yin* and *yang* served on their own to account for all changes. It is hard even to imagine a philosophy of "change" or "transformation" whose point of departure was something other than this initial contrariety (or *enantiōsis*).

But the difference between Greek and Chinese thought arises when Aristotle, adapting an argument from the *Phaedo*, adds a third term to support and accommodate the two contrary principles (*antikeimena*). This is the *substratum* or *subject* ("what underlies," *hupokeimenon*), which underlies the other two and receives them into itself. It is "posited," along with the "opposites" that replace each other, as the permanent principle of change. Let us follow the example set by the *Physics* and pause to consider the two contrary terms "density" and "rarity." "A man might well be at a loss to conceive how 'density' itself... could possibly make 'rarity's' self into anything, or 'rarity' 'density's,'" so "must we not necessarily posit a third principle as the subject on which the antithetical principles act?"[47] Aristotle frequently returns to this argument, always in an equally systematic fashion. Thus, in the *Metaphysics*:

> Sensible substance is liable to change. Now if change proceeds from opposites or intermediates — not however from all opposites (for speech is not white) but only from the contrary — then there must be something underlying which changes into the opposite contrary; for the contraries do not change.[48]

And this "something" that "underlies" (*hupomenei*) the transformation is "matter."

Why this logical necessity for a third principle conceptualized as a "substratum or subject"? As Aristotle declared, contraries "cannot act upon each other," "do not change into each other," and "are mutually destructive."[49] In logical terms, they are mutually exclusive. In contrast, the entire Chinese tradition insists that contraries both oppose each other and "contain each other mutually": within *yin* there is *yang*, just as within *yang* there is *yin*; or, one might say, as the *yang* penetrates the density of the *yin*, the *yin* opens up to the dispersion of the *yang*.[50] Both constantly proceed from the same primordial unity and reciprocally give rise to each other's actualization. So Aristotle's statement could be literally reversed: there certainly *is* a "natural disposition" through which contraries interact, and that interaction is both spontaneous and continuous (continuous, in fact, because it is spontaneous).

"There is no being whose substance is seen to be constituted by contraries," Aristotle also tells us. In China, all the energy fueling actualization is constituted by both *yin* and *yang*. Those two are thus not only the limiting terms of change; they *together* form all that exists. There is thus no need to posit a "third term" to support their relation. Even the regulating principle does not exist over and above the two contraries: it simply expresses their harmonious relation. The two contraries form on their own a self-sufficient configuration; as we have certainly seen by now, the propensity that stems on its own from their interdependence orients the process of reality. Even as energy is ceaselessly divided between *yin* and *yang*, it is constantly led to actualize itself, functioning in a balanced and regular fashion: there is constantly *materialization* but, strictly speaking, no matter. In Aristotle, in contrast, the dynamic insufficiency of contraries goes hand in hand with his doctrine of substance: reality is not conceived as a particular arrangement providing its own dynamic from disposition; rather, it is conceived as a relation between matter and form, based on the concept of essence (which is why contraries can only be "inherent" to a subject as "accidents"). It also follows that change can no longer be interpreted in terms of spontaneous tendency, as in a bipolar structure, but instead implies the elaboration of a complex system of causality.

The following formula, taken from the *Metaphysics*, may appear culturally neutral, a simple statement of fact: "All change is of some subject by some agent into some object."[51] However, it is perhaps now easier to see to what extent the generality of the definition in fact conceals a theoretical a priori (i.e., the many assumptions masked by the platitudinous nature of the expression). It might even seem to border on a tautology, yet the minimal explanation provided by the definition already involves everything that has subsequently served to orient our thinking. Over and above the two contraries (here converted into the opposition of "form" and "privation") is implied the idea of a subject serving as matter for the change and an agent "through which the change comes about." With no interaction between these contraries, as soon as one introduces a third principle that serves to support their relation, one is automatically led to introduce a fourth element, an external factor, to serve as the efficient cause of change. After the "subject or substratum," it was necessary to introduce a "mover" (*to kinoun*), "matter," on the one hand, and "form," which is also an "end," on the other. The theory of the four causes was now complete and seemed to go without saying. In other words, the Western *epistēmē* was ready.[52]

Aristotelian thought marked the culmination of the development of Greek philosophy; and although Western science from the Renaissance on made progress through a break with the authority of his theories, his thought seems nonetheless to have served as the basic framework of the West's quest for knowledge — a framework that would later even fuel its own critique on a theoretical level. All things considered, this endeavor involved very particular choices, regardless of its general domination over other later cultures.

All of this ought to encourage us to reinterpret our own philosophy from an external perspective. Instead of perpetually repeating the same old story, we should retrace our steps to a point earlier than the first exercises in logic, to bases of which philosophy may not even be conscious. By going upstream in this way, we may find the link between the system of causality and the "preconception" of substance. For once "physics" became based on substance, the static order could not adequately explain the dynamic order, requiring the introduction of a mover. Conversely, Chinese thought, which dispensed with the need for a subject, could with equal logic dispense with external causality. Within the disposition of things, the efficient cause that brings about the movement is not something external but is always totally immanent. The static order is also dynamic; the structure of reality is always in process.

Propensity through Spontaneous Interaction or Aspiration to God

However, it is tempting to approach the comparison from the other side. Does the dynamism that Western physics also conceives as being immanent in nature not overlap to a degree with the tendency inherent in processes, namely, the Chinese *shi*? It is certainly on the basis of an opposition such as "potentiality" and "actuality" (*dunamis* and *energeia*) that we have earlier been led to interpret, within the framework of our own thought, the great alternation that punctuates the Chinese vision of process (for example, we have employed terms such as "latency" and "actualization"; cf. p. 231). That assumption is furthermore justified by a more general convergence. As we know, Chinese thought differs essentially from Greek thought in its inclination to operate

253

not in terms of being (that which is eternal), but in terms of becoming (change). The notion of *potentiality* is precisely the means by which Greek thought tried to escape from the *aporia* of "being" into which the Eleatics had led it (being, they said, can come from neither "being" nor "nonbeing"). Potentiality, a relative "nonbeing" in between "being" and "not-being," makes the very possibility of becoming thinkable (all of which justifies our returning once again to Aristotle, the theorist of genesis).

This comparison seems to be one we cannot afford to decline, for it appears objectively most likely to reveal a common preoccupation and convergent perspectives. Yet once again, the comparison collapses on closer inspection. In fact, it may be easier to understand Chinese propensity by *opposing* (rather than likening) it to the Greek *dunamis*. According to the Greek idea, actualization stems not from "potentiality" itself but from the "form" that serves as the end (*telos*); "actuality" is thus ontologically superior to "potentiality," since it can be assimilated to form, whereas "potentiality" is attached to matter. For this reason, according to Aristotle, "it can happen that that which has potentiality does not pass on to action."[53] In contrast, according to the Chinese view, actualization is completely dependent on potentiality; potentiality implies actualization. The *shi* is ineluctable; the stages of potentiality and actualization are correlative, one becomes the other, there is parity between them.

In Greek thought, the primacy ascribed to the final cause was so general that it even influenced the concept of natural movements. Both Greek and Chinese thinkers became aware early on that certain bodies have a propensity to rise and others a propensity to fall. Aristotle, criticizing the notion of undifferentiated space favored by the Atomists, tells us that "these terms,...'above' and 'below,' not only indicate definite and distinct positions, but also produce distinct effects."[54] Could it be that in this context of physical space structured in a bipolar fashion (above and below) and in connection with phenomena of weight (conceived as an ineluctable tendency), we have finally found a possible equivalent for the Chinese concept of the deployment of things and its propensity (since "position" corresponds here to "potentiality" and *thesis* to *dunamis*)? But according to Aristotle, fire tends naturally to rise and stones to fall, because their "form" (*eidos*) predestines them to do so. Their "form" also confers a proper place on them. (We should further note a significant difference vis-à-vis the dispositional dimension of *shi*; cf. the most common Chinese example of a round stone at the top of a slope.) Once again, in Greek thought tendency is understood not on the basis of a particular functional disposition but in teleological terms. This leads me, in conclusion, to pinpoint two essential aspects in which the Greek concept of tendency differs from Chinese thought. First, it opposes natural tendency to spontaneity, whereas Chinese thought conflates the two. Second, it conceives of tendency as aspiration or desire, which leads to an ontological hierarchization of reality, and provides it with a metaphysical orientation. Chinese thought, meanwhile, takes no account of "degrees of being" and has no need for a prime mover.

According to Aristotle, the third kind of coming-to-be of reality, in contrast to natural engendering and human fabrication, happens of its own accord, "by itself" (*automaton*), and involves neither forms nor ends. In such cases the natural properties of matter arrive at the result that would ordinarily be produced through form, but here in the absence of form; a material cause happens on its own without any end to fulfill. However, Aristotle, refuting Democritus, maintains that it is exceptional for a spontaneous combination of elementary actions to simulate organization through form (whereas finality is expressed by constant and regular effects), and he declares that those exceptional instances only involve phenomena low in the order of reality: the engendering of insects, parasites, and maggots, changes of direction in certain water courses, corruption, rotting, the growth of nails and hair, and so on.[55] In these instances what would normally happen *a natura* happens *sponte sua*. A "privation of nature" (*sterēsis phuseōs*) is involved, in the same manner as the effects of chance must be conceived as "a privation of art." In the causalist explanations of Western philosophy, the role of spontaneity is no more than residual. In contrast, as we have seen, the entire Chinese tradition not only conceives of what is natural as whatever is spontaneous, but furthermore uses this as the ideal both for the course of the world and for human behavior. As the Western view is founded on ontological hierarchization, it is logical that it would value above all the ability to free oneself from material causality; this leads triumphantly to liberty. But it is equally logical, in the Chinese view of the deployment of things, that supreme value should be attached to the spontaneity of propensity, in which whatever is disposed in a certain manner should proceed regularly by itself and of its own accord. Individual attempts to become free from this automaticity of the functioning of things should be ruled out, and any play within the deployment of things is an irregularity; for this reason, Chinese thought was never concerned with liberty.

What then, in our view, is the tension that animates reality, given that dynamism cannot be produced simply from the interaction of two poles, as it can in the Chinese view? As we have seen, the initial contrariety that both of these traditions took as their point of departure was later converted by Aristotle into an unequal relation between "form" and "privation": the third principle, that of subject/matter, tends toward form as to the good, just as "female does to male" (or the ugly does to the beautiful).[56] Tendencies inherent in reality are thus not conceived as an objective and ineluctable propensity, as in Chinese thought, but instead are seen as a subjective and teleological "desire" or "aspiration" (*ephiesthai kai oregesthai*). At the summit of the hierarchy of reality, that tendency is conceived as God, the prime mover: at the final end of the causal chain, God "moves without being moved." He does not act mechanically (it would be necessary, then, to backtrack even further in the chain of causality) but, as in a famous formula, through the "desire" (or "love") he elicits (*kinei hōs erōmenon*).[57] All other beings, in a mere state of potentiality, *tend toward the fullest mode of Being*, aspiring to its eternity; at the higher level of the sphere of the fixed stars, they do so via circular rotation while, at the bottom of the ladder, they do so simply through the perpetuation of the species, the reciprocal transmutation of elements, and the equilibrium of physical forces. God, *ens realissimum*, pure actuality and form, is the *single pole* for all the movements and transformations of the world, so that the heavens and all of nature "are dependent on him." In the bipolar system of Chinese thought, in contrast, natural movements and changes stem only from an immanent logic, derive from no divine *energeia*, and tend toward nothing other than a continuous renewal of the process. For the Chinese, tendency is oriented only by its initial implication. It never culminates in that absolute abolition of any tendencies that define God through the elimination of all matter and potentiality. In the one system, tendency has been conceived tragically, as the expression of a lack: motivated by an insufficiency of being, it thirsts to be rejoined with God. In the other, it is regarded positively as the internal regulating motor and is fully justified by the logic of its functioning.

For the Greeks, the "supremely desirable" is also the "supremely intelligible": the wisdom that stems from this aspiration toward Being is to imitate God in his eternal and perfect life, through contemplation, the sole source of beatitude. In China, while wisdom also means imitating Heaven, it entails conforming with the way Heaven is disposed and to allow oneself to be advantageously carried along by the spontaneity of its propensity, to become one with the reason for things.

CHAPTER ELEVEN

Conclusion III:

Conformism and Efficacy

Neither Tragic Heroism nor Disinterested Contemplation
Two models of human fulfillment have come down to us from
ancient Greece and have helped to fashion our aspiration toward
the ideal. The first is that of a heroic commitment to action, conceived in the tragic mode: an individual decides to take part in
the course of things, resolutely assuming responsibility for his initiative despite all the contrary forces that he encounters in the
world and even at the risk of being destroyed and swept away. The
second is the model of a vocation to contemplation, conceived in
a philosophical and religious mode: having seen through the illusion of all that is "perceptible" and having understood that everything here on earth is ephemeral and doomed, the soul aspires
to eternal truths and conceives of no "sovereign good," and hence
no "happiness," other than the world of the intelligible, which
it may reach by drawing closer to the divine absolute.

In contrast, ancient Chinese thought is above all concerned
with avoiding *confrontation*, which is exhausting and sterile. It
conceives of a model of efficacy based on correlation and detectable at the heart of the objective processes. This is the only kind
of efficacy valid on the human level. Chinese thought is, furthermore, unassailed by *the doubt about the perceptible realm* that is

the source of the opposition between appearance and truth in Western thought and that has oriented our philosophical activity toward abstraction aimed at description and disinterest. In Chinese thought, the level of knowledge is not separate from that of action: a wise man, yielding to an intuition of the dynamism implied in the course of things (revered as the *Dao*), takes care not to go against it, and instead lets it it operate fully in all situations.

The Closed System of Disposition Evolving Solely as a Result of the Interaction of Poles

What we have learned about the word *shi* demonstrates this last point. Because it implies no dissociation between practice and theory, it never becomes detached from its initial strategic meaning and always helps us to think about the processes to which it is applied from the perspective of *how to use them*. Since the principles of dynamism are fundamentally the same across reality, the word *shi* can serve equally well in the analysis of nature and in the analysis of history; in the field of political management and in that of artistic creation. Reality always presents itself as a particular situation that results from a particular *disposition* of circumstances that is, in turn, inclined to produce a particular *effect*: it is up to the general, and equally to the politician, the painter, and the writer, to avail himself of the *shi*[a] (the same expression is repeated in all fields) so as to exploit it to its maximum potentiality.

Chinese thought, then, may not be inclined toward speculation, but it is from early on inclined toward systematization. It tends to exclude as far as possible any form of external intervention (such as supreme modes of causality that cannot initially be grasped: not only "God," in the sense of the prime mover of nature, but also "destiny" in warfare and "inspiration" in poetry). To this extent, it repeatedly conceives of reality as a closed *system* that *evolves* from a single principle of interaction and necessarily

refers back to two poles. Those two essential features of any configuration of factors, which stand in opposition to each other and
at the same time function correlatively, are to be found at every
level of reality, from the relation between *yin* and *yang* (or Earth
and Heaven) in the order of nature to the relation between sovereign and subject (or man and woman) in the social order, and
similarly from the relation between above and below (or dark and
light, slow and rapid, etc.) in the art of writing to the relation
between emotion and landscape (or empty and full, flat tones and
oblique tones) in poetic composition. From the established bipolar system stems *variation through alternation*, the tendency toward
engendering that is implied by the very deployment of things, and
it is that variation that makes it possible for "reality," whatever
that might be, to continue to come about. This variation can be
found both shaping the relief of the land and punctuating time:
we can contemplate it in the sequence of mountains and valleys
in the landscape and equally in the unfolding of times of achievement and decline in the course of history. Everything oscillates
between two poles, changes, and is renewed. This is the model
that the general must emulate, as he switches constantly from one
tactic to its opposite in as sinuous a fashion as a "snake-dragon"
to keep his power to attack always fresh. It is also the model for
the poet, who makes a poetic text "undulate" like "the folds in a
draped canopy" to maintain vitality in his expression of emotion.

This is an utterly general concept, as valid for the great process of the world as it is for human activities, as relevant to the
order of *phusis* as to the order of *techne*. An artist who "creates
shi," be he painter or poet, is simply using particular means to
his own advantage; he is using the logic that presides over the
whole of existence that it is his task to reveal. But even though
it is universal, this model makes it possible to acquire understanding that is *always particular* and qualified. Since it is always the

situation that matters initially and since, in every case and at every instant, that situation is unique and never ceases evolving, the propensity that rules reality is necessarily different in each case and is never repeated. "What is real" is never fixed, never stereotyped, and it is this very fact that preserves it as reality. The only exception to this is *shi* as Legalist authorities strove to fix it, in their anxiousness to arrest the way in which power is disposed and to frustrate any chance at evolution. But as for art and nature, they never cease to renew their ability to function, and for this reason they both possess an unfathomable or "marvelous"[b] dimension that eludes any rational explanation, which would be both generalizing and simplifying. For this reason as well, *shi* can never be treated abstractly. Not only is Chinese thought profoundly unified; it is also striking in its deep sense of the concrete.

Wisdom or Strategy: Conforming with Propensity

Conceiving, as they do, of all reality as a deployment, the Chinese are not led to backtrack along a necessarily infinite series of possible causes. Convinced as they are of the ineluctable nature of propensity, they are not inclined to speculate on ends, which can never be anything more than probable. Neither cosmogonical stories nor teleological suppositions interest them. They are concerned neither to recount the beginning nor to imagine the end. All that exists, has always existed, and will always exist are interactions that are constantly at work, and reality is never anything other than their ceaseless process. Thus, the problem that concerns the Chinese is not that of "being," in the Greek sense (i.e., being as opposed to becoming and the perceptible world); rather it is the problem of the capacity to function: the source of the efficacy that is at work everywhere in reality and the best way to profit from it.

As soon as one believes, as the Chinese do, that all oppositions

262

interact correlatively as a matter of principle, any idea of antagonism dissolves; reality can never be dramatic. Even in the case of
strategic deployment, in which the conflictual aspect is the most
marked (since one is face-to-face with the enemy), the advice of
Chinese thinkers is always to aim to evolve, to adapt totally to
the movements of the enemy, rather than attack him head on. A
general should always act with a view to profiting from the dynamism of this partner, his enemy, for as long as it operates, so as
to allow himself to be renewed by it at the expense of his opponent and at no cost to himself. In this way he will maintain his
own energy as completely as at the beginning. Any head-on attack
will be costly and possibly risky. All one needs to do is always
respond and react to the incitement of one's opponent, just as
water constantly adapts to the variations in land levels. In this way
one can preserve one's own dynamism and remain safe. (And the
essential word in this context is *always*, for any break in the process of correlation would put us in a new position by making us
independent of the other party at a cost to ourselves; in this position our opponent, finding us face to face but now unconnected,
would reassume power over us and possibly win the day.)

In China, "practical reason" thus lies in adapting to the propensity at work so as to be carried along by it and exploit it. No
initial alternative between good and evil is involved, since the status of both is ontological. It is simply a matter of either "going
along with" the propensity and thereby profiting from it or "going
against it" and being ruined. For what is valid for the general is
also valid for the sage. He does not abstract from some ephemeral codification of reality a norm that can be set up as a goal for
his will (e.g., orders and rules of conduct). Instead, he "conforms"[c] with the initiative of the continuous course of things
("Heaven" being seen as the inexhaustible fount of the process)
so as to tap into its efficacy. From a subjective perspective, he

does not aim to assert his liberty, but simply follows the inclination toward the good that exists in embryonic form in every conscious mind (in a sense of solidarity with all that exists, i.e., the Confucian *ren*); this leads to perfect morality. Far from seeking to reconstruct the world on the basis of some order or another, attempting to impose his own designs on it and force the course of things, all he does is respond and react to whatever reality prompts within him. And this he does not do partially or at particular moments, when it is in his interest to do so, but in all situations and continuously. In this way his power to change reality is checked by no obstacles or limits. He does not "act," does nothing himself (on his own initiative), and the degree of the efficacy of this behavior is determined by the extent to which he refrains from trying to manage things. His cooperation with reality as a whole results in a power of influence that can be at once invisible, infinite, and perfectly spontaneous.

In contrast to action and causality, which are transitive, the only kind of efficacy that is recognized is intransitive, and "Heaven," set up as transcending the human horizon, is itself simply the totalization, or absolutization, of that immanence.

It is therefore hardly surprising that Chinese thought is so *conformist*. It does not seek to distance itself from the "world," does not question reality, is not even surprised by it. It has no need of myths (and we, for our part, know that the most farfetched myths are always the most powerful) to save reality from absurdity and confer meaning on it. Instead of inventing *myths* that attempt to explain the enigma of the world through fabulous flights of fancy, the Chinese devised *rites* to embody and express by signs, at the level of human behavior, the functioning inherent in the world's disposition. Reality was not regarded as a problem but presented itself from the beginning as a credible process. It did not need to be deciphered like a mystery but simply to be understood in its *functioning*. There was no need to project a "meaning" onto the world or to satisfy the expectations of a subject/individual, for its meaning stemmed in its entirety, without requiring any act of faith, from the propensity of things.

In the West, the monopolizing tension created by the ideal produced the saint or genius – for instance, Prometheus, "the stealer of fire," the epitome of a martyr. In the interstices between the anguish of dereliction and the fervor of discovery and between the despair of nothingness and the jubilation of the "god within oneself," a feverish and ardent quest developed. In contrast, the bipolarity of the Chinese system produces centrality and equilibrium, which gives rise to serenity. And from alternation, which ensures the constancy of the functioning of reality, a vital rhythm flows. Any opening out to some Beyond, instead of leading to an endless outpouring of emotion and dizzying ecstasy, is immediately compensated with a corresponding closure. Such is the essence of the whole process and what makes it breathe. There is no need to forge a morality of sublimation. Between joy and fear, there is no need to invent salvation. It is enough to go along with change, change that is also forever regulation, change that helps to create harmony.

Notes

INTRODUCTION

1. The term *shi* (勢) is the same as the word *yi*, which is believed to represent a hand holding something, a symbol of power to which the diacritic radical for force (*li* 力) was later added. Xu Shen thinks that what is held in the hand is a clod of earth, which could symbolize something put in position or a "positioning." As such, the word *shi*, in terms of its spatial connotation, corresponds to the word *shi* (時), with its temporal associations in the sense of "opportunity" or "chance"; in fact, the latter term is sometimes used in place of the former.

NOTICE TO THE READER

1. François Jullien, *Procès ou création* (Paris: Seuil, 1989).

CHAPTER ONE: POTENTIAL IS BORN OF DISPOSITION
IN MILITARY STRATEGY

Ancient China's principle text on military strategy is the *Sunzi*, usually dated to the fourth century B.C. I have used it as the basis of this chapter. To complement this, I have also used the *Sun Bin bingfa*, also from the fourth century B.C., whose fragmentary text was discovered in a tomb in Shandong in 1972, and chapter 15 of the *Huainanzi*, a later compilation dating from the early Han period (end of the second century B.C.), which preserved or developed this concept of *shi*. The text of the *Sunzi* I have used is the *Sunzi shijia zhu, Zhuzi jicheng* (Shanghai shudian; repr. 1986), vol. 6. The *Huainanzi* is cited from the same edition, *Zhuzi jicheng*, vol. 7. The *Sun Bin* is cited from the edition by Deng Zezong, *Sun Bin bingfa zhuyi* (Beijing: Jiefangjun chubanshe, 1986).

1. *Sunzi*, ch. 4, "Xing pian," pp. 59–60.

2. *Ibid.*, pp. 58–59.

3. *Ibid.*, pp. 60–61.

4. *Ibid.*, ch. 3, "Mou gong," p. 35; *Huainanzi*, ch. 15, "Bing lüe xun," p. 257.

5. For a systematic study of the various uses of *shi* "as a special military term," see Roger T. Ames, *The Art of Rulership: A Study in Ancient Chinese Political Thought* (Honolulu: University of Hawaii Press, 1983), p. 66; see also D.C. Lau, "Some Notes on the Sun Tze," *BSOAS* 27 (1965), pt. 2, in particular p. 332.

6. *Sun Bin bingfa*, ch. "Cuanzau," p. 26.

7. *Sunzi*, ch. 4, p. 64.

8. *Ibid.*, ch. 5, "Shi pian," p. 71.

9. *Ibid.*, ch. 10, "Di xing pian."

10. *Huainanzi*, ch. 15, pp. 259–60.

11. *Sun Bin bingfa*, ch. "Wei wang wen," p. 13.

12. *Huainanzi*, ch. 15, p. 261.

13. *Sunzi*, ch. 11, "Jiu di pian."

14. *Ibid.*, ch. 5, p. 72.

15. *Sun Bin bingfa*, ch. "Shi bei," p. 38; another characteristic image (ch. "Bing qung," p. 41) is of the arrow referring to the troops, the crossbow to the general, and the hand that draws it to the sovereign.

16. *Sunzi*, ch. 5, p. 80. As D.C. Lau has noted ("Some Notes," p. 333), the same image of rolling down is used for both *xing* and for *shi* at the end of chapters 4 and 5. However, it seems that the aspect of the effect that results from manipulation (stones that *are made* to roll or, as above, pebbles carried along by the course of water) is more emphasized, even in *Sunzi*, in relation to *shi* than to *xing*.

17. *Sunzi*, ch. 5, p. 79.

18. *Ibid.*, commentary by Li Quan and Wang Xi.

19. *Huainanzi*, ch. 15, p. 262.

20. *Ibid.: suoyi jue sheng zhe, qian shi ye* (*qian* for *quan*; cf. Ames, *The Art of Rulership*, p. 223 n.23).

21. *Huainanzi*, ch. 15, p. 263. This chapter of the *Huainanzi*, which is influenced by the cosmological speculation that became ubiquitous under the Han, is not always as categorical in its negation of "supernatural" factors, which are based on the interrelation between Heaven, Man, and the Five Phases, as it is in the example given here. It does not go so far as the ideas of the strategic treatises of Antiquity (cf. *Sunzi*, ch. 11, "Jiu di," and 18, "Yong jian").

22. *Sunzi*, ch. "Ji pian," p. 12. This "outside" (*qi wai*) has been understood in two ways by commentators: either as that which is outside the "constant rules" (*chang fa*, Cao Cao's interpretation) or as the outside constituted by the battlefield as opposed to the inside of the temple, where the strategy is decided (*Mei Yaochen* [1002-1060]); but the two interpretations amount to the same thing.

23. The principle of *xing ren er wo wu xing*, *Sunzi*, ch. 6, "Xu shi pian," p. 93.

24. *Huainanzi*, ch. 15, p. 253.

25. *Sunzi*, ch. 6, pp. 101-102.

26. *Ibid.* In the *Sun Bin* (ch. "Jian wei wang," p. 8), we find the formula *fu bing zhe, fei shi heng shi ye*, which can be understood in this sense (cf. the edition by Fu Zhenlun [Chengdu: Bashu shushe, 1986], p. 7).

27. Treatises on the game of *go* resort to this concept to explain the evolving relation of the forces represented on the checkerboard. *Go* is well known as a game that illustrates the fundamental principles of Chinese strategy.

28. See the beginning of ch. 15, "Yi bing," by Xunzi or in the summary chapter, "Yao lüe," of the *Huainanzi*, pp. 371-72. The bibliographic chapter of the *Hanshu* ("Yiwenzhi") refers to one of the four categories of works relating to strategy as that produced by *shi* specialists (*bing xing shi*); for an appreciation of this rubric, based on such works as have survived, see Robin D.S. Yates, "New Light on Ancient Chinese Military Texts: Notes on Their Nature and Evolution, and the Development of Military Specialization in Warring States China," *T'oung Pao* 74 (1988), pp. 211-48.

29. "Lun chijiuzhan" (On prolonged warfare), para. 87, in *Mao Zedong xuanji*, vol. 2, p. 484.

30. A way of rendering the notion of *linghuoxing*, which is not adequately conveyed by the usual translation of "flexibility" (cf. Mao Zedong, *Oeuvres choisies*, vol. 2, p. 182).

31. Victor Davis Hanson, *The Western Way of War* (London: Hodder & Stoughton, 1989), Introduction.

32. *Ibid.*, p. 224.

33. Karl von Clausewitz, *On War*, trans. J.J. Graham (Harmondsworth, UK: Penguin Classics, 1968), ch. 2. This relation between means and ends is the subject in particular of ch. 2 of the first book of *On War*, which is of considerable interest. On the importance of this concept in Clausewitz, see Michael Howard, *Clausewitz* (New York: Oxford University Press, 1983), ch. 3; Raymond Aron, *Penser la guerre* (Paris: Gallimard, 1977), *Sur Clausewitz* (Paris: Complexe, 1987).

CHAPTER TWO: POSITION AS THE DETERMINING FACTOR IN POLITICS

The principal texts used in this chapter are ch. 1 of Shen Dao (fourth century B.C.), the *Guanzi* (in particular ch. 67), a composite work generally dated to the third century B.C., and the *Hanfeizi* (280? to 234 B.C.), which is the most profound and most fully developed in the Legalist tradition. These are complemented by the *Shangjunshu (Book of the Lord Shang)* by Shang Yang, fourth century B.C. (ch. 24), and the *Lüshi chunqiu*, ch. "Shen shi." The reference edition is the *Zhuzi jicheng*, vols. 5 and 6. With respect to the *Hanfeizi* and the *Lüshi chunqiu*, the references to the Chen Qiyou edition, *Hanfeizi jishi* (Shanghai renmin chubanshe, 1974), 2 vols., and *Lüshi chunqiu xiaoshi* (Xuelin chubanshe, 1984), 2 vols., are also given in brackets.

1. *Zhuangzi*, ch. 33, "Tian xia," a paragraph devoted to Shen Dao. This is a difficult as well as fascinating passage, the translation of which is more of an interpretation; cf. Arthur Waley's comments in his *Three Ways of Thought in Ancient China* (London: Allen & Unwin, 1939), p. 237.

2. On the problem of the relation between the "Daoist" Shen Dao, as presented in the *Zhuangzi*, and the Legalist *Shen Dao*, as in the *Hanshu*, see

P.M. Thompson, *The Shen Tzu Fragments* (New York: Oxford University Press, 1979), p. 3; Léon Vandermeersch, *La Formation du légisme* (Paris: Ecole française d'Extrême-Orient, 1965), p. 49; for a study on the principal references for the term *shi* in this political context, see Roger T. Ames, *The Art of Rulership: A Study in Ancient Chinese Political Thought* (Honolulu: University of Hawaii Press, 1983), p. 72.

3. Shen Dao, ch. i, "Weide," 5.1-2; cf. Thompson, *The Shen Tzu Fragments*, p. 232.

4. *Shangjunshu*, ch. 24, "Jin shi," p. 39.

5. *Hanfeizi*, ch. 40, "Nan shi," p. 297 [p. 886].

6. Same comparison in *Hanfeizi*, ch. 34, p. 234 [p. 717].

7. Chen Qiyou (p. 894 n.27) considers that this second passage is not by Han Fei, but his arguments do not seem to me conclusive. In any case, this argument is too well developed not to provoke in itself the keenest interest.

8. See, e.g., *Guanzi*, ch. 31, "Jun chen," p. 177.

9. *Ibid.*, ch. 78, "Kui duo," p. 385.

10. *Ibid.*, ch. 16, "Fa fa," p. 91.

11. *Ibid.*, ch. 67, "Ming fa jie," p. 343.

12. *Hanfeizi*, ch. 14, p. 68 [p. 245].

13. *Guanzi*, ch. 64, "Xing shi jie," p. 325.

14. *Ibid.*, ch. 31, "Jun chen," p. 178; *Hanfeizi*, ch. 48, 3rd canon, p. 332 [p. 1006]; cf. also chs. 34, 38.

15. *Lüshi chunqiu*, ch. "Shen shi," 6.213 [p. 1108].

16. *Hanfeizi*, ch. 38, p. 288 [p. 864].

17. See, on this subject, Vandermeersch, *La Formation du légisme*, p. 225.

18. *Hanfeizi*, ch. 48, 4th canon, p. 334 [p. 1017].

19. *Ibid.*, ch. 14, p. 71 [p. 247].

20. *Huainanzi*, ch. 9, pp. 133, 145.

21. *Hanfeizi*, ch. 48, 2nd canon, p. 331 [p. 1001].

22. *Ibid.*, ch. 28, p. 155 [p. 508].

23. *Ibid.*, ch. 38, p. 284 [p. 849].

24. *Ibid.*, ch. 48, 1st canon, p. 330 [p. 997].

25. *Ibid.*, ch. 28, p. 155 [p. 508].

26. *Ibid.*, ch. 48, p. 330 [p. 997].

27. Depending on which of the two equally possible interpretations of the expression *tian ze bu fei* (cf. Chen Qiyou, p. 999 n.10).

28. Depending on whether one reads *kun* or *yin*; cf., on this point, Chen Qiyou, p. 999 n.11, and Vandermeersch, *La Formation du légalisme*, p. 246.

29. On this natural character of manipulation, see Jean Lévi, "Théories de la manipulation en Chine ancienne," *Le Genre humain* 6 (1986), p. 9f., and "Solidarité de l'ordre de la nature et de l'ordre de la société: 'loi' sociale dans la pensée légiste de la Chine ancienne," *Extrême-Orient – Extrême-Occident* 8.3 (1983), p. 23f.

30. On this Daoist interpretation of Legalist thought, see Vandermeersch's excellent analyses in *La Formation du légisme*, p. 257.

31. *Hanfeizi*, ch. 34, p. 231 [p. 711], p. 234 [p. 717].

32. *Ibid.*, ch. 49, pp. 342–43 [p. 1051].

33. *Ibid.*, ch. 14, p. 74 [p. 249].

34. *Ibid.*, ch. 38, p. 285 [p. 853].

35. *Ibid.*, ch. 48, 5th canon, p. 335 [p. 1026], ch. 8, p. 29 [p. 121].

36. While it may never have occurred to the Chinese to question the monarchical principle, they did come to criticize the Legalist model of the monopolization of power, citing the need for reciprocity: the power stemming from the political setup should not be thwarted by being made to operate in one direction only, i.e., from above to below, as the Legalists so keenly wanted. Instead, its operations should be left open to interaction, which presupposes two poles, not just one: interaction *between* above and below, *between* the sovereign and his vassal, and *between* the prince and his people. As we will see below, this principle of duality is common to every aspect of Chinese thought, and as a result, under the influence of the *literati*, the imperial ideology was corrected.

The Legalist concept of *shi* is thus important here to the extent that it was the subject of the most sustained theoretical analysis. At the same time, though, it represents an impoverishment in relation to the intuition of efficacy commonly expressed through the term *shi*, for while the Legalists certainly focused on the dimension of objective conditioning peculiar to *shi* and likewise on its automatic nature, they wound up stripping their representation of *shi* of its essential variability. By immobilizing it in this way, they rendered it sterile.

37. Machiavelli, *Le Prince* (Paris: Garnier, 1987), ch. 18.

38. Michel Foucault, *Discipline and Punish: The Birth of the Prison*, trans. Alan Sheridan (New York: Vintage, 1979), pp. 195–200.

39. *Ibid.*, pp. 200–209.

40. *Ibid.*, p. 202.

41. Jeremy Bentham, *The Panopticon*, in *Works*, ed. John Bowring (Edinburgh: W. Tait, 1843), pp. 202–204.

CHAPTER THREE: CONCLUSION I

The texts used in this chapter are those of Mencius, second half of the fourth century B.C. (in particular, VII, A, 8 and VI, A, 2), Xunzi, about 289–235 B.C. (in particular, chs. 9, 15, 16), and the compilation dating from the beginning of the empire, the *Huainanzi* (chs. 9, 15). The references to the *Mencius* are taken from James Legge, *The Chinese Classics* (Hong Kong: Hong Kong University Press, 1960), vol. 2; those for the *Xunzi* and the *Huainanzi* are taken from the *Zhuzi jicheng*, vols. 2, 3.

1. See, e.g., *Mencius*, III, B, 5, p. 271; cf. on this subject my own study, "Fonder la morale, ou comment légitimer la transcendance de la moralité sans le support du dogme ou de la foi," *Extrême-Orient – Extrême-Occident* 8.6 (1985), p. 62.

2. *Mencius*, VII, A, 8, p. 452.

3. *Ibid.*, VI, A, 2, p. 396. For an opposite but common use of *shi* to evoke the natural course of water, see, e.g., the *Guanzi*, ch. 31, p. 174. Mencius is also familiar with the ordinary use of the term *shi*, as is attested by the proverb from the region of Qi that he cites at II, A, 1, p. 183: "However great one's wisdom and discernment, it is better to depend on *shi*."

4. *Xunzi*, ch. 11, "Wangba," p. 131.

5. On this reflection relating to *shi* in Xunzi, see the meticulous study by

Roger T. Ames, *The Art of Rulership* (Honolulu: University of Hawaii Press, 1983), p. 85.

6. *Xunzi*, ch. 11, "Wangba," p. 131.

7. *Ibid.*, ch. 9, "Wangzhi," p. 96.

8. *Ibid.*, ch. 11, "Wangba," p. 131.

9. *Ibid.*, ch. 16, "Qiangguo," p. 197.

10. *Ibid.*, pp. 194–95.

11. *Ibid.*, ch. 11, "Wangba," p. 140.

12. *Ibid.*, ch. 15, "Yibing," p. 177.

13. *Huainanzi*, ch. 15, "Binglüexun," pp. 251–53.

14. *Ibid.*, pp. 259, 261, 262–63.

15. *Ibid.*, ch. 9, "Zushuxun," pp. 142–44.

16. *Ibid.*, pp. 137, 141–42.

17. *Ibid.*, p. 136.

18. See, e.g., the fine article by Tzvetan Todorov, "Eloquence, morale et vérité," *Les Manipulations*, in *Le Genre humain* 6 (1986), p. 26f.

19. *Shuihuzhuan* (*Water Margin*), ch. 51; cf. English translation by Sidney Shapiro, *Outlaws of the Marsh* (Bloomington: Indiana University Press, 1981). The same type of manipulation is to be found in other scenes in the novel: to lure Xu Ning to the den (vol. 2, ch. 56); to force Lu Yunyi to join the band (*ibid.*); and to compel the doctor An Daoquan to come and cure Song Jiang (*ibid.*).

20. Commentary by Jin Shengtan, *Shuihuzhuan huipingben* (Beijing: Beijing daxue chubanshe, 1987), vol. 2, p. 944.

CHAPTER FOUR: THE FORCE OF FORM, THE EFFECT OF GENRE

The aesthetic texts on calligraphy cited in this chapter can be found in the *Lidai shufa lunwenxuan* (Shanghai: Shuhua chubanshe, 1980) (hereafter *Lidai*); those on the aesthetics of painting are in Yu Jianhua, ed., *Zhongguo hualan leibian* (Hong Kong, 1973) (hereafter *Leiban*); finally, in the field of literary "theory," the *Wenxin diaolong* is cited from the edition by Fan Wenlan (Hong Kong: Shangwu yinshuguan).

1. On this subject, see my study, *La Valeur allusive: Des catégories originales de*

l'interprétation poétique dans la tradition chinoise (Paris: Ecole Française d'Extrême-Orient, 1985), ch. 1.

2. Kang Youwei, *Lidai*, p. 845.

3. "Force-form," as John Hay aptly puts it: "It is the form of becoming, process and, by extension, movement" ("The Human Body as a Microcosmic Source of Macrocosmic Values in Calligraphy," in *Theories of the Arts in China*, ed. Susan Bush and Christian Murck [Princeton, N.J.: Princeton University Press, 1983], p. 102 n.77).

4. Cai Yong, "Jiu shi," *Lidai*, p. 6.

5. Wang Xizhi, "Bishilin shi er zhang," *Lidai*, p. 31.

6. Wei Heng, "Si ti shu shi," *Lidai*, p. 13.

7. *Ibid.*, p. 15.

8. Hence the importance of pairs of terms, at once contrasted and correlated, which organize traditional aesthetic thought in China; see, e.g., in the *Wenxin diaolong*: *bi* (analogous similarity)/*xing* (evocative theme), *feng* ("wind")/*gu* ("armature"), *qing* (emotion)/*cai* (ornamentation), *yin* (the buried richness of meaning)/*xiu* (visible splendor), etc.

9. Yang Xin, *Lidai*, p. 47.

10. The famous judgment made by Taizong of the Tang dynasty, cited in William Acker, *Some T'ang and pre-T'ang Texts on Chinese Painting* (Leiden: E.J. Brill, 1954), 1.xxxv.

11. Wei Heng, *Lidai*, p. 12.

12. *Ibid.*, p. 14.

13. Zhang Huaiguan, "Lun yong bi shi fa," *Lidai*, p. 216.

14. Jiang Kui, "Xushupu," *Lidai*, p. 394.

15. Zhang Huaiguan, "Lun yong bi shi fa," *Lidai*, p. 216.

16. Cai Yong, "Jiu shi," *Lidai*, p. 6.

17. Zhang Huaiguan, "Lun yong bi shi lun," *Lidai*, p. 216.

18. Cf. the "Lunhua" by Gu Kaizhi cited in the *Lidai minghuaji* (cf. Acker, *Some T'ang and pre-T'ang Texts*, vol. 2, p. 58). On the sense of "disposition," *zhi chen bu shi*; in the sense of "surge," *you ben teng da shi* (note also the interesting expression, *qing shi*). It is probably the sense of "disposition" that is

also to be found at the beginning of the "Xuhaua" by Wang Wei, *qiu rong shi er yi.*

19. Gu Kaizhi, "Hua yuntai shan ji," *Leibian*, pp. 581–82. For a study on this text that is crucial for an understanding of the birth of landscape painting in China, see the excellent work by Hubert Delahaye, *Les Premières Peintures de paysage en Chine. Aspects religieux* (Paris: Ecole française d'Extrême-Orient, 1981) (for the four occurrences of the term *shi* in this text, see pp. 16, 18, 28, 33).

20. Gu Kaizhi, "Hua yuntai shanjim," *Leibian*, pp. 581–82. This notion of "danger" characterizing an extreme tension and a maximum of potential calls to mind the *Sunzi*, ch. 5, "*shi gi shan zhan zhe, qi shi xian*," which should, I believe, be translated as, "The good general exploits to its extreme the potential born of the situation." The term *shi* itself is well translated by Susan Bush and Hsio-yen Shih, *Early Chinese Texts on Painting* (Cambridge, MA: Harvard University Press, 1985), p. 21: "The term *shi* (dynamic configuration) is used here to describe such a 'momentum' or 'effect.' "

21. Zhang Yanyuan, *Leibian*, p. 603.

22. Huang Gongguang, *Leibian*, p. 697.

23. Da Chongguang, *Leibian*, p. 802.

24. *Ibid.*, p. 801.

25. *Shan shui* (mountain-water) means "landscape" – TRANS.

26. Tang Zhiqi, *Leibian*, pp. 738, 744.

27. Wang Zhideng, *Leibian*, p. 719.

28. Gu Kaizhi, *Leibian*, p. 582 (Delahaye, p. 28); Li Cheng, *Leibian*, p. 616.

29. Jing Hao, *Leibian*, pp. 605–608 (cf. French translation in Nicole Vandier-Nicolas, *Esthétique et peinture de paysage en Chine* [Paris: Klincksiek, 1982], p. 71).

30. The high value set on tension in painting is also strikingly reflected – and still expressed in terms of *shi* – in the concave line of a roof (curving slightly up at the lower edge), a characteristic of traditional architecture of the Far East. (But even here there is no single, predetermined form, for this line depends on the calculations made in each particular case as to the "degree of the angle."

Those calculations depend on such variables as the type of building, the breadth of each bay, the dimensions of the horizontal projections of each rafter, etc. As such, they enable the joints of the differently sloping rafters to give the roof its uptilted aspect.) See *Yingzao fashi*, ch. 4; Mo Shilong, *Leibian*, p. 713; Tang Zhiqi, *Leibian*, p. 744.

31. The treatise by Fang Xun, "Shanjingju lun hua shanshui" (*Leibian*, p. 912) is particularly interesting in this respect and provides a rich illustration of the term *shi* in painting.

32. Fang Xuan, *Leibian*, p. 913.

33. Shitao, para. 12; cf. *Shitao hua yulu* (Beijing: Renmin meishu chubanshe, 1962), p. 53, and the French translation by Pierre Ryckmans, *Les Propos sur la peinture du moine Citrouille-amère* (Brussels: Institut belge des hautes études chinoises, 1970), p. 85.

34. Li Rihua, *Leibian*, p. 134.

35. Shitao, para. 17; cf. *yulu*, p. 62, and Ryckmans, *Les Propos sur la peinture du moine Citrouille-amère*, p. 115.

36. See this interesting expression in Han Zhuo (*Leibian*, p. 674): "*xian kan fengshiqiyun*," whereas it is clear (see p. 672) that Han Zhuo certainly, in conformity with this whole tradition, does ascribe a supreme value to *qiyun*. On this affinity between wind and *shi* in the evocation of landscape painting in Han Zhuo, see *Leibian*, pp. 668–69.

37. Gong Xian, *Leibian*, p. 784.

38. Fang Xun, *Leibian*, p. 914.

39. Yu Shinan, *Lidai*, p. 112.

40. *Wenxin diaolong*, "Ding shi pian," p. 529. On the possible relationship of this literary concept of *shi* with the concept distinguishable in pictorial and calligraphic theory, see the brief notes of Tu Guangshe, "Wenxin diaolong de dingshilun" ("Essay on the Meaning of *shi* in the *Wenxin diaolong*"), in *Wenxin shi lun* ([Shengyan: Chunfeng wenyi chubanshe, 1986], p. 62), although the analysis is inadequate.

41. On the influence of the *Sunzi* on this chapter, see the important study by Zhan Ying, "Wenxin diaolong de dingshilun" reprinted in *Wenxin diaolong*

de fengge xue (Beijing: Renmin wenxue chubanshe, 1982), p. 62, which has helped to promote understanding of this chapter; cf. the erroneous interpretation of Fan Wenlan regarding the "round" and the "square," in relation to Heaven and Earth, p. 534 n.3.

42. For a typical interpretation of this, see, e.g., Kou Xiaoxin, "Shi ti shi" ("Interpretation of *ti* and *shi*") in *Wenxin diaolong xuekan* 1 (Jinan: Qilu shushe, 1983), p. 271.

43. Pierre Guiraud, "Les tendances de la stylistique contemporaine," in *Style and Literature* (The Hague: Van Goor Zonen, 1962), p. 12; Roland Barthes, *Le Degré zéro de l'écriture* (Paris: Seuil, 1953), p. 19.

44. See ch. "Fuhui," p. 652; ch. "Xuzhi," p. 727.

CHAPTER FIVE: LIFELINES ACROSS A LANDSCAPE

The principal texts cited in this chapter come from the *Zhongguo hualan leibian* (hereafter *Leibian*).

1. Heidegger, "Comment se détermine la *phusis*," *Questions II* (Paris: Gallimard, 1968), pp. 181–82.

2. *Ibid.*, p. 183.

3. The most commonplace and unexceptional concept in the Chinese tradition. The citiations are taken from the beginning of the *Book of Funerals* (*Zangshu*) attributed to Guo Pu.

4. On this geomancy tradition, still very much alive in China today, see the classic studies by Ernest J. Eitel, "Fengshoui ou Principes de science naturelle en Chine," *Annales du musée Guimet* 1 (1880), p. 205; J.J.M. de Groot, *The Religious System of China* (Leiden: E.J. Brill, 1967), vol. 3, ch. 12, p. 935; and Stephan D.R. Feuchtwang, *An Antropological Analysis of Chinese Geomancy* (Ventiane, Laos: Vithagna, 1974), in particular p. 111.

5. The term *shi* already had this particular topographical sense at the end of Antiquity, e.g., in the *Guanzi*; cf. ch. 76, p. 371; ch. 78, p. 384. This sense is specified in the bibliographical chapter of the *Hanshu* ("Yiwenzhi"), in the rubric devoted to "configurationists" (*xing fa liu jia*).

6. Guo Pu, *Zangshu*; *idem* for the citations that follow.

7. This point has been forcefully made in the important study by Yonezawa Yoshio, *Chugokû kaigashi kenkyû* (Tokyo: Heibonsha), p. 76.

8. I have chosen the expression "lifeline" to convey this aspect of *shi* because it relates directly to the notion of the *vital breath* on which it is based and because it is reminiscent of our own chiromancy, closely related to geomancy. I have, furthermore, noticed that in the West certain contemporary schools of drawing and painting (such as that of Martenot) are now distancing themselves from traditional training methods and utilizing this expression in their own teaching.

9. Jing Hao, *Leibian*, p. 607; cf. Susan Bush and Hsio-yen Shih, *Early Chinese Texts on Painting* (Cambridge, MA: Harvard University Press, 1985), p. 164; "The different appearances of mountains and streams are produced by the combinations of vital energy and dynamic configuration"; and Nicole Vandier-Nicolas, *Esthétique et peinture de paysage en Chine* (Paris: Klincksiek, 1982), p. 76.

10. Zong Bing, "Introduction to Painting Landscapes" ("Hua shanshui xu"), *Leibian*, p. 583; see the detailed study by Hubert Delahaye in *Les Premières peintures de paysage en Chine: Aspects religieux* (Paris: Ecole Française d'Extrême-Orient, 1981), p. 76.

11. Guo Xi, *Du haut message des forêts et des sources (Lin quan gao zhi)*, *Leibian*, p. 634. This is a common distinction, see Jing Hao, *Leibian*, p. 614.

12. Rolf A. Stein, "Survey of Themes," in *The World in Miniature: Container Gardens and Dwellings in Far Eastern Religious Thought*, trans. Phyllis Brooks (Stanford, CA: Stanford University Press, 1990).

13. *Ibid.*, p. 49.

14. Zong Bing, p. 583.

15. "Brilliance," *xiu*; "spirituality," *ling*; the idea of "reflection" is introduced in the very first sentence of the text, *Han dao ying wu*.

16. On the importance of Buddhism in Zong Bing, the author of the *Mingfolun*, see the pertinent analysis by Delahaye, *Les Premières peintures de paysage en Chine*, p. 80.

17. This is the etymology of the word *hua* given by the *Shuowen jiezi* to

which Wang Wei seems to be referring at the beginning of his treatise; see Delahaye, *Les Premières peintures de paysage en Chine*, p. 117.

18. Wang Wei, "On painting" ("Xu hua"), *Leibian*, p. 585. But the term *shi*, which is used at the beginning of the treatise (*jing qiu rong shi er yi*), here means no more than "disposition" and has not yet acquired the later, stronger sense. In his above-cited study, Yonezawa Yoshio is, in my opinion, wrong to attribute this stronger, positive sense to *shi*. I believe the sense of the passage to be: "seek out only the aspect and the disposition. But the Ancients..."

19. Du Fu, "Xi ti Wang Zai hua shanshui tu ge"; see William Hung, *Tu Fu, China's Greatest Poet* (New York: Russell & Russell, 1969), p. 169.

20. See, e.g., Tang Zhiqi, *Leibian*, p. 733.

21. The nature and function of the "wrinkles" have been very clearly described by Pierre Ryckmans in several notes in *Les Propos sur la peinture du moine Citrouille-amère* (Brussels: Institut belge des hautes études chinoises, 1970), on which I have drawn here.

22. Tang Zhiqi, *Leibian*, p. 742.

23. Fang Xun, *Leibian*, p. 914.

24. Mo Shilong, *Leibian*, p. 712.

25. Tang Zhiqi, *Leibian*, p. 743.

26. On the whole of this passage, see the important dissertation attributed to Zhao Zuo, *Leibian*, p. 759, which is devoted exclusively to *shi* (see also Qian Du, *Leibian*, p. 929).

27. Tang Dai, *Leibian*, pp. 857–59 (the whole paragraph is devoted to the importance of *shi*).

28. Da Chongguang, *Leibian*, pp. 809, 833.

29. Wang Shizhen (Wang Yuyang), *Daijingtang shihua* (Beijing: Renmin wenxue chubanshe, 1982), vol. 1, ch. 3, "Zhu xing lei," para. 3, p. 68. Wang Shizhen also reused the pictorial theory of distance (see the "three distances" of Guo Xi) to explain the poetic effect, see p. 78, para. 6; pp. 85–95, para. 15.

30. *Ibid.*, para. 4.

31. *Ibid.*

32. Wang Fuzhi, *Jiangzhai shihua* (Beijing: Renmin wenxue chubanshe, 1981), ch. 2, para. 42, p. 138.

33. *Ibid.*

CHAPTER SIX: CATEGORIES OF EFFICACIOUS DISPOSITIONS

In this chapter, the texts of calligraphy are cited, as above, from the anthology *Lidai shufa lun wenxuan*; those concerning the lute are cited from the *Great Treatise on Supreme Sound* (*Taiyin daquanji*), an anonymous textbook of the fourteenth century (ch. 3); those concerning the "art of the bedroom" are from the (Tang) *Dongxuanzi*, as reconstructed in the *Shuang mei jing an congshu* by Ye Dehui; for *taiji quan*, the texts have a number of different origins (which is understandable, given the late and secondary character of this literature). My analysis of the poetic *shi* is based on the thought of poeticians of the Tang period, Wang Changling and Jiaoran, as expressed in the *Wenjing mifulun* (Japanese *Bunkyô hifuron*), ed. Wang Liqi, *Zhongguo shehui kexue chubanshe* (Beijing: Xinhua shudian, 1983), and in the critical work of Jiaoran, *Jiaoran shishi jixiao xinbian*, ed. Xu Qingyun (Taiwan: Wenshizhe chubanshe, 1983).

1. A more general application could probably be given to the remark made by Dong Qichang, according to which the Tang calligraphers were particularly interested in technique (*fa*), while those of the Six Dynasties period stressed the "internal resonance" (*yun*) and the Song calligraphers stressed the expression of "individual feeling" (*yi*); see Jean-Marie Simonet, *La Suite au "Traité de calligraphie" de Jiang Kui*, unpublished thesis (Paris: Ecole nationale des langues orientales, 1969), pp. 94–95.

2. This is particularly true, in the field of poetics, of the *Wenjing mifulun* (*Bunkyô hifuron*) compiled by Kûkai, the founder of the Shingon, and completed in 819; and, in the field of medicine, of the *Yixinfang* (*Ishimpô*), compiled by Tamba Yasuyori between 982 and 984 (on the history of this text and the reconstruction of ch. 28, devoted to the "bedroom" (*fangnei*) by the modern Chinese scholar Ye Dehui, see the classic work by Robert Van Gulik, *Sexual Life in Ancient China* (Leiden: E.J. Brill, 1961).

3. Cai Yong, "Jiu shi," *Lidai*, p. 6. This is a matter of an apocryphal attri-

bution made by the *Shuyuan Jinghua* by Chen Si of the Song period. Other lists of the *shi* of calligraphy, relating to the movement of the brush, are to be found in Wang Xizhi's "Bishulun," *Lidai*, p. 34; and lists relating to the graphic elements (in a sense that was then almost the equivalent of *fa*) can be found in Zhang Huaiguan, *Lidai*, p. 220.

4. On this question, see R.H. Van Gulik, *The Lore of the Chinese Lute* (Tokyo: Sophia University, 1940), p. 114; Kenneth J. De Woskin, *A Song for One or Two, Music and the Concept of Art in Early China* (Ann Arbor: University of Michigan Press, 1982), ch. 8, p. 130. The plates that are commented on here are borrowed from the *Taiyin daquanji*.

5. On this subject, see the work by Catherine Despeux, *Taiji quan, Art martial, technique de longue vie* (Paris: G. Trédaniel, 1981) (Chinese text, p. 293). It is also thought that these two series correspond to the "five paces" and the "eight entries," which are distributed according to the eight cardinal and collateral points.

6. Associations of this type are already to be found in connection with the *shi* of geomancy; see the *Zangshu* of Guo Pu, cited above.

7. *dongxuanzi*; see Van Gulik.

8. On this subject, see the remarks of Simonet, p. 113.

9. See, e.g., the graphic reconstructions proposed by Akira Ishihara and Howard S. Levy, *The Tao of Sex* (Yokohama: Shibundo, 1969), p. 59.

10. This idea has been excellently summarized by Jean François Billeter in *L'Art chinois de l'écriture* (Geneva: Skira, 1989), pp. 185–86.

11. This point on the playing of music and those that follow are taken from Van Gulik, *The Lore of the Chinese Lute*, p. 120.

12. Qi Ji (Hu Desheng), *Fengsao zhige*, in *Wenjing mifulun* (Beijing: Xinhua shudian, 1983), "Shi you shi shi."

13. *Wenjing mifulun (Bunkyô hifuron)*, the "Earth" section, "The seventeen *shi*," ed. Wang Liqi, p. 114. It has long been recognized that this chapter ought to be attributed to Wang Changling (in view of the quotations from poems and the many overlaps with the *Lunwenyi*). A good philological study of the text has been made by Hiroshi Kôzen, in the edition of the complete works of Kûkai

(Tokyo: Chikuma Shobô, 1986). But there is no translation of this chapter in any Western language. In his Ph.D. thesis on this work (*Poetics and Prosody in Early Mediaeval China: A Study and Translation of Kûkai's Bunkyô hiruron* [Cornell University, Ithaca, N.Y., 1978, University Microfilms]), Richard Wainwright Bodman does not translate the chapters in the "Earth" section because he considers their interpretation to be a tricky matter, although he does recognize that this chapter is particularly interesting. However, his translation of the title as "Seventeen Styles" is unsatisfactory (as was Vincent Shih's earlier translation of the title of the chapter in the *Wenxing diaolong*, "On choice of style"), particularly as he also translates *ti* as "style" (see p. 89).

14. An attempt to order the series according to modern criteria has been made by Luo Genze, in his *Histoire de la critique littéraire chinoisee, Zhongguo wenxue pipingshi* (Dianwen chubanshe), pp. 304–308.

15. A comparison between this chapter of the "Seventeen *shi*" and the following lists of the *Bunkyô hifuron*'s "Earth" section is instructive in this respect; see the study by François Martin, "L'énumération dans la théorie littéraire de la Chine des Tang," in *L'Art de la liste, Extrême-Orient – Extrême-Occident* 8 (1990), p. 37f.

16. Jiaoran, *Pinglun*, "San by tong yu yi shi," p. 28. A brief commentary on this passage is to be found in the study by Xu Qingyun, *Jiaoran shishi yanjiu* (Taiwan: Wenshizhe chubanshe), p. 130.

17. *Bunkyô hifuron*, "Lunwenyi," p. 317; the poems are cited from the *Shijing* (poems 3 and 226).

18. The meaning does not seem to me well rendered by Bodman, who has failed to analyze the passage properly (see Bodman, p. 409), and renders it "although the natural image is different, the forms are alike"; likewise in the following passage, in which the expression *gao shou zuo shi* is translated simply as "when a superior talent works." Similarly, *chôshi*, in the Japanese translation by Kôzen (p. 449), also seems to fail to render the meaning of *shi*, which is extremely revealing here.

19. The fact that the *shi* is regarded as identical despite the difference between the two situations, and thus rates as a specific factor in itself, is often

noted in a wide range of fields. We have already noted one such remark in the context of thought on calligraphy – "the same *shi*, whatever the body [form] of the writing" (cf. p. 77) – and it reappears in a mathematical text dating from the same period (third century) as the treatise on calligraphy: "the *shi* is similar, while the [operational] situation is different." Here, the remark relates to an identity of *procedure* (Liu Hui's commentary on the *Jiuzhang suanshu* [*The Nine Chapters on the art of calculation*], compiled in the first century A.D., is considered the classic par excellence not only of the Chinese but also of the entire Far Eastern mathematical tradition); and in both examples this identity of procedure is revealed at the operational level, by means of a deep analysis.

20. See the old but still pertinent analyses in *Sound and Symbol in Chinese* (Hong Kong: Hong Kong University Press, repr. 1962), in particular p. 74.

21. *Bunkyô hifuron*, "Lunwenyi," p. 283.

22. Du Fu, "Deng Yueyang lou."

23. *Bunkyô hifuron*, "Lunwenyi," pp. 296, 317.

24. On this subject, see the various studies collected in *Extrême-Orient – Extrême-Occident: Parellélisme et Appariement des choses* 11.8 (1989), and in particular the article by François Martin, p. 89.

25. Jiaoran, *Pinglun*, p. 33.

26. Jiaoran, *Shishi*, para. "Ming shi," p. 39. Guo Shaoyu (Luo Genze, *Histoire de la critique littéraire chinoise, Zhongguo wenxue pipingshi*, vol. 1, p. 207) detects in this imagistic expression an anticipation of the poetic critique of Sikong Tu. See also the remarks of Xu Fuguan (*Zhongguo wenxue lunji xubian*, Xinya yanjiusuo congkan, Xuesheng shuju, p. 149) on the distinction between *shi* and *ti*, conceived as the effect of the difference between a static point of view and a dynamic one. Xu Qingyun, p. 124, does not seem adequate to me in this respect.

27. Jiaoran, *Pinglun*, p. 19.

28. Jiaoran, *Shishi*, para. "Shi you si shen," p. 41.

29. *Bunkyô hifuron*, "Lunwenyi," p. 283.

30. *Ibid.*, p. 317.

Chapter Seven: Dynamism Is Continuous

As above, in the field of calligraphy, the references are to the *Lidai shufalun wenxuan* and, in the field of painting, to the *Zhongguo hualun leibian*. Again as above, the edition of the *Wenxin diaolong* that is cited is the one by Fan Wenlan, and that of the *Wenjing mifulun* is by Wang Liqi; likewise, the *shihua* of Wang Shizhen (Wang Yuyang) and Wang Fuzhi are cited from the edition by Dai Hongsen, in the *Oeuvres de critique et de théories littéraires classiques de la Chine* (Beijing: Renmin wenxue chunanshe, 1981, 1982). Finally, with regard to the critical work of Jin Shengtan, the commentary of Du Fu refers to the *Dushijie* edited by Zhong Laiyin (Shanghai: Shanghai guji chubanshe, 1984); that of the novel *The Water Margin* refers to the *Shuihuzhuan huipingben*, University of Beijing edition, 1978. The reference to the French translation by Jacques Dars (Paris: Gallimard, 1978), on which the English translations in the present work are directly based, follows.

1. See, e.g., the analysis of Shen Zongqian, *Leibian*, p. 907.

2. See *Sunzi*, ch. 5, "Shipian," end.

3. Zhang Huaiguan, "Liu ti shu lun," *Lidai*, pp. 214–15.

4. Zhang Huaiguan, "Lun yong bi shi fa," *Lidai*, p. 216.

5. This is the first of the nine *shi* mentioned by Cai Yong; see *Lidai*, p. 6.

6. This is the defect of "double heaviness," *shuang zhong*; see Catherine Despeux, *Taiji quan, Art martial, technique de longue vie* (Paris: G. Trédaniel, 1981), p. 57.

7. Jiang Kui, "Bi shi," *Lidai*, p. 393.

8. *Ibid.*, "Zhen shu," *Lidai*, p. 385.

9. Zhang Haiguan, *Shuyi, Lidai*, p. 148. This is a good example of the way in which the arts of calligraphy and that of poetry are conceptualized according to the same logic: the expression "the column of characters is completed but the impetus carries on beyond" repeats the famous idea of *xing* in poetry (i.e., an introductory theme with a symbolic meaning, and the implicit richness of the poem that is "beyond words").

10. Zhang Huaiguan, *Shuduan, Lidai*, p. 166.

11. Jiang Kui, "Caoshu", *Lidai*, p. 387. (There is a good analysis in Jean-Marie Simonet, *La Suite au "Traité de calligraphie" de Jiang Kui*, unpublished

thesis [Paris: Ecole nationale des langues orientales, 1969], pp. 145–46).

12. Jiang Kui, p. 386.

13. *Ibid.*, p. 387; on this subject, see the remarks of Hsiung Ping-Ming, *Zhang Xu et la calligraphie cursive folle* (Paris: Institut des hauts études chinoises, 1984), pp. 154, 158, 180.

14. In this sense, the art of cursive writing sums up the art of Chinese calligraphy in general: if calligraphy is not engendered by alternation and change, all that is produced is an "appearance of calligraphy," with no savor at all (see Wang Xizhi, "Shun lun," *Lidai*, p. 29).

15. Jiang Kui, "Xuemai," p. 394; see analysis in Simonet, pp. 223–24.

16. Shen Zongqian, *Leibian*, p. 906. The long passage devoted to *shi* in this treatise is without a doubt one of the most explicit and most systematic instances of reflection on this subject in all Chinese literary criticism.

17. Da Chongguang, *Leibian*, p. 802. This method of increasing the tension that leads to the effect is not a principle solely of the arts of writing and painting. The same formula is valid for literary composition, since here too "the priority is to acquire *shi*" (Zhu Rongzhi, *Wenqilun yanjin* [Taiwan: Xuesheng shuju, 1985], p. 270). Rather than prosaically develop the text in conformity with the theme, as one initially learns to do, "it is better to confer some relief on the text" ("like waves swelling up, like the mountain summits rising," according to the Chinese comparisons) "by moving the brush in the opposite direction." I understand this to mean that, instead of tackling the subject directly, it should be approached by creating the diversion of a contrasting effect, then greeting it head on, thus rendering it more striking. It would be impossible to assimilate these different forms of art more closely than by using this common argument of the *shi* of the brush.

18. Shen Zongqian, *Leibian*, p. 906.

19. Fang Xun, *Leibian*, p. 915. This famous analogy is for the first time here attributed to the great painter Lu Tanwei (late fifth through early sixth centuries). It was inspired by the calligraphy of Wang Xianzhi, the son of the famous calligrapher Wang Xizhi, who was himself famous for his radical attempts to exploit the potentialities of cursive writing.

20. Shen Zongqian, *Leibian*, p. 907.

21. *Ibid.*, p. 905.

22. *Ibid.*, p. 906.

23. Although this is, of course, "just a manner of speaking" (the expression *zhongshi* calls to mind the *Book of Changes*) (*Zhouyi*, "Xici," pt. 1, para. 4), it is nonetheless significant. In particular, it helps us to understand why Chinese culture is impervious to tragedy (i.e., the essence of tragedy). For a tragic vision to be conceivable, one must believe in a final end, imagined as a screen beyond which it is impossible to pass. It also helps us to understand why classical Chinese thought (even before Buddhism) found unnecessary the idea of "another world," separate from this one and compensating for it, since the world is always in the process of becoming other and death itself is simply a transformation.

24. Liu Xie, *Wenxin diaolong*, ch. "Fuhui," vol. 2, p. 652. The logic of this image does not seem to have been sufficiently recognized by contemporary Chinese commentators (the meaning of *zhen*: to lift up). See the complete editions of Lu Kanru and Mou Shijin (Qilu shushe, 1981), vol. 2, p. 297, and of Zhou Zhenfu (Beijing: Renmin wenxue chubanshe, 1981), p. 465. On the other hand, it is well conveyed by Vincent Yu-chung Shih, *The Literary Mind and the Carving of Dragons* (Taipei: Chung Hwa Book Company, 1975), p. 324.

25. The notion of *wenshi* is different from that of *wenzhang*. See, e.g., the significant uses of the term in the *Wenjing mifulun*, ch. "Dingwei," p. 341.

26. Liu Xie, *Wenxin diaolong*, ch. "Shenglü," vol. 2, pp. 553–54. This image is known to be taken from the *Sunzi*, ch. "Shipiau."

27. *Wenjing mifulun*, "Lunwenyi," p. 308; "Dingwei," p. 340.

28. *Ibid.*, "Dingwei," pp. 343–44.

29. Wang Shizhen, *Daijingtang shihua*, "Zhenjuelei," vol. 3, para. 9, p. 79.

30. Wang Fuzhi, *Jiangzhai shihua*, p. 222, para. 33. When "the conscious mind truly tends to express itself" here conveys the notion of *yi*.

31. *Ibid.*, p. 48.

32. In my opinion, this concept of poetic *shi* has not received the attention that it deserves, particularly from the commentators of Wang Fuzhi. See, in particular, the work by Yang Songnian, *Wang Fuzhi shilun yanjiu* (Studies on the poet-

ics of Wang Fuzhi) (Taiwan: Wenshizhe chubanshe, n.d.), in particular pp. 39, 47. This passage on Wang Fuzhi's concept of the poetic process uses analyses that I have published elsewhere, in *La Valeur allusive* (Paris: Ecole française d'Extrême-Orient, 1985), p. 280, and *Procès et Création* (Paris: Seuil, 1989), p. 266.

33. *Jiangzhai shihua*, p. 228. The notion of *jingju* has been important in Chinese literary criticism ever since the *Wenfu* by Lu Ji (the notion of *jingce*), but in that text its meaning was different from the one usually conferred on it by the later tradition here criticized by Wang Fuzhi: "Let one word, coming at the crucial point in a passage / Be for the entire text as it were a crack of the whip that astonishes us" (not simply to reinforce the meaning – cf. Li Shan's interpretation – but also, it seems to me, here, to impel the text forward). On changes in the meaning of this idea, see, in particular, Qian Zhongshu, *Guanchuipian* (Zhonghua shuju, 1979), vol. 3, p. 1197.

34. *Ibid.*, p. 61.

35. *Ibid.*, p. 19.

36. Jin Shengtan, *Dushihie*, "Ye ren song zhu ying," p. 122.

37. *Ibid.*, "Song ren cong jun," p. 91.

38. *Ibid.*, "Lin yi she di shu zhi...," p. 23.

39. The Chinese critics tell us that, whoever reads silently, solely with his eyes, "remains outside the text." One should recite it "aloud and with an accelerated rhythm" so as to "apprehend the *shi*," as well as read it to oneself "slowly," so as to apprehend "its invisible savor." The two readings should be mutually supportive (Yao Nai, "Letter to Chen Shuoshi," discussed in Zhu Rongzhi, *Wenqilun Yanjiu* [Taiwan: Xuesheng Shuju], p. 300).

40. See, in particular, the commentary that Jin Shengtan devotes to the long poem by Du Fu, "Beizheng," in which the effects of *shi*, within the composition, are carefully pinpointed (p. 67).

41. *Shuihuzhuan (huipingben)*, text, p. 149 (Dars, p. 146).

42. *Ibid.*, text, p. 254 (trans., p. 280).

43. *Ibid.*, text, p. 547 (trans., p. 635); see also text, p. 57 (trans., p. 29); text, pp. 275–76 (trans., p. 311), etc.

44. *Ibid.*, text, p. 339 (trans., p. 391); see also text, p. 111 (trans., p. 105).

45. *Ibid.*, text, p. 308 (trans., p. 350).

46. *Ibid.*, text, p. 502 (trans., p. 586).

47. *Ibid.*, text, p. 192 (trans., p. 200).

48. *Ibid.*, text, p. 667 (trans., p. 798).

49. *Ibid.*, text, p. 1124 (trans., II, p. 360).

50. *Ibid.*, text, p. 301 (trans., p. 343).

51. *Ibid.*, text, p. 358 (trans., p. 415); cf. also text, p. 295 (trans., p. 336).

52. *Ibid.*, text, p. 669 (trans., p. 801).

53. *Ibid.*, text, p. 197 (trans., p. 207).

54. *Ibid.*, text, p. 1020 (trans., II, p. 214).

55. *Ibid.*, text, p. 470 (trans., p. 551).

56. *Ibid.*, text, p. 512 (trans., p. 597).

57. *Ibid.*, text, p. 503 (trans., p. 587).

58. *The Three Kingdoms, Sanguo yanyi (huipingben)*, commentary by Mao Zonggang, ch. 43, p. 541.

59. Mao Zonggang, commentary on the *Three Kingdoms*, "Du sanguozhi fa," in *Zhongguo lidai xiashuo lunzhuxuan*, ed. Huang Lin (Shanghai: Jiangxi renmin chubanshe, 1982), p. 343.

60. *Ibid.*, p. 14. On this question, see the few, inadequate, remarks made by Ye Lang, *Aesthetics of the Chinese Novel (Zhongguo xiaoshuooo meixue)* (Beijing: Beijing daxue chabanshe), pp. 146–47.

61. On this subject see various "reading techniques" (*dufa*) suggested by Jin Shengtan for the *Shuihuzhuan*, by Mao Zonggang for the *Sanguo yanyi*, and by Zhang Zhupo for the *Jinpingmei*. I am most grateful to Rainier Lanselle for his helpful information on this point.

CHAPTER EIGHT: CONCLUSION II

The references are the same as for the earlier chapters (3–6); on the dragon motif, see the general and exhaustive study by Jean-Pierre Diény, *Le Symbolisme du dragon dans la Chine antique* (Paris: Institut des hautes études chinoises, 1987).

1. Guo Pu, *Zangshu*; see, e.g., the significant overlap between expressions such as "*shi* that comes from far away" and "the dragon that comes from thou-

sands of *li* away" (*yuan shi zhi lai, qian li lai long*). On the theme of the dragon as "what all topographical formations resemble," cf. Stephan D.R. Feuchtwang, *An Anthropological Analysis of Chinese Geomancy* (Ventiane, Laos: Vithagna, 1974), p. 141.

2. Gu Kaizhi, "Hua yuntai shan ji," *Leibian*, p. 581.

3. Jing Hao, "Bi fa ji," *Leibian*, p. 665.

4. Han Zhuo, "Shanshui chun quanji," *Leibian*, p. 665.

5. *Ibid.*, p. 666.

6. Suo Jing, "Caoshushi," *Lidai*, p. 19.

7. Wang Xizhi, "Ti Wei furen 'Bichentu' hou," *Lidai*, p. 27.

8. Commentary of Jin Shengtan, *Shuihuzhuan*, p. 113 (trans. Jacques Dars, *Au bord de l'eau* (Paris: Gallimard, 1978), p. 107.

9. *Ibid.*, p. 163 (see Dars trans., p. 196).

10. Diény, *Le Symbolisme du dragon*, pp. 205–207.

11. Jin Shengtan's commentary, *Shuihuzhuan*, p. 189 (cf. for this passage, the Dars trans., p. 196).

12. Yang Xiong, *Fayan*; as cited in Diény, *Le Symbolisme du dragon*, pp. 242–43.

13. *Zuozhuan*; cf. Diény, *Le Symbolisme du dragon*, p. 1.

14. *Shiji* (Beijing: Zhonghua shuju), vol. 7, ch. 63, p. 2140.

15. *Huainanzi*, ch. 15, p. 266.

16. Han Zhuo, *Lidai*, p. 6655.

17. Du Fu, "Bei zheng"; Jin Shengtan's commentary, *Dushijie*, p. 71.

18. *Shuihuzhan*, Jin Shengtan's commentary, p. 645 (for the passage cited, cf. Dars trans., p. 770).

19. *Ibid.*, p. 504 (Dars trans., p. 588); also p. 543 (Dars trans., p. 630).

20. Jiaoran, on the calligraphy of Zhang Xyu; see Hsiung Ping-Ming, *Zhang Xu et la Calligraphie cursive folle*, p. 181.

21. Wang Fuzhi, *Jianfzhai shihua*, p. 48. In Wang Fuzhi's view, this peak of the poetic art has only been achieved by Xie Lingyun; see, e.g., his commentary on the poem "You nan ting" in the *Gushi pingxuan*.

22. Wang Fuzhi's way of conveying more precisely the notions of *qixiang*

("aura of meaning") and *jing* ("poetic world"), which, since the Tang period, have been used to characterize the poetic experience of China.

CHAPTER NINE: SITUATION AND TENDENCY IN HISTORY

In this chapter, the texts cited from the *Xunzi*, the *Shangjunshu*, the *Guanzi*, and the *Han Feizi* refer to the *Zhuzi jicheng*, vols. 2 and 5. The *Fengjianlun* by Liu Zongyuan is cited from the *Liu He Dongji* edition (Shanghai: Renmin chubanshe, 1974) (2 vols.), the *Rizhilu* by Gu Yanuu (Taipei: Shangwu Yinshuguan), vol. 3. For Wang Fuzhi, I used principally *Dutong jianlun* (Beijing: Zhongua shuju, 1975) (2 vols.) and the *Songlun* (Taipei: Jiusi congshu, 1976). Finally, the references to Chinese literary history are for the most part to the anthology by Guo Shaoyu, *Zhongguo lidai wenlunxuan* (Hong Kong: Zhonghua shuju, repr. 1979), vol. 2.

1. Etienne Balazs has suggested rendering this use of *shi* in a historical context as "power of prevailing conditions, tendency, trend" or even "necessity." See *Political Theory and Administrative Reality in Traditional China* (London: School of Oriental and African Studies, 1965). In his study *Nation und Elite im Denken von Wang Fu-chih* (Hamburg: Mitteilungen der Gesellschaft für Natur un Völkerkunde Ostasiens, 1968), vol. 49, p. 87, Ernst Joachim Vierheller renders it as "die besonderen Umstände, die Augenblickstendenz, die zu diesen Zeiten herrscht"; and Jean-François Billeter ("Deux études sur Wang Fuzhi," *T'oung Pao* [Leiden: E.J. Brill, 1970], vol. 56, p. 155) writes as follows: "More simply, one might suggest, provisionally, 'situation or the course of things.' The course of things is clearly inseparable from their structure." In effect, it means both "course" and "situation" at once, and it is to this ambivalence (as we see it) that the term owes its philosophical richness.

2. *Xunzi*, ch. "Zidao," p. 348.

3. On this use of *shi*, in the sense of a determining factor, at once "forces" and "conditions," see the *Shangjunshu*, ch. 11, "Li ben," p. 21 (*xing san zhe you er shi*: "to establish these three points, there are two conditions, which are its determining factors"); further on, see also *er shi yu bei shi*: "manifests itself in the fact of making the potential of the situation complete").

4. *Shangjunshu*, ch. 20, "Ruo min," p. 35.

5. *Ibid.*, ch. 18, "Hua ce," p. 32. For an analogous idea in the *Guanzi*, see Roger T. Ames, *The Art of Rulership: A Study in Ancient Chinese Political Thought* (Honolulu: University of Hawaii Press, 1983), pp. 77, 224 n.39.

6. *Shangjunshu*, ch. 26, "Ding fen," p. 43. The force of this term does not, in general, seem to me to be adequately rendered in the translation by Jean Lévi, *Le Livre du prince Shang* (Paris: Flammarion, 1981), pp. 112, 146, 160, 177, 185.

7. *Guanzi*, ch. 23, p. 144.

8. *Mencius*, ch. 3, "Tengwengong," pt. 1, para. 4 (trans. by Legge, p. 250).

9. Zhuangzi, ch. "Daozhipian" (trans. by Liou Kia-hway, "Connaissance de l'Orient," 1973, p. 239).

10. Han Feizi, ch. 2, "Wu du," p. 339.

11. *Shangjunshu*, ch. 7, "Kai sai," p. 16. This concept of *shi* is henceforth part of the theory of the modernists; see, e.g., the beginning of the famous letter to Renzong from Wang Anshi, *Wang Wen gong wenji* (Shanghai: Shanghai renmin chubanshe, 1974), 1.2.

12. Jia Yi, "Guoqinlun." This text is so important that it is cited several times in *Shiji* by Sima Qian: in the "Biography of the first emperor" (Beijing: Zhonghua shuju), 1.282 and in ch. 48, "House of Chen She," 6.1965. The difference between the translations is symptomatic of the ambivalence of the term *shi*: Chavannes (*Mémoires historiques*, vol. 2, p. 231) renders the term as "conditions" ("since the conditions for conquering and the conditions for preserving are different") and Burton Watson (*Records of the Grand Historian of China*, vol. 1, p. 33) renders it as "power" ("the power to attack and the power to retain").

13. Liu Zongyuan, "Fengjianlun" ("On feudality"), p. 43. Contemporary native historians of Chinese philosophy have stressed the "progressive" character of the concept of *shi* in Liu Zongyuan and have set it up as a theory (see Hou Wailu, "La philosophie et la sociologie matérialistes de Liu Zongyuan," in *Liu Zongyuan yanjiu lunji* [Hong Kong, repr. 1973], p. 16). This systematization of a historical theory of *shi* was pushed to the limit at the end of the Cultural Revolution, when the "Fengjianlun" was suggested for "the study of the masses" (Liu Zongyuan, the new Legalist, was opposed to the reactionary Han Yu

in a battle "between the two lines"; cf. the biography devoted to Liu Zongyuan by the Department of History of the University of Shanxi [Shanxi: Renmin chubanshe, 1976], p. 53f.). For an appreciation of what was historically at stake in such a debate at the time of Liu Zongyuan, see in particular David McMullen, *State and Scholars in T'ang China* (Cambridge: Cambridge University Press, 1987), pp. 196–97, and "Views of the State in Du You and Liu Zongyuan," in *Foundations and Limits of State Power in China*, ed. S.R. Schram (London: SOAS, and Hong Kong: CUHK, 1987), in particular pp. 64 and 79–80.

14. Han Yu, "Yuandao" ("On the origin of the Way"). Of course, one cannot reduce this famous founding essay of the Confucian revival to a formula such as this, as the commentators of the Cultural Revolution tried to do. Nevertheless, this text can be compared with the historical ideas of the *Mencius*, to the detriment of an interpretation of history based on the idea of internal necessity. On the relationship between Liu Zongyuan and Han Yu, see Charles Hartman, *Han Yu and the T'ang Search for Unity* (Princeton, NJ: Princeton University Press, 1986).

15. Wang Fuzhi, first page of the *Dutongjianlun*. This text has been much used by modern commentators on Wang Fuzhi; see in particular Ji Wenfu, *Wang Chuanshan xueshu lunji*, p. 122. It has been translated by Ian McMorran in his unpublished thesis, *Wang Fu-chih and His Political Thought* (Oxford University, 1968), pp. 168–71.

16. This is the point of view not only of Wang Fuzhi but also, in the same period, of a scholar such as Gu Yanwu; cf. *Rizhilu*, "Junxian" ("On administrative constituencies"), ch. 7, p. 94.

17. Wang Fuzhi, *Dutongjianlun*, ch. 2, "Wendi," p. 40.

18. *Ibid.*, ch. 3, "Wudi," p. 66.

19. *Ibid.*, ch. 20, "Taizong," p. 684; cf. also Gu Yanwu, ch. 7, p. 96.

20. *Ibid.*, ch. 2, "Wendi," pp. 46–47.

21. *Ibid.*, ch. 3, "Wudi," pp. 56–58.

22. *Ibid.*, ch. 5, "Chengdi," p. 122. But man, for his part, does not have to evolve in the same way; cf. ch. 6, "Guangwu," p. 150.

23. *Ibid.*, ch. 12, "Huaidi," p. 382. The attention payed by Chinese think-

ers to slow, progressive change dissolves individual events into historical continuity. However sudden and spectacular an event may seem, invariably it is simply the logical end result of a tendency that, when it started, was probably barely perceptible (on this subject, cf. the *wenyan* commentary on the first line of the *Kun* hexagram in the *Book of Changes*).

24. *Ibid.*, ch. 20, "Taizong," pp. 692–94.

25. *Siwenlu (waipian)* (Beijing: Zhonghua shuju, 1956), p. 72. This aspect is all too frequently passed over in silence by Wang Fuzhi's Chinese commentators, who are determined to turn him into a progressive thinker: see, e.g., Li Jiping, *Wang Fuzhi yu Dutongjianlun* (Jinan: Shandong jiaoyu chubanshe, 1982), p. 153.

26. *Siwenlu*, pp. 72–73.

27. See, e.g., Huang Mingtong and Lü Xichen, *Wang Chuanshan lishiguan yu lishi yanjiu* (Changsha: Hunan renmin chubanshe, 1986), p. 10.

28. This idea is already explicit in the *Mencius*, ch. 3, "Tengwengong," pt. 2, para. 9 (Legge, p. 279): in Mencius, it is Yao and Shun, the king Wu, the duke of Zhou, Confucius, in his capacity as the author of the *Chunqiu*, and Mencius himself who, in one period or another, intervene to cure disorder.

29. This idea was inherited from Zou Yan (in the third century B.C.) and was later theorized by Dong Zhongshu (175–105 B.C.) in the *Chunqiu fanlu*; see Anne Chang, *Etude sur le confucianisme Han* (Paris: Institut des hautes études chinoises, 1985), vol. 26, p. 25.

30. Wang Fuzhi, *Dutongjianlun*, ch. 16, "Wudi," pp. 539–40.

31. *Ibid.*, "Xulun," 1.1106.

32. *Ibid.*, ch. 19, "Yangdi," pp. 656–57.

33. Wang Fuzhi, *Zhangzi zhengmeng zhu* (Beijing: Zhonghua shuju, 1975), p. 68.

34. *Dutongjianlun*, ch. 15, "Xiaowudi," p. 511. The expression frequently recurs in Wang Fuzhi's historical thought, e.g., *Dutongjianlun*, ch. 12, p. 368, or *Songlun*, ch. 3, p. 62; ch. 14, p. 252.

35. *Dutongjianlun*, ch. 27, "Izong," p. 957.

36. *Songlun*, ch. 8, p. 155.

37. The theme of the *bi wang zhi shi*: see, e.g., *Dutongjianlun*, ch. 8, "Huandi," p. 245, and ch. 12, "Mindi," p. 385.

38. *Songlun*, ch. 8, p. 155.

39. *Ibid.*, ch. 14, p. 252.

40. It is only thanks to this distinction that it is possible to understand how Wang Fuzhi can speak on the one hand of a tendency that, "carried to its extreme," "is difficult to reverse" (cf. *Songlun*, ch. 4, p. 74) and, on the other, of a tendency that, "carried to its extreme," becomes fragile and is therefore "easy to reverse" (see, e.g., *Songlun*, ch. 7, p. 134). In the second case, *zhong* (heavy) is opposed to *qing* (light), and this tendency is often described as *qing zhong zhi shi* (see, e.g., *Dutongjianlun*, p. 263).

41. *Songlun*, ch. 7, pp. 134-35.

42. Toynbee picks an early date for the beginning of this reversal which would bring with it the decline of Greek civilization: 431 B.C. His justification for so doing strikes me as being very close to the Chinese intuition, in which decline becomes detectable at the stage of the hexagram of prosperity (in the third and – especially – the sixth strokes); the same goes for the way in which he conceives of that which is "shattered"; see, e.g., the explanation that he provides in Raymond Aron, ed., *L'Histoire et ses interprétations* (discussions on the work of Arnold Toynbee) (Paris: Mouton, 1961), p. 118: "What is shattered by the breakdown, what has broken down, is harmony, cooperation between the human beings who possess creative power within the ruling minority, those who had in effect participated actively in the growth of civilization."

43. In his *Internal Commentary* on the *Book of Changes* (the hexagrams *tai* and *pi*), Wang Fuzhi skillfully expresses in terms of *shi* the ineluctable nature of each phase in a manner totally analogous to the account of the great social and political changes of China that he advances in his historical *oeuvre*. History is but one of many illustrations of this absolutely general logic (expressed by every process).

44. *Songlun*, ch. 15, p. 259.

45. Wang Fuzhi, *Chunqiu shilun*, ch. 4.

46. *Songlun*, ch. 7, p. 135.

THE PROPENSITY OF THINGS

47. *Ibid.*, ch. 6, p. 118.

48. *Dutongjianlun*, ch. 4, "Yuandi," pp. 106–107.

49. See, e.g., for these expressions, and in order, *Dutongjianlun*, ch. 13, "Wudi," p. 405; *Songlun*, ch. 15, p. 259; *Dutongjianlun*, ch. 20, "Taizong," p. 691; *Ibid.*, ch. 13, "Chengdi," p. 411.

50. *Songlun*, ch. 7, p. 135.

51. *Ibid.*, ch. 8, p. 155.

52. *Ibid.*, ch. 7, p. 134.

53. *Ibid.* On this interpretation of the historical role of Huo Guang in Chinese historiography, see Michael Loewe, *Crisis and Conflict in Han China* (London: George Allen, 1974), pp. 72, 79, 118.

54. *Dutongjianlun*, ch. 8, "Lingdi," p. 263.

55. *Songlun*, ch. 10, p. 193. On this "myth" for which Yue Fei sacrificed so much, see the study by Hellmut Wilhelm, "From Myth to Myth: the Case of Yüeh Fei's Biography," in *Confucian Personalities*, ed. Arthur F. Wright and Denis Twitchett (Stanford, CA: Stanford University Press, 1962), p. 156. This theme of "opportunism" (in the most positivist sense of the term, of course) is already to be found in Mencius, who takes Confucius as his model (*Mencius*, ch. 5, "Wanzhang," pt. 2, para. 1; see Legge, pp. 369–72).

56. *Dutongjianlun*, ch. 28, pp. 1038–39.

57. The leaders of twentieth-century China have always displayed this kind of wisdom. When no longer able to fight off the encircling forces of the Guomindang, Mao Zedong withdrew, at the cost of a "long march," to the caves of Shenxi; once there, out of the way, he rebuilt his forces, established his first "bases," and patiently waited for the situation to allow him to regain the initiative (first during the Japanese invasion, then during World War II), return to the attack, and eventually emerge victorious. His rival, Chang Kai-shek, employed similar tactics: having been beaten by the Communist forces, he withdrew to Taiwan, which became the launching pad for a new rise.

Modern Chinese political observers frequently explain the situation in terms of alternation: first the doors are "opened up," then "closed shut"; the party blows first "hot," then "cold." Those threatened by the current tendency "withdraw" for a while, but only to prepare for their "return." They retire to the country, pretend to be "ill," even embark obligingly on self-criticism, the better to bounce back later on, when the situation is once again favorable to them.

58. Wang Fuzhi, *Chunqiu jiashuo*, ch. 1. The last sequence in the passage, *ran er you bu ran zhe cun yan*, has been interpreted in a number of different ways; see Vierheller, *Nation und Elite*, p. 88; J.F. Billeter, "Deux études sur Wang Fuzhi," p. 155 (n.1 above).

59. *Dutongjianlun*, ch. 2, "Wendi," pp. 49–50.

60. *Songlun*, ch. 4, p. 94.

61. *Ibid.*, ch. 14, p. 244.

62. On Wang Fuzhi's activities in resistance to the Manchu invasion, see the study by Ian McMorran, "The Patriot and the Partisans: Wang Fu-chih's Involvement in the Politics of the Yung-li Court," in *From Ming to Ch'ing*, ed. Jonathan D. Spence and John E. Wills (New Haven, CT: Yale University Press, 1979), p. 135.

63. Liu Xie, *Wenxin diaolong*, ch. "Dingshi," ed. Fan Wenlan, p. 531.

64. Jiaoran, "Pinglun"; this passage is cited in the *Wenjing mifulun (Bunkyô hifuron)* in ch. "Lunwnyi," ed. Wang Liqi, p. 321; see Bodman, *Poetics and Prosody in Early Medieval China*, p. 414; the Japanese translation of *shi* by *chôshi*, frequent in Kôzen (p. 458) does not seem adequate to me here.

65. Li Zhi, "Tongxinshuo," in Guo Shaoyu, 2.332. This primacy given to the spontaneity of consciousness comes of course from Wang Yangming's philosophy; and we know that Li Zhi, the heir to Wang Yangming, exerted a direct influence on Yuan Hongdao.

66. Yuan Hongdao, "Préface au *Pavillon des vagues de neige*" in Guo Shaoyu, 2.396. On this modernist declaration of the Gong'an school, see the rich study by Martine Valette-Hémery, *Yuan Hongdao. Théorie et pratique littéraires* (Paris: Institut des hautes études chinoises, 1982), vol. 28, p. 56; and Chih-P'ing Chou, *Yüan Hung-tao and the Kung-an School* (Cambridge, UK: Cambridge University Press, 1988), p. 36. In this text, the particle *er* seems to me to convey transition from one state to another (the ineluctable passage from the past to the present) rather than concession (the translation cannot be: "If literature can-

not not be modern as well as ancient...."). On this theme of the radical difference between different periods, expressed by the opposition between summer clothes and winter clothes, see also Wang Fuzhi, *Dutongjianlun*, ch. 3, p. 56.

67. Yuan Hongdao, "Letter to Jiang Jinzhi," in Guo Shaoyu, vol. 2, p. 401.

68. Gu Yanwu, *Rizhilu*, "Shiti daijiang" ("Evolution of Poetry"), ch. 7, p. 70.

69. The first option is illustrated by the preface of the *Wenxuan*; the second haunts a theorist such as Liu Xie (see my study "Ni écriture sainte ni oeuvre classique: du statut du texte confucéen comme texte fondateur vis-à-vis de la civilisation chinoise," *Extrême-Orient — Extrême-Occident* 8.5 [1984], p. 75).

70. Ye Xie, *Yuanshi*, the opening passage, ed. Huo Songlin (Beijing: Renmin wenxue chubanshe, 1979). On the difference between this concept of literary history and Western periodization, see the excellent study by Maureen Robertson, "Periodization in the Arts and Patterns of Change in Traditional Chinese Literary History," in *Theories of the Arts in China*, ed. Susan Bush and Christian Murck (Princeton, NJ: Princeton University Press, 1983), pp. 6, 17–18.

71. The expression recurs frequently in Wang Fuzhi's thought; see *Songlun*, ch. 4, p. 93, and ch. 10, p. 169; and, in the general conclusion of the *Dutongjianlun*, "Xulun," vol. 2, p. 1110.

72. *Songlun*, ch. 15, p. 260; see also ch. 4, p. 105.

73. *Dutongjianlun*, ch. 12, "Mindi," p. 386; see also ch. 14, "Andi," p. 455.

74. *Songlun*, ch. 4, p. 106.

75. Hegel, *Vorlesungen über der Geschichte*; see trans. by J. Gibelin, *Leçons sur la philosophie de l'histoire* (Paris: Vrin, 1987), p. 23; "der vermünftige notwendige Gang des Weltgeistes."

76. *Ibid.*, p. 26.

77. *Ibid.*, p. 35.

78. See, e.g., Wang Fuzhi, *Dutongjianlun*, ch. 1, p. 2, "*Yi zhe qi tian hu.*"

79. Hegel, *Leçons sur la philosophie de l'histoire*, p. 36; Wang Fuzhi, *Dutongjianlun*, p. 2.

80. On this "economy" of the divine plan in human history according to the Chinese tradition, see, e.g., Henri-Irénée Marrou, *Théologie de l'histoire* (Paris: Seuil, 1968), p. 31.

81. See the study by Paul Veyne (which provided my inspiration), *Comment on écrit l'histoire?* (Paris: Seuil, 1971 [repr. 1979]), p. 24.

82. See the now-classic analysis by Raymond Aron, "Le Schéma de la causalité historique," in *Introduction à la philosophie de l'histoire* (Paris: Gallimard, 1981), p. 201.

83. See Veyne, ch. 8.

84. That is the formula used by Wang Fuzhi to define the overall task of the historian: *tui qi suoyi ran zhi you* (you should here be understood in the sense of "from"); see *Dutongjianlun*, ch. 2, "Xulun," p. 1110.

85. The closed nature of the system is often indicated in Chinese thought (particularly in the historical thought of Wang Fuzhi), by the term *shu* ("number"; cf. ch. 8). To mark the contrast, it is worth citing Raymond Aron: "An integral reality is unthinkable. A necessary relation can only apply in a closed system or an isolated series. In relation to what is concrete any law is probable; circumstances external to the system or ignored by science are in danger of interrupting or changing the unfolding of foreseen phenomena" ("Le Schéma," p. 206).

86. The idea of "corruption," developed in the traditional, moral sense in ch. 10 of Montesquieu's *Considerations on the Causes of the Greatness of the Roman Empire and their Decline* (New York: Free Press, 1965), had been taken in its logical sense of a necessary reversal a little earlier: "There exists in the world at this moment a republic that hardly anyone knows about and that – in secrecy and silence – increases its strength every day. Certainly, if it ever attains the state of greatness for which its wisdom destines it, it will necessarily change its laws. And this will not be the work of a legislator but of corruption itself" (ch. 9, p. 94). It was this idea of corruption that Montesquieu was to develop in connection with the different types of government (as indeed the thinkers of Antiquity had) in *The Spirit of Laws* (Book VIII). But what was involved now was a dissociation of political principles, not an evolution inherent in the process of becoming.

87. Montesquieu, *Considerations on the Causes of the Greatness of the Roman Empire*, ch. 18, p. 169.

88. *Ibid.*, p. 168. The idea of a subterranean tendency suddenly erupting is

to be found in the comparison with which ch. 14, p. 130, opens: "As a river slowly and silently undermines the dikes erected against it and finally overthrows them in a moment, flooding the countryside they protected, so in the same way the sovereign power that acted insensibly under Augustus overthrew things violent under Tiberius." This idea of the "accumulation" of a tendency is common in Wang Fuzhi (*shi yi ji*; see *Dutongjianlun*, ch. 3, p. 66), and in the *Songlun* (ch. 7, p. 135) it gives rise to a comparison similar to the one used by Montesquieu. Similarly, the idea of a reversal through a tendency to reaction and compensation (on the tension-relaxation model) is to be found in ch. 15, p. 136: "Caligula reestablished the comitia, which Tiberius had done away with, and abolished the arbitrary crime of lèse-majesté which he had established. From this we may judge that the beginning of the reign of bad princes is often like the end of the reign of good ones. What good princes do from virtue, bad ones can do from a desire to run counter to the conduct of their predecessor. And to this spirit of contrariety we owe many good regulations and many bad ones as well." Montesquieu then goes on to generalize this point in a tragic (rather than a logical) mode: "What! This Senate had brought about the extinction of so many kings only to fall into the meanest enslavement to some of its most contemptible citizens, and to exterminate itself by its own decrees! We build up our power only to see it the better overturned!" (p. 138).

89. Aron, *L'Histoire et ses interprétations* (Paris: Mouton, 1961), p. 18.

90. *Ibid.*, p. 119.

91. See, e.g., Albert Rivaud, *Le Problème du devenir et la notion de la matière dans la philosophie grecque depuis les origines jusqu'à Théophraste* (Paris: Félix Alcan, 1905), p. 15. A simple "then" (*epeita*) is generally used to link the various verses in the cosmogony: all it means is that various gods come *after* other gods and belong to different ages; it does not suggest that they "are linked by a common substance, through the unity of a single development."

92. *Ibid.*, p. 461.

93. From Plato (*Republic*, Books VII and XI) and Aristotle (*Politics*, Books III and IV) down to Montesquieu (*The Spirit of Laws*, bk. VIII), Western philosophers regarded historical becoming purely as the passage from one poitical

regime to another: from monarchy to tyranny, from tyranny to democracy (or vice versa), etc. (see, e.g., Raymond Weil, *Aristotle et l'Histoire: Essai sur la "Politique"* [Paris: Klincksieck, 1960], p. 339). Yet again, becoming is envisaged on the basis of the *forms*, themselves immutable (the forms of the various constitutions regarded from the perspective of their basic principles). It never is considered from the point of view of an internal logic of change.

CHAPTER TEN: PROPENSITY AT WORK IN REALITY

As in the preceding chapters, the Chinese texts from Antiquity are, for the most part, cited from the *Zhuzi jicheng* (vols. 2, 3, 7); those by Wang Fuzhi, at the other end of the tradition, are from the Beijing edition, *Zhonghua shuju* (1975, 1976, and 1981).

1. Aristotle, *Physics*, 194b, trans. Philip H. Wickstead and Francis M. Cornford (London and Cambridge: The Loeb Classical Library, 1963); *Posterior Analytics*, 71b, trans. E.S. Forster (London and Cambridge: The Loeb Classical Library, 1966); *Metaphysics*, 982a, trans. Hugh Tredennick (London and Cambridge: The Loeb Classical Library, 1968).

2. Léon Vandermeersch, "Tradition chinoise et religion," *Catholicisme et Sociétés asiatiques* (Paris: L'Harmattan, 1988), p. 27; see also the important passages devoted to this question by the same author in *Wangdao ou la Voie royale* (Paris: Ecole française d'Extrême-Orient, 1980), vol. 2, in particular p. 267f., "Ritualisme et morpho-logique." Vandermeersch has shed excellent light on the extent to which Chinese logic differs from the "teleo-logic" of the West. However, reconsidering his analyses, I am not convinced that it is the notion of "form" that best points up the difference of Chinese thought: the internal dynamic aspect of the configuration is perhaps not sufficiently emphasized and, besides, Western thought, from its Aristotelian foundations on, itself tends to confuse form and finality (rather than set them in opposition). "Any morphology" usually implies that a "syntax" is added to it. But in China, the configuration itself serves as the functioning system, which is why I have stressed the idea of "the way in which things are disposed."

3. "Lettre à M. de Rémond," *Discours sur la théologie naturelle des Chinois*

(Paris: L'Herne, 1987), pp. 93–94; see also Olivier Roy, *Leibnitz et la Chine* (Paris: Vrin, 1972), p. 77.

4. *Book of Changes*, hexagram *kun*. This is the meaning favored by Wang Bi's commentary.

5. *Laozi*, para. 5, p. 31.

6. *Guiguzi*, ch. 7, "Chuaipian."

7. *Ibid.*, ch. 10, "Moupian."

8. On this subject, see the study by Charles Le Blanc, *Huai Nan Tzu, Philosophical Synthesis in Early Han Thought* (Hong Kong: Hong Kong University Press, 1985), p. 6.

9. *Huainanzi*, ch. 1, p. 131.

10. *Guiguzi*, ch. 8, "Mopian."

11. *Huainanzi*, ch. 1, p. 6.

12. *Ibid.*, ch. 9, pp. 134–35.

13. *Ibid.* ch. 19, p. 333 (cited in J. Needham, *Science and Civilisation in China* [Cambridge, UK: Cambridge University Press, 1956], vol. 2, pp. 68–69).

14. *Ibid.*, ch. 1, p. 5.

15. See the essential role given, in this type of expression, to the "empty word," *er*, meaning transition from one stage to another.

16. It is interesting in this respect to note the perfect overlap of the beginnings of Wang Chong's two chapters, "Wushi" ("On the propensity of things") and "Ziran" ("On what is natural," i.e., whatever happens *sponte sua*), even if the term *shi* is not yet used by Wang Chong as a concept in itself (cf. the common and secondary uses of it at the end of the "Wushi" chapter). It seems to me that a philosophical elaboration of the notion of *shi*, with a view to explaining natural phenomena, did not really begin until Liu Yuxi.

17. The meaning of *gu* opposed to *zi*.

18. Wang Chong, "Wushi."

19. On this major subject, see the excellent remarks of Vandermeersch, *Wangdao*, vol. 2, p. 275.

20. *Xunzi*, "Tianlun," p. 208.

21. Liu Zongyuan, "Tianshuo." In reply to Han Yu, who denies man the right

to complain to Heaven, given that he has committed so many affronts to it (by spoiling nature, just as worms make holes in fruit; what a staunch Green!), Liu Zongyuan argues that Heaven is just as insensitive to the good or the harm that one does to it as the fruit is. And Liu Yuxi, a close friend of Liu Zongyuan both personally and politically (they both belonged to Wang Shuwen's party) produced a more elaborated philosophical rendering of Liu Zongyuan's "naturalist" thesis. Thus, this was an important debate of the period, and it was through it that the term *shi* came to acquire its theoretical significance (cf. the same central use of this term in Liu Zongyuan's thought on history, apropos the developments that led to feudalism). On the "materialist" interpretation of his thought by Chinese historians of philosophy, see Hou Wailu, "La philosophie et la sociologie matérialistes de Liu Zongyuan," p. 7.

22. Liu Yuxi, "Tianlun", pt. 1.

23. *Ibid.*, pt. 3, end.

24. *Ibid.*, pt. 2.

25. *Jingxiu xiansheng wenji*, "Tuizhaiji."

26. This logic of reversal is certainly present in the founding text, *Laozi* (cf. in particular paragraphs 7, 9, 22, 36). By withdrawing into the background, the sage reaches the forefront and, because he lacks personal ambition, he can bring about what is in his own interest. Wang Bi, in the third century, interprets this in terms of *shi* (commentary on para. 9 of the *Laozi, Wang Bi jixiaoshi* [Beijing: Zhonghua shuju, 1980], 1.21).[gg] Significantly, from the time of Laozi's teaching, the thinker has in mind the compensation inherent in the tendency of things, which is implied by that very tendency and is therefore "logically" necessary. It is not a matter of recompense handed out in some Beyond, outside this world, through the good will of some deity (as in a religious perspective, particularly Christianity).

27. *Ibid.*

28. Wang Fuzhi, *Zhangzi zhengmeng zhu*, ch. 1, "Taihe," pp. 1–2.

29. *Ibid.*, p. 5.

30. *Ibid.*, p. 13.

31. *Ibid.*, ch. "Canliang," p. 39 (text by Zhang Zai).

32. *Ibid.*, p. 41.

33. *Ibid.*, p. 42.

34. Wang Fuzhi, *Dusishu daquanshuo*, vol. 2, pp. 599–601.

35. See Jacques Gernet, *Annuaire du Collège de France: Résumé des cours et travaux*, 1987–1988, Paris, p. 598.

36. *Ibid.*, pp. 601–602.

37. Wang Fuzhi, *Shiguangzhuan*, "Xiao ya," para. 41, pp. 97–98. A brief analysis of this text is to be found in the study by Lin Anwu, *Wang Chuanshan renxingshi zhexue zhi yanjiu* (Taipei: Dongda tushugongsi, 1987), p. 123. In general, the subject of the reversibility of *li* and *shi* is one of those most frequently tackled these days in relation to Wang Fuzhi by Chinese historians of philosophy. But it is treated too simplistically, in my opinion, because they search too directly for an equivalent to our Western "dialectic" without following up any philosophical interest in the subject on its own account.

38. Wang Fuzhi, *Shangshu yinyi*, "Wu cheng," pp. 99–102. I am unable to accept the interpretation of this chapter suggested by Fang Ke in his *Wang Chuanshan bianzhengfa sixiang yanjiu* [Studies on the dialectic thought of Wang Fuzhi] (Changsha: Hunan renmin chubanshe, 1984), pp. 140, 144. Fang Ke considers, I believe mistakenly, that the expression "to espouse the effective propensity that is favorable to one's power in such a way as to accord with the regulating principle" corresponds to the case of King Wu (and the battle of Mu). But in truth, at this point in the text, this is simply a general theoretical formulation. The entire chapter seeks to distinguish between the work of King Wu and that of King Wen by criticizing, through the former, all policies, however well intentioned, that separate principle from propensity and conceive of the assumption of power without regard to the moral exigency necessary for the preservation of that power.

39. On the history of this tradition, see Michel-Pierre Lerner, *La Motion de la finalité chez Aristote* (Paris: PUF, 1969), p. 11.

40. See, e.g., Aristotle, *On the Parts of Animals*, 639b.

41. See, e.g., the presentation of the mechanistic theory in Aristotle, *Physics*, 199a.

42. See, e.g., Aristotle, *Physics*, 199a.

43. See, e.g., Aristotle, *Physics,* 199a, and *On the Parts of Animals*, 640a; on this subject, see Joseph Moreau, *Aristote et son école* (Paris: PUF, 1962), p. 109; and among more recent studies, Lambros Couloubaritsis, *L'Avènement de la science physique: Essai sur la "Physique" d'Aristote* (Brussels: Ousia, 1980), ch. 4; Sarah Waterlow, *Nature, Change and Agency in Aristotle's Physics* (Oxford, U.K.: Clarendon, 1982), chs. 1, 2.

44. Even for Aristotle in his guise as a "naturalist," the good is not immanent in the world; it emanates from God, who is its source, as is attested by a comparison with the general and his army; see *Metaphysics*, 50, 1075a: "The efficiency of an army consists partly in the order and partly in the general; but chiefly in the latter because he does not depend upon the order, but the order depends upon him."

45. On this point, see my earlier work, *Procès ou création* (Paris: Seuil, 1989), p. 149.

46. Aristotle, *Physics*, ch. 1, 188b.

47. *Ibid.*, 189a.

48. *Metaphysics*, 50, 1069b; see *De generatione et corruptione*, 314b and 329a.

49. *Ibid.*, 1075a; see Albert Rivaud, *Le Problème du devenir et la notion de la matière dans la philosophie grecque depuis les origines jusqu'à Théophraste* (Paris: Felix Alcan, 1905), p. 386.

50. These formulae are common in the entire Chinese tradition; see, e.g., Wang Fuzhi, *Zhangzi zhengmeng zhu*, ch. 2, "Canliang," pp. 30, 37, 40.

51. Aristotle, *Metaphysics*, 50, 1069b–1070a.

52. The idea of *epistēmē* is here used in Foucault's sense but turned against him, for the discursive configuration essential to *epistēmē*, which can be perceived from the "heterotypic" perspective of another culture (such as China, faced with the European culture), depends on a "long-term view" and prompts us to reintroduce the traditional representations so severely criticized by him. (Yet did not Foucault's last works, on the history of sexuality, also in a way make us recognize that longer term?)

53. *Metaphysics*, 50, 1071b.

54. *Physics*, 4, 208b; on this subject see the study by J. Moreau, *L'Espace et le Temps selon Aristote* (Padua: Editrice Antenore, 1965), p. 70.

55. Aristotle, *Physics* 2, 196a–198a; *Metaphysics*, A, 984b, and Z, 1032a; *Parts of Animals*, 1, 640a.

56. *Physics*, 1, 192a.

57. *Metaphysics*, 50, 1072b.

Glossary of Chinese Expressions

a. *Qi zhan sheng bu te* 其战胜不忒

b. *Sheng yu yi sheng zhe ye* 胜于易胜者也

c. *Qi qiao zai yu shi* 其巧在于势

d. *Qi shi, di shi, yin shi* 气势，地势，因势

e. *Shi zhe, suoyi ling shi bi dou ye* 势者，所以令士必斗也。

f. *Ren sui zhong duo, shi mo gan ge* 人虽众多，势莫敢格。

g. *Shi ru kuo nu* 势如矿弩

h. *Qiu zhi yu shi, bu ze yu ren* 求之于势，不责于人。

i. *Yong qie, shi ye* 勇怯，势也。

j. *Shi sheng ren* 势胜人

k. *Ji li yi ting, nai wei zhi shi, yi zuo qi wai* 计利以听，乃为之势，以佐其外。

l. *Shi zhe, yin li er zhi quan* 势者，因利而制权。

m. *Suoyi wu zhen zhe, yi qi wu chang xingshi ye* 所以无朕者，以其无常形势也。

n. *Bing wu chang shi, shui wu chang xing* 兵无常势，水无常形。

o. *Shen shi du shi* 审时度时

p. *Shi* and *li* 势利

CHAPTER TWO: POSITION AS THE DETERMINING FACTOR IN POLITICS

a. *Qu wu er bu liang* 趣物而不两

b. *Shi wei zu yi qu xian* 势位足以屈贤

c. *Bu shi qi qiang er shi qi shi* 不恃其强而恃其势

d. *Yi shi wei zu shi yi zhi guan* 以势为足恃以治官

e. *Wu suo wei yan shi zhe, yan ren zhi suo she* 吾所为言势者，言人之所设。

f. *Wei wu shi ye, wu suo li* 威无势也，无所立。

g. *Fan ren jun zhi suoyi wei jun zhe, shi ye* 凡人君之所以为君者，势也。

h. *Chu shi* 处势

i. *Ren jun shi shi, ze chen zhi zhi* 人君失势，则臣制之。

j. *De cheng xin xing zhi shi* 得乘信幸之势。

k. *Duo jian feng, suoyi bian qi shi ye* 多建封，所以便其势也。

l. *Can and wu* 参伍

m. *Guan ting zhi shi* 观听之势

n. *Cong ming zhi shi xing* 聪明之势兴

   is qualified by *ming zhu* 明主

o. *Fa and shu* 法术

p. *Yi zhong wei shi* 以众为势

q. *Chu shi er bu neng yong qi you* 处势而不能用其有

r. *Zhi bing yi chu shi* 执柄以处势

s. *De shi wei ze bu jin er duo cheng* 得势位则不进而多成。

t. *Ming zhu zhi xing zhi ye tian, qi yong ren ye gui* 明主之行制也天，其用人也鬼。

u. *Shi xing jiao yan (ni) er bu wei* 势行教严（逆）而不违。

v. *Jie (he) she shi zhi yi ye er dao xing zhi nan* 皆（合）舍势之易也而道行之难。

w. *Fei huai qi yi, fu qi shi ye* 非怀其义，服其势也。

x. *Shan chi shi* 善持势

308

CHAPTER THREE: CONCLUSION I

   a. *Hao shan er wang shi* 好善而忘势

   b. *Shi qi shui zhi xing zai, qi shi ze ran ye* 是其水之性哉，其势则然也。

   c. *Shi qi ze bu yi* 势齐则不一

   d. *Ren fu er shi cong zhi* 人服而势从之

     Ren bu fu er shi qu zhi 人不服而势去之

   e. *Bi*, on the one hand; *mo bu*, on the other 必，莫不

   f. *Bi bi zuo qi gui jue ren zhi shi* 笔笔作奇鬼攫人之势

CHAPTER FOUR: THE FORCE OF FORM, THE EFFECT OF GENRE

   a. *Gai shu, xing xue ye; you xing ze you shi* 盖书，形学也；有形则
     有势

   b. *De shi bian, ze yi cao sheng suan* 得势便，则已操胜算

   c. *Bi shi, zi shi* 笔势，字势

   d. *Yi ti tong shi* 异体同势

   e. *Qi shi – xing shi* 气势一形势

   f. *Shi yi sheng zhi* 势以生之

   g. *Xu qiu dian hua shang xia yan yang li he zhi shi* 须求点画上下偃仰离
     合之势

   h. *Yan yang xiang bei* 偃仰向背

   i. *Xing shi di xiang yingdai* 形势递相映带

   j. *Xu qiu yingdai, zi shi xiongmei* 须求映带，字势雄媚

   k. *Qu shi, de shi – shi shi* 取势，得势一失势

   l. *Hua xian jue zhi shi* 画险绝之势

  m. *Jian de shanshi gao bu ke ce* 见得山势高不可测

   n. *Yi shou fu yi fang, shan jian kai er shi zhuan* 一收复一放，山渐开而
     势转

   o. *Qi shui shi yu jian pi* 其水势欲溅壁

   p. *Shi shi xiang wei* 势使相偎

   q. *Shi gao er xian* 势高而险

309

r. *De cenci zhi shi* 得参差之势

s. *Yi shi du zhi, fang de qi miao* 以势度之，方得其妙。

t. *Zhi xu xu shi qu shi* 只须虚实取势

u. *You qu shi xu yin chu* 有取势虚引处

v. *Bing wu chang chen, zi wu chang ti* 兵无常阵，字无常体

w. *Shi duo bu ding* 势多不定

x. *Ji ti cheng shi* 即体成势

　　Xun ti er cheng shi 循体而成势

y. *Shi zhe, cheng li er wei zhi* 势者，乘利而为制

z. *Bing zong qun shi* 并总群势

aa. *Zong yi zhi shi* 总一之势

bb. *Wen zhi ren shi* 文之任势

cc. *Shi shi xu ze* 势实须泽

dd. *Yuan qi wei ti, e shi suo bian* 原其为体，讹势所变。

ee. *Yi shi yu yan, yu feng bu chang* 遗势郁淹，余风不畅

　　tu feng shi 图风势

CHAPTER FIVE: LIFELINES ACROSS A LANDSCAPE

a. *Qi xing ye, yin di zhi shi* 其行也，因地之势

　　Qi ju ye, yin shi zhi zhi 其聚也，因势之止

b. *Di shi yuan mai, shan shi yuan gu* 地势原脉，山势原骨

c. *Qian chi wei shi, bai chi wei xing* 千尺为势，百尺为形

d. *Shan shui zhi xiang, qi shi xiang sheng* 山水之象，气势相生

e. *Yuan wang zhi yi qu qi shi* 远望之以取其势

f. *Jin zhe wan xi bu neng jiu cuozong qizhi zhi shi* 近者玩习不能究错纵起止之势

g. *You gong yuan shi gu mo bi* 尤工远势古莫比

h. *Yao zhi qu shi wei zhu* 要之取势为主

i. The notion of *lishi* 理势

310

j. *Fan yi cao yi mu ju you shi cun hu qi jian* 凡一草一木具有势存乎其间

k. *De shi ze sui yi jingying, yi yu jie shi* 得势则随意经营，一隅皆是。

l. *Shi zhi tui wan zai yu ji wei* 势之推挽在于几微

m. *Zhi qu xinghui shendao (chaomiao)* 只取兴会神到（超妙）

CHAPTER SIX: CATEGORIES OF EFFICACIOUS DISPOSITIONS

a. *Chansi jing* 缠丝劲

b. *Ge qi shi* 割其势

c. *Shi* as distinct from *fa* 势法

d. *Shoushi* as distinct from *zhefa* 手势，指法

e. *Xing sui bie er shi tong* 兴虽别而势同

f. *Gao shou zuo shi, yi ju geng bie qi yi* 高手作势，一句更别其意

g. *Xia ju ruo yu shang ju, bu kan xiangbei* 下句弱于上句，不看向背

h. *Ruo yu shi you dui* 若语势有对

i. *Shi you tongsai* 势有通塞

j. *Hou shi te qi, qian shi si duan* 后势特起，前势似断

k. *Yu yu xing qu, shi zhu qing qi* 语与兴驱，势逐情起

l. *Qixiang yinyun, you shen yu tishi* 气象氤氲，由深于体势

m. *Gao shou you hubian zhi shi* 高手有互变之势

CHAPTER SEVEN: DYNAMISM IS CONTINUOUS

a. *Qi yi cheng shi, shi yi yu qi* 气以成势，势以御气。

b. *Shi ke jian er qi bu ke jian* 势可见而气不可见

c. *Shi you yu* 势有余

d. *Wu ning zhi zhi shi* 无凝滞之势

e. *Shi qi xingshi dixiang yingdai, wu shi shi bei* 使其形势递相映带，无使势背

f. *Di er san zi cheng shang bi shi* 第二三字承上笔势

g. *Cao ze hang jin shi wei jin* 草则行尽势未尽

h. *Fei dong zeng shi* 飞动增势

i. *Qi xiang lian chu, te shi yin dai* 其相连处，特是引带

j. *Heng xie qu zhi, gou huan pan yu, jie yi shi wei zhu* 横斜曲直，钩环盘纡，皆以势为主。

k. *Ru bi jiang yang, bi xian zuo fu shi* 如笔将仰，必先作俯势

l. *Ni qi shi* 逆其势

m. *Qi shi guan chuan* 气势贯串

n. *Zong zhi tong hu qi yi cheng qi huodong zhi qu zhe, shi ji suowei shi ye* 总之统乎气以呈其活动之趣者，是即所谓势也。

o. *Yi bi zhi qi shi mao wu zhi ti shi* 以笔之气势貌物之体势

p. *You suo cheng jie er lai, you suo tuo xie er qu* 有所承接而来，有所脱卸而去。

q. *Shi* and *li* agree 势理

r. *Wenshi* as different from *wenzhang* 文势，文章

s. *Fan qie yun zhi dong, shi ruo zhuan huan* 凡切韵之动，势若转圜

t. *Shi bu xiang yi, ze feng du wei zu* 势不相依，则讽读为阻

u. *Cheng jie er ju you gui de shi* 承接二句尤贵得势

v. *Wu fu you neng xing zhi shi* 无复有能行之势

w. *Shi zhe, yi zhong zhi shenli ye* 势者，意中之神理也。

x. *Wei neng qu shi, wanzhuan qushen yi qiu jin qi yi* 为能取势，宛转屈伸以求尽其意

y. *Sui dang cheng yi pian zhi shi* 遂宕成一篇之势

z. *Qian jie shi shengqi hou jie zhi shi* 前解实生起后解之势

aa. *Fu xian you jin gong nu ma zhi shi* 伏线有劲弓怒马之势

bb. *Bi shi qi wu* 笔势奇兀

cc. *Wenshi weiyi quzhe zhi ji* 文势逶迤曲折之极

dd. *Die cheng qi shi, bian xia wen zou de xun ji ke xiao* 叠成奇势，便下文走得迅疾可笑

ee. *Zhi shi bi mo yi yang, yi cheng wenshi* 只是笔墨抑扬，以成文势。

ff. *Zuozhe te yu wei hou wen qu shi* 作者特欲为后文取势

gg. *Bi xu bie shi yi jian zhi, er hou wen shi nai cuozong jin bian* 必叙别事以间之，而后文势乃错综尽变。

CHAPTER EIGHT: CONCLUSION II

a. *Shi weiyi quzhe, qian bian wan hua, ben wu ding shi*
势委蛇曲折，千变万化，本无定式。

b. *Di shi yuan mai, shan shi yuan gu, weiyi dongxi huo wei nanbei*
地势原脉，山势原骨，委蛇东西或为南北

c. *Shi shi wanshan ru long* 使势蜿蟺如龙

d. *Pan qiu zhi shi, yu fu yun han* 蟠虬之势，欲附云汉。

e. *Chong she qiu liao, huo wang huo huan* 虫蛇虬缪，或往或还。

f. *Ziti xingshi, zhuang ru long she, xiang goulian bu duan* 字体形势，状如龙蛇，相钩连不断

g. *Bishi yaojiao* 笔势夭矫

h. *Qi shi wan zhuang, bian tai mo ce* 其势万状，变态莫测

i. *Zhen ru long xing yaojiao, shi ren bu ke zhuonuo* 真如龙行夭矫，使人不可捉搦

CHAPTER NINE: SITUATION AND TENDENCY IN HISTORY

a. *Fei wu li, shi bu ke* 非无力，势不可

b. *Jiu chu li shi bi wang* 久处利势必王

c. *Shi bu neng wei jian, shi de wei jian* 势不能为奸，势得为奸

d. *Shi zhi zhi dao ye, shi luan zhi dao ye* 势治之道也，势乱之道也

e. *Xiu jin ze sai yu shi* 修今则塞于势

f. *San dai yi shi er jie ke yi wang* 三代异势而皆可以王

g. *Gong shou zhi shi yi ye* 攻守之势异也

h. *Fengjian fei shengren yi ye, shi ye* 封建非圣人意也，势也。

i. *Shi zhi lai* 势之来

j. *Shi zhi suo qu, qi fei li er neng ran zai* 势之所趋，岂非理而能然哉。

k. *Shi suo bi lan* 势所必滥

l. *Shi suo bi ji* 势所必激

m. *Shi xiang ji er li sui yi yi* 势相激而理随以易

n. *Shi you suo bu de ju ge* 势有所不得遽革

o. *Fengjian zhi bi ge er bu ke fu ye, shi yi ji er si zhi yi zhao* 封建之必革而不可复也，势已积而俟之一朝。

p. *Jian you he yi zhi shi* 渐有合一之势

q. *Min li zhi suo bu kan er shi zai bi ge* 民力之所不堪而势在必革

r. *Shi sui shi qian er fa bi bian* 事随势迁而法必变

s. *Yi gu jin zhi tong shi er yan zhi* 以古今之通势而言之

t. *Tian xia zhi shi, yi li yi he, yi zhi yi luan er yi* 天下之势，一离一合，一治一乱而已。

u. *Wu xing xiang sheng* or *xiang sheng* 五行相胜，相生

v. *Zheng tong* 正统

w. *Li er he zhi, he zhe bu ji li* 离而合之，合者不继离。

x. *Shen qi zhe, shi zhong xiang guan, wu ju sheng ju mie zhi lishi* 神气者，如终相贯，无遽生遽灭之理势。

y. *Yi dong er bu ke zhi zhe, shi ye* 一动而不可止者，势也。

z. *Jie ziran bu ke zhong zhi zhi shi* 皆自然不可中止之势

aa. *Ji zhong nan fan zhi shi, bu neng ni wan yu yi zhao* 极重难返之势，不能逆挽于一朝

bb. *Wu yi er fei bi wang zhi shi* 无一而非必亡之势

cc. *Wu ji bi fan* 物极必反

dd. *Ji zhong zhi shi, qi mo bi qing, qing ze fan zhi ye yi, ci shi zhi biran zhe ye* 极重之势，其末必轻，辅则反之也易，此势之必然者也。

ee. *Shun biran zhi shi zhe, li ye; li zhi ziran zhe, tian ye* 顺必然之势者，理也；理之自然者，天也。

ff. *Tai* and *pi* 泰，否

gg. *Qu er neng shenzhe, wei qi shi ye* 屈而能伸者，惟其势也。

hh. *Ji er bi fan zhi shi cheng hu tian* 极而必反之势成乎天

314

ii. *Pi ji er qing, tian zhi suo bi dong, wu dai ren ye* 否极而倾，天之所必动，无待人也。

jj. *Cheng da chi er shi qie qiu zhang zhi ri* 承大弛而势且求张之日

kk. *Xiang reng zhe zhi bi xiang bian ye, shi ye* 相仍者之必相变也，势也。

ll. *Zhang-chi; shen-qu; zhi-luan; sheng-shuai; yi-yang* 张弛，伸屈，治乱，盛衰，抑扬

mm. *Ju zhen yi si, xu qi er shun zhong zhi yi tu cheng* 居贞以俟，徐起而顺众志以图成。

nn. *Yin qi jian shuai zhi shi* 因其渐衰之势

oo. *Tian zhe, li er yi yi; li zhe, shi zhi shun er yi yi* 天者，理而已矣，理者，势之顺而已矣。

pp. *Qing zhong zhi shi, ruo bu ke fan, fan zhi ji zheng zai shi ye* 轻重之势，若不可返，返之几正在是也。

qq. *Qu yu ci zhe, shen yu bi, wu liang de zhi shu, yi wu bu fan zhi shi* 屈于此者，伸于彼，无两得之数，亦无不反之势。

rr. *Sheng zhi yu si, cheng zhi yu bai, jie lishi zhi bi you* 生之与死，成之与败，皆理势之必有。

ss. *Li zhe gu you ye, shi zhe fei shi ran; yi shi wei biran, ran er you bu ran zhe cun yan* 理者固有也，势者非适然；以势为必然，然而不然者存焉。

tt. *Ji* 几

uu. *Shi liu bu fan* 势流不反

vv. *Ci suowei shi bu tong er wu moni zhi neng* 此所谓势不同而无模拟之能

ww. *Gu zhi bu neng wei jin zhe ye, shi ye* 古之不能为今者也，势也。

xx. *Ci li ye, yi shi ye* 此理也，亦势也。

Shi bu neng bu bian 势不能不变。

yy. *Du qi shi* 度其势

Shi yi er shi yi, shi yi er li yi 时异而势异，势异而理异

zz. *Zhi shi yi shen shi, yin shi er qiu he yu li* 知时以审势，因势而求合于理。

Chapter Ten: Propensity at Work in Reality

a. *Di shi kun* 地势坤

b. *Shi cheng zhi* 势成之

c. *Ji zhi shi* 几之势

d. *Yin qi shi yi cheng jiu zhi* 因其势以成就之

e. *Shi zhi ziran* 势之自然

f. *Wu lei xiang ying yu shi* 物类相应于势

g. *Tui (er) bu ke wei zhi shi* 推（而）不可为之势

h. *Shu cun, ranhou shi xing hu qi jian yan* 数存，然后势形乎其间焉

i. *Shi dang qi shu cheng qi shi* 适当其数乘其势

j. *Tian guo xia yu shi ye* 天果狭于势耶

k. *Yi li zhi xiang dui, shi zhi xiang xun* 以理之相对，势之相寻。

l. *Jiao zhi shi bi wu* 皦之势必污

m. *Lishi* 理势

n. *Xiang dang, qi biran zhi lishi* 相荡，其必然之理势。

o. *Jie sheng jiang fei yang ziran zhi lishi* 皆升降飞扬自然之理势

p. *Jing ji lishi* 精极理势

q. *Li dangran er ran, ze cheng hu shi* 理当然而然，则成乎势

r. *Shi jiran er bu de bu ran* 势既然而不得不然

s. *Shi zhi shun zhe, ji li zhi dangran zhe yi* 势之不顺者，即理之当然者已。

t. *Qi, li* 气，理

u. *Li yi zhi qi, qi suo shou cheng, si wei zhi tian* 理以治气，气所受成，斯谓之天

v. *Zhi zai shi zhi biran chu jian li* 只在势之必然处见理

w. *Li cheng shi* 理成势

x. *Shi cheng li* 势成理

y. *Yi shi zhi fou cheng li zhi ni* 以势之否成理之逆

z. *Li zhi shun ji shi zhi bian* 理之顺即势之便

aa. *Gong shou yi shi* 攻守异势

bb. *Yin li yi de shi* 因理以得势

cc. *Yi shun shi yi xun li* 亦顺势以循理

dd. *Feng shou zhi li yi gong, cun gong zhi shi yi shou* 奉守之理以攻，存攻之势以守

ee. *Bu neng yu chi hou shi* 不能豫持后势

ff. *Li shi wu li, li li wu shi* 离事无理，离理无势

gg. *Shi bi qing wei* 势必倾危

 Shi bi cui nü 势必摧衄

CHAPTER ELEVEN: CONCLUSION III

a. *Cheng shi* 乘势

b. *Miao* 妙

c. *Shun* 顺

Photo Credits:

1. From *The Garden of the Mustard-seed*.
2. From *The Garden of the Mustard-seed*.
3. From *The Garden of the Mustard-seed*.
4. From *The Garden of the Mustard-seed*.
5. From *The Garden of the Mustard-seed*.
6. Evolution of the structure of a roof, from the *Grand Atlas de l'architecture mondiale* (Paris: Encyclopaedia Universalis, 1981).
7. Bell tower, Xi'an, from the *Grand Atlas de l'architecture mondiale*.
8. From the plates of the *Great Treatise on Supreme Sound*.
9. From the plates of the *Great Treatise on Supreme Sound*.
10. From *The Garden of the Mustard-seed*.
11. From *The Garden of the Mustard-seed*.
12. From Jean-François Billeter, *L'Art chinois de l'écriture* (Geneva: Editions d'art Albert Skira, 1989).
13. From *L'Art chinois de l'écriture*.
14. From Nicole Vandier-Nicolas, *Peinture chinoise et tradition lettrée* (Paris: Seuil, 1983).
15. Francis Gardner Curtis Fund. Courtesy, Museum of Fine Arts, Boston.

Zone Books

The Organism
By Kurt Goldstein

Third Sex, Third Gender
Edited by Gilbert Herdt

The Movement of the Free Spirit
By Raoul Vaneigem

The Society of the Spectacle
By Guy Debord

A Vital Rationalist
*Selected Writings from
Georges Canguilhem*
Edited by François Delaporte

The Invention of Pornography
Edited by Lynn Hunt

Etienne-Jules Marey
By François Dagognet

La Jetée
By Chris Marker

The Accursed Share
Volume I
By Georges Bataille

The Accursed Share
Volumes II & III
By Georges Bataille

Perspective as Symbolic Form
By Erwin Panofsky

Fragmentation and Redemption
By Caroline Walker Bynum

**Expressionism in Philosophy:
Spinoza**
By Gilles Deleuze

The Poetic Structure of the World
Copernicus and Kepler
By Fernand Hallyn

The Life of Forms in Art
By Henri Focillon

The Normal and the Pathological
By Georges Canguilhem

Masochism
Coldness and Cruelty
By Gilles Deleuze
Venus in Furs
By Leopold von Sacher-Masoch

Theory of Religion
By Georges Bataille

**Myth and Society in
Ancient Greece**
By Jean-Pierre Vernant

**Myth and Tragedy in
Ancient Greece**
By Jean-Pierre Vernant and
Pierre Vidal-Naquet

Mitra-Varuna
By Georges Dumézil

Bergsonism
By Gilles Deleuze

Matter and Memory
By Henri Bergson

Your Money or Your Life
By Jacques Le Goff

Foucault/Blanchot
*Maurice Blanchot: The Thought
from Outside*
By Michel Foucault
Michel Foucault as I Imagine Him
By Maurice Blanchot

Society Against the State
By Pierre Clastres

This edition designed by Bruce Mau
Type composed by Archetype
Chinese composed by Han Lin
Printed and bound Smythe-sewn by Maple-Vail
using Sebago acid-free paper